Advances in Planning and Management of Watersheds and Wetlands

in Eastern and Southern Africa

Advances in Planning and Management of Watersheds and Wetlands

in Eastern and Southern Africa

John E. FitzGibbon, editor

Published by:

Weaver Press, P O Box A1922, Avondale, Harare, Zimbabwe

Cover design: Danes Design, Harare

Layout: Fontline Electronic Publishing, Harare

Printed in Zimbabwe by Mazongororo Paper Converters.

ISBN 0 7974 2017 7

Environmental Capacity Enhancement Project

Environmental Roundtable Series

John Devlin, series editor

TABLE OF CONTENTS

SERIES PREFACE

The Environmental Capacity Enhancement Project (ECEP) has sought over the past four years to contribute to improved regional environmental management in Eastern and Southern Africa. The project has involved participants from 13 countries (Angola, Botswana, Kenya, Lesotho, Malawi, Mozambique, Namibia, South Africa, Swaziland, Tanzania, Uganda, Zambia, Zimbabwe) and has concentrated upon six environmental areas: ecotourism, ecological agriculture. land use planning, small scale mining, waste management and watershed management. The project has not sought to develop a narrow set of regional environmental experts. Rather it has sought to bring together development practitioners, activists, analysts, researchers and policymakers so that all could become familiar with the policy options and technology choices available to respond to the complex range of environmental problems shared across the region.

The regional training courses, the collaborative research projects, and the professional exchanges supported by ECEP have created multistakeholder venues where representatives from governmental and nongovernmental institutions, the private sector and academic institutions could build linkages for mutual support and on-going information exchange. During its four years of operation ECEP has graduated 180 from its training courses and funded 53 collaborative research projects involving 125 principal researchers. It has also supported 35 professional enhancement attachments of which 27 have involved exchanges between different countries. Having brought environmental practitioners together ECEP then sought to establish the conditions for continued networking among them so that the regional and multistakeholder perspective would be maintained over the long term. Six networks of researchers and practitioners have been created. And all have had an opportunity to meet during the networking conference held in Harare from May 13-15, 1998 to exchange papers, discuss their future organizational efforts and evaluate what had been achieved to date.

The final outputs of the project are the five volumes of collected papers comprising the Environmental Roundtable Series. These five volumes represent the best of documents and reports that have been produced by ECEP participants. They will serve not only as valuable collections for environmental policy makers, environmental educators and environmental activists but also as catalysts for future initiatives dedicated to building an effective environmental management culture in the region. The preparation of this series has been made possible by two important groups. First, the Canadian International Development Agency, which has generously funded ECEP over the past four years. Second, the many ECEP participants who have generously donated their time and energy to making this project a success. Their contributions are acknowledged with thanks.

Dr. R.J. McLaughlin
Dean, Ontario Agricultural College, University of Guelph, Canada
March 1999

CONTRIBUTORS

Farokh Afshar
   Associate Professor, School of Rural Planning and Development
   University of Guelph
   Guelph, Canada

Aggrey J.D. Ambali
   Lecturer, Department of Biology
   Chancellor College, University of Malawi
   Zomba, Malawi

James Bogart
   Professor, Department of Zoology
   University of Guelph
   Guelph, Canada

Laura Brown
   M. Sc. Student
   Department of Geography, University of Guelph
   Guelph, Canada

Robert Brown
   Professor, School of Landscape Architecture
   University of Guelph
   Guelph, Canada

Alan Channing
   Professor, Department of Biochemistry
   University of the Western Cape
   Belleville, South Africa

Stephen Chapman
   M. Sc. Student (since completed)
   Department of Geography, University of Guelph
   Guelph, Canada

Mary Jane Conboy
   Ph. D. Student (since completed)
   Department of Land Resource Science, University of Guelph
   Guelph, Canada

John E. FitzGibbon
    Professor & Director, School of Rural Planning and Development
    University of Guelph
    Guelph, Canada
Nina Gruntkowski
    Researcher
    Desert Research Foundation of Namibia
    Swakopmund, Namibia
Johannes Henschel
    Coordinator, Research and Resources
    Desert Research Foundation of Namibia
    Swakopmund, Namibia
Meya P. Kalindekafe
    Lecturer, Department of Biology
    Chancellor College, University of Malawi
    Zomba, Malawi
Brian (Bruce) E. Kelbe
    Professor, Department of Hydrology
    University of Zululand
    Kwa Dlangezwa, South Africa
Ray Kostaschuk
    Professor, Department of Geography
    University of Guelph
    Guelph, Canada
Reid Kreutzwiser
    Professor, Department of Geography
    University of Guelph
    Guelph, Canada
Alfred O. Maluwa
    Senior Fisheries Research Officer
    National Aquaculture Centre, Department of Fisheries
    Domasi, Malawi

Chimwang'a Maseka
Hydrogeologist
Department of Water Affairs
Lusaka, Zambia

Vilho Mtuleni
Research Assistant
Desert Research Foundation of Namibia
Swakopmund, Namibia

Imasiku Nyambe
Lecturer, Department of Geology
School of Mines, University of Zambia
Lusaka, Zambia

Mary K. Seely
Director
Desert Research Foundation of Namibia
Windhoek, Namibia

Elias Shanyengana
Researcher
Desert Research Foundation of Namibia
Swakopmund, Namibia

Abdi Siad Omar
M. Sc. Student (since completed)
School of Rural Planning and Development, University of Guelph
Guelph, Canada

Moira Simpson
M. Sc. Student (since completed)
School of Rural Planning and Development, University of Guelph
· Guelph, Canada

Nina Snyman
Researcher, Department of Hydrology
University of Zululand
Kwa Dlangezwa, South Africa

An Introduction to Watershed and Wetland Ecosystem Management in Eastern and Southern Africa

by John FitzGibbon

Introduction

As we enter into the 21st century we face the challenge of the growing demand for land and water to meet the needs of our growing populations. At the same time we face the increasing uncertainty of the impacts of climate change and loss of resource capacity due to loss of water quality. Our ability to secure adequate clean water is a function of our ability to manage both water and land and to manage our activities so that the water secured is clean and used in the most efficient way. In addition to human need for water there is the need for water to support the ecosystem; to maintain natural functions, plant and animal diversity and productivity and the capacity of the environment to store and retain water and to cleanse it.

The challenge faced is to understand the natural system and the goods and services provided by it to both the human population and to the plants and animals in the environment. To this end there are a number of well known functions of the water system that we need to understand with greater depth and precision. These include the water balance, the pathways of water movement and the pathways of the movement of contaminants, patterns and processes of water capture and use and the habitat functions which water provides. In addition we need to improve our understanding and management of water use and conservation at local, regional, national and international levels. This includes the legal, institutional, social and economic structures and processes which form the basis of the management system.

Sustainable development of watersheds and wetlands has become the objective to which improved science is being applied. Sustainable development requires that we consider not only the human use objectives of water management but also the maintenance and improvement of the ecosystem which supports the plant and animal populations with which we share the system. Sustainable development of watersheds also requires that we deal with the long term well being of the system in a climate of change and uncertainty. This is indeed a complex challenge which requires that we alter not just our approach to management but also our objectives and the values which condition those objectives. The traditional approach of one solution fits all has been shown to fail because it does not respond to the context of the resource environment nor does it adapt to change. As a result the use of adaptive management strategies which recognize the context and that can change through learning are increasingly necessary to provide for sustainable development.

WATERSHED AND WETLAND ISSUES IN SOUTHERN AFRICA

In some senses the issues related to watersheds and wetlands in Eastern and Southern Africa are typical of those that plague all regions. There are however a number of dimensions of this region that make the understanding and management of water unique. Water in the region is probably more spatially and temporally variable than in most regions of the world. It ranges from the extreme aridity of the Namibian coast to the humid tropics of the mountain rainforests of the headwaters of many of the major rivers. It forms the great lakes of the rift valley, the large rivers such as the Zambesi and the immense wetlands such as the Okavango. This variability means that the management of the resource needs to be based on a good understanding of the dynamics and the complexity of the linkages between hydrologic systems at local, national and regional scales.

The most important issues in the region are the development of water supply for domestic use, for industrial and agricultural development and for the maintenance of the ecosystem. Several factors contribute to the problem of adequate water supply. The first is the growth of urban areas concentrating demand in small areas exceeding the supply capacity of the local system. This has contributed to the need to move water from one area to another in order to meet the demand. However it is not without adverse impact on both the donor basin and the receiving basin.

The second major problem is scarcity due to either episodic or perpetually limited precipitation. This is the major challenge for the region as a whole.

Responses to this condition have included improved water capture through construction of large dams, interbasin transfers, and displacement of people and productivity due to drought. Given the increasing probability that climate change will result in exacerbation of the problems of aridity and drought there is a clear need to make further adjustment to water management. This will need to be done in a way that will put emphasis on the protection of the ecosystem that provides the water. This will include the improvement of agricultural and forestry practice to maintain the soil so that runoff is moderated and ground water recharged. It will also require management of demands so that water is used efficiently and the optimum economic, social and environmental value is achieved.

Third there are the problems of contamination by both conventional contaminants (nutrients and organics), toxins and pathogenic organisms. These are derived from the increased discharge of domestic waste into surface and groundwater, the development of industry, the use of commercial pesticides in intensive agriculture and the development of habitat conditions which harbour pathogenic orgasms. Contamination is greatest in the urban areas but is also found in the intensive agricultural areas. Throughout the region problems with water borne disease and vector organisms are endemic including astro-intestinal infections, parasites and malaria. Occasional outbreaks of other diseases particularly during drought suggest that the problems could become more pronounced with climate change and increasing concentration of population in unserviced urban areas. Clearly the development of safe water supply and the containment of disease vectors is a priority. Contamination results in further restriction in the supply of water by making available water unusable or imposing risks to health and well being upon the user.

A fourth major issue relates to the degradation of the ecosystem. Clearing and drainage of wetlands for agricultural use has resulted in the loss of storage capacity in the watersheds and reduction of recharge to groundwater as well as the loss of habitat for plants and wildlife. The damming of rivers has modified the natural flow regime and developed habitat for disease organisms while eliminating habitat for fish and wildlife. Removal of forest cover and over exploitation of land for agriculture has resulted in loss of moisture holding capacity and resulted in more extreme runoff and soil erosion. All of these actions have resulted in the decreased availability of water and degraded the system that provides the water.

The response to these issues has been the development of a great deal of scientific knowledge and management capacity to mitigate the impacts of development and to improve the availability and quality of water . It is also aimed at the protection and enhancement of the ecosystem so that the impacts of future stresses will not result in further loss and damage to the system. Sustainable watershed management is evolving from a concept and a debate, to a science which provides an approach to management that responds to the complex issues that face the region.

WATERSHED AND WETLAND SCIENCE AND APPROACHES TO MANAGEMENT

Watersheds as ecosystems

The watershed has become the fundamental geographic and functional unit for both understanding and managing water resources. The advantage of the watershed as a unit of analysis and management is that all of the functions of the hydrologic system and many of the hydrobiological system are integrated within the watershed. This is expressed through the water balance and related sediment and nutrient balances . It is also dynamically integrated through the routing of water through the pathways in the watershed. Wetlands form a special component within the watershed being areas where the presence of water on or near the surface creates a transitional environment between the terrestrial component of the watershed and the aquatic. Wetlands represent a critical element in maintaining the stability of the runoff regime of a watershed and because of the abundance of water and nutrients that are stored in the wetland they are among the most productive and diverse areas. In biological terms wetlands are integrated in habitat systems that exist within and between watersheds which support the life cycle of the species and communities that derive their well being from the environment.

Watersheds and wetlands can be viewed in a number of ways; as resources, as utilities, as habitats, or as ecosystems. There is a trend to employ the ecosystems approach as an over arching holistic view of the watershed for the purposes of integrated watershed management. It incorporates the concepts of the watershed as habitat, as well as the concept of the watershed as a provider of environmental goods and services. The advantage of the ecosystems approach is that of linking the critical functional elements of the watershed system in a way that human action and natural changes or shifts in the environment can be understood and the implications assessed for all affected elements of the system. This approach reduces the potential for unanticipated or unintended effects which may result in degradation of the watershed system.

Human ecosystems science

The concept of human ecosystems science was put forward by Naveh and Liberman (1984). It encompasses not only the physical and biological nature of human habitat and human activity but the ethical, social, economic and political dimensions of human organization and development. Mazer (1999) has set out a prime directive for sustainable human ecosystem science. The prime directive emphasizes the need to live with the ecosytem and where possible enhance it. Mazer (1998) identifies a number of key characteristics of human ecosystems that provide for sustainability. They include community identity, community citizenship, organization, ethics, intelligence and status. Community identity is the understanding we have of our selves and our environment. It influences how we represent ourselves and expresses our key values both to our selves and to other communities. Community citizenship is how we participate in the decisions that determine our interactions with each other and with the environment. It influences the degree to which we are enfranchised in the decision making process and determines the degree to which we support or resist decisions. Organization refers to the structures within which decision making and action are undertaken. It influences the pathways of exchange of communication and social and economic activity. Ethics is the set of rules which guide the application of our values to our actions. They are not always consistent but differ depending on the local or global application. Much of the conflict that needs to be resolved within human ecosystems stems from the resolution of the differences between our local and global ethics. Intelligence refers to not only having information that is relevent to a problem but the appropriate application of that information through an understanding of the problem. Intelligence is exercised both individually and collectively in making decisions about action. Status refers to the recognition of worth of the individual or group and the accordance of respect for the needs and actions of the individual or group. It influences how others react. These characteristics focus on how human beings interact with each other in their decision making. These characteristics recognize that human action is a critical factor in the sustainability of the natural as well as the human ecosystem.

Natural ecosystems functions

In order to understand and develop natural watersheds and wetlands in a fashion that is sustainable it is necessary to understand and work with the key functions of these systems. Savory (1988) identified what he considered the key ecological functions of an ecosystem to be: "Succession/life cycling", "Hydrologic cycling", "Mineral cycling", and "Energy cycling". Water clearly plays a key role in the functioning of any ecosystem providing a key link between energy nutrients and living plants and animals. Conway (1991) identified the critical characteristics of an ecosystem that provides for sustainability. These characteristics include productivity, stability, diversity, and resilience. Productivity refers to the ability of the ecosystem to support the growth of organisms. Stability refers to the range of conditions that are maintained within the ecosystem by the inertia or positive feedback within the system. Diversity refers to the range of opportunities for adaptation of organisms that are developed within the ecosystem. Diversity tends to link to stability in most ecosystems. Resilience is the ability of the ecosystem to adjust to a stable state after severe disturbance.

Implications of the whole ecosystems approach

In the development of science and management of sustainable watersheds and wetlands it is necessary to have an understanding that integrates all of the functional characteristics identified for both sustainable human and natural ecosystems. The challenge is to develop knowlege that provides an understanding of the implications of decisions and actions made in the human ecosystems for the sustainability of the natural ecosystem and in turn the necessary characteristics of sustainable natural ecosystems for supporting sustainable human ecosystems. In order to link human ecosystems science with natural ecosystems science there are a number of areas where our capacity to understand and act need to be improved.

NEW INFORMATION AND INFORMATION MANAGEMENT

In the past much emphasis in water resource development and management was focused on information required to design and implement structural solutions to quantity and quality problems. Conceptualization of the watershed as an ecosystem requires more than a disciplinary approach to the understanding of the system. It requires science which includes a much greater scope of information both in terms of the subject matter (physical hydrology, water quality, aquatic biology, terrestrial

6

biology, engineering, economics, sociology and environmental psychology) but also it requires data which provides for an understanding of the temporal and spatial dynamics of these phenomena. This has given rise to the need for integrated databases which are linked through relational structures referenced with respect to both space and time.

In addition to the transdisciplinary nature of the ecosystems approach we can no longer ignore the vast amounts of data, information and knowledge that are available from "local indigenous sources". Traditionally there has been a tendency to discount this knowledge as being too qualitative, inconsistent and imprecise to be of utility in a scientific understanding of the ecosystem. However it is being discovered that this information can be valid and reliable as well as precise and accurate for use in defining the ecosystem and its functioning. It can be used in the development of interventions for the management of water by extending the usually limited (spatially and temporally) scientific measurements that we are able to make. A further advantage to the incorporation of local indigenous knowledge in the development of watershed initiatives is that it immediately involves the local community, who will be impacted by development, in meaningful participation in the development process. This becomes even more significant if local people are further able to influence decision making through the influence of their knowledge.

Information technology has had a major impact on the development and management of watersheds and wetlands. The development of digital data base systems allows the assembly, storage and retrieval and analysis of massive amounts of technical data to improve our ability to model and predict the future condition of the resource and the demands that will be placed on it. The incorporation of Geographically referenced Information Systems (GIS) and the incorporation of remotely sensed information has provided greater ease of access to current data at scales of precision only dreamed of in the past. This has not only improved our precision and accuracy as a positive impact but raised the negative implication of data overload for both data management, analysis and decision making. The "front end" cost in terms of time and effort for development of these systems has led to difficulty in many cases. However when the linking of the data systems to advanced models and decision software is achieved it results in a marvelous tool for the testing of the impacts of alternative management scenarios. This provides for much greater understanding of the impacts of intervention prior to final decisions being made. Thus we avoid many of the mistakes that might have been made and many unintended adverse effects being mitigated after the fact of development.

A continuing challenge is the integration of the newly recognized body of indigenous knowledge with the body of scientific knowledge in an effective fashion. This will require the quantification of some qualitative information and the use of some qualitative data with quantitative data in analytical models. There has been a schism between qualitative and quantitative analysis in science which reflects the split between that which is called social science and what is traditionally thought of as science. The new data based systems have gone some way in providing for integrated storage and retrieval but the area of integrating qualitative with quantitative models lags behind.

NEW AND APPROPRIATE TECHNOLOGIES

Technology will play a key role in the development of sustainable watershed and wetlands. In the past we have thought of technology primarily in terms of engineering technology used to extract, transport, store, process and deliver water and wastewater. This technology will continue to be important in managing water. However alternative technologies which include the development of small scale integrated water systems at the household and village level will become more important in the future. These technologies will be by their nature appropriate to the capacity of the household and community in terms of development and maintenance. They will include new approaches to the development of ground water, new approaches to water capture and storage, new pump technologies, new approaches to sanitation with respect to both water supply and waste water treatment. In addition they will include soft technologies such as demand management especially in urban areas, community based management systems and multiple use systems. Many of these improvements will stem from the laboratory but many more will be developed in the community laboratory through participatory development which will incorporate local and scientific knowledge.

A further refinement of technology which is part of sustainable water resources development is the development of eco-technology. This is manifest on two fronts; the use of natural systems and modified natural systems to improve the management of water and the enhancement and rehabilitation of natural systems to improve their functioning. Examples of eco-technology are the development of artificial wetlands which are used to receive and process wastewater. Many of these can also be designed to provide habitat for fish and wildlife at the same time though

8

they may lack the capacity to provide for biodiversity and the quality of productivity found in natural systems. The development of habitat for natural populations of fish and wildlife can provide alternative income and food through enhanced harvesting and other activities. The development of habitat systems that provide for biological control of many insect and disease threats represents a potential safe means of controlling these vectors using eco-technology. Eco-technology offers a great opportunity to integrate the rest of the ecosystem with the needs of the human community in a way that provides for a broad range of benefits for both.

Participation

It has been stated that the environment does not have problems - people do. While one may not agree with this completely the statement emphasizes the importance of the role of involvement of the community of interest in the process of development and management of the environment. In the past the mode of operation of development has been one of institutionally initiated development under "top-down" policies. With the restructuring of central governments and delegation of responsibility to local governments and non-governmental groups here has been an increasing requirement for support of local people in developing and managing watersheds and wetlands. Local people have been involved in the planning, design and implementation of development and the management and maintenance of the undertakings.

The result has been a change in the way that development proceeds. Environmental impact assessments are increasingly being required to include the interested and affected public at the earliest stages of development. Indeed progressively we will see locally initiated development with the government and NGO agencies facilitating and supporting these initiatives. The use of local knowledge in the process of design, construction and management of projects will in the future become more normal. The challenge for the research and management community will be to make these complicated multi-stakeholder processes more efficient while maintaining effective participation.

The Current Volume

This volume contains the results of some of the research supported by the ECEP project. The scope of the research is very broad and encompasses every thing from innovative technology and information technology, to biology to community and local knowledge research. This is demonstrative of the complexity of the requirements of sustainable development. Much progress has been made but much is yet to be discovered. Improvements suggested by the research need to be made operational so that the benefits can reach the practitioner and the community .

Projects like ECEP that provide for this multidisciplinary research on a broad front aimed at development, that provide for the dissemination of this knowledge and advance the transfer of skills and knowledge to a wide range of professionals and practitioners play a key role in the effective development of sustainability for the water resources of the region. There is clearly great capacity in the region that, when mobilized, will provide much of the means necessary to succeed in developing Eastern and Southern Africa's water resources for a sustainable future.

REFERENCES

Conway, G. R. 1991: *Sustainability in Agricultural Development: Tradeoffs with Productivity, Stability and Equitability*. A paper presented at the 11th Annual AFSR/E Symposium, Michigan, Oct. 5-10.

Mazer, C. 1998: *Setting the Stage for Sustainability: a Citizen's Handbook*. Boca Raton, Fl.: Lewis Publishers.

Mazer, C. 1999: *Vision and Leadership in Sustainable Development*. Boca Raton, Fl.: Lewis Publishers.

Naveh, Z. and Liberman A. 1984: *Landscape Ecology: Theory and Application*. New York, NY.: Springer Verlag.

Savory, A. 1988: *Holistic Resource Management*. Covello, Calif.: Island Press.

Chapter 2

THE DEVELOPMENT OF A HYDROLOGICAL DECISION SUPPORT SYSTEM FOR THE MHLATUZE RIVER CATCHMENT AREA IN KWAZULU-NATAL.

by Bruce Kelbe, Ray Kostaschuk, Nina Snyman and Laura Brown

INTRODUCTION

Developments in the computer software industry have shown that highly complex systems can be developed into packages which make their applications much easier to use. The Windows Operating System (OIS) converted DOS into an operating system which is now routinely used by many people who don't have any knowledge of computer programming. This project is based on the belief that similar tools can be developed which incorporate models of complex environmental issues for easy use by planners and managers. These tools form a Decision Support System (DSS) that links numerical models of the environment and a detailed information database into a single system which is capable of presenting the spatial information through a Graphical User Interface (GUI).

Recent designs of computer hardware and software have enabled PC-based Geographic Information Systems (GIS) to become accessible and affordable tools for research and planning. Every computerized office uses one of many Office Suites of computer programmes, and environmental software tools (expert systems) abound for predicting aspects of catchment management and environmental issues. Here we aim to build a DSS around selected components of these three common computerized systems (Figure 2.1) as a single tool that planners and managers can apply for sustainable development of river catchments. In this project, we focus on the Mhlatuze River in KwaZulu-Natal, South Africa.

Figure 2.1 Schematic of the DSS components

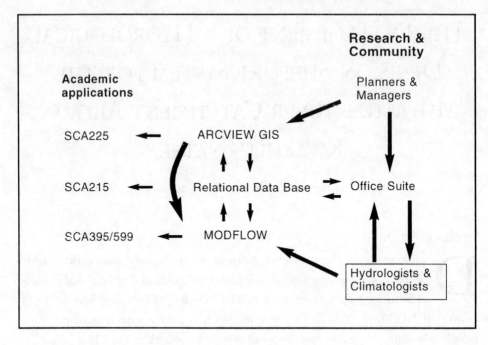

numerical systems and integrating them into a single system. This will require considerable capacity building in the Department of Hydrology at the University of Zululand, through the assistance of other institutions (University of Guelph and the Institute of Water Research at Rhodes University). The system being developed will be used in the teaching and learning programmes of the Department of Hydrology at both undergraduate and postgraduate levels, particularly if the DSS becomes an integral part of local management of the regional water resources in KwaZulu-Natal.

Aims and objectives

This project has two broad aims:
- To develop a hydrological decision support system (DSS) for the Mhlatuze catchment. This will include methodologies for integrating information storage, retrieval and dissemination together with expert opinion.
- To develop the capacity at the University of Zululand for appropriate postgraduate training of hydrologists and water resource managers for the Zululand region.

This report focuses on the selection and application of the catchment hydrologic model that is the integral component of the DSS. The objectives of the research are to:

▶ Acquire, assimilate and capture all relevant spatial and temporal information into a GIS. The information data base will be used to derive the parameter set for inclusion into the hydrologic model.

▶ Select a suitable catchment hydrologic model. The model must be PC-based with networking abilities and have the capability of determining the groundwater and transmission losses that are major elements of the Mhlatuze system.

▶ Validate the discharge and water quality simulations for the estimated Mhlatuze parameter set during normal and extreme hydrological conditions. The severe floods of 1984 and 1987 together with the present drought should provide a full range of conditions for model validation.

▶ Assess the problems of data intensity and field data collection imposed by the model. This will allow evaluation of the model as a planning and decision tool for developing countries in the southern Africa region.

GEOGRAPHIC INFORMATION SYSTEM

Acquire, assimilate and capture all relevant spatial and temporal information on each subcatchment into a Geographic Information System (GIS). The information data base will be used to derive the parameter set for inclusion into the hydrologic model.

Three basic types of data have been collected. Sequential-temporal data at specific locations has been sourced, acquired and captured. Geographically-referenced spatial information has been purchased in various forms from different organizations and a variety of reports have been consulted. The groundwater information is presently being captured into a form compatible with the SA National Groundwater Database (HYDROCOM). Data sources are summarized in Table 2.1.

A Geographic Information System is being used to manage and analyze data and is a fundamental component of this project. A GIS can handle spatial co-ordinates, topological information and the attributes associated with geometric entities (McDonnell, 1993), but data must be converted to digital format before simulation of processes and variable interactions can begin (Nyerges, 1991). GIS can be used for overlay mapping where information such as soils, geology, elevation and precipitation are stored in separate layers. GIS is also used to assess hydrological phenomena and determine hydrological parameters for input into the model.

Table 2.1 Data sets acquired and included in the Mhlatuze DSS

DATA	TYPE	INFORMATION & SOURCE
Sequential data	Rainfall	69 daily station series from the CCWR (University of Natal)
	Flow data	8 Monthly & Daily evaporation series from the DWAF data base
	Evaporation data	8 Monthly & Daily evaporation series from the DWAF data base
	Farm dams	Position of registered dams from maps, DWAF data base and field trips
	River extractions	Pumping rates for 1997 from Mhlatuze Water Board
	Irrigation	KwaZulu Farmers scheme
		Heatonville scheme
		Mfuli scheme
		Nkwaleni scheme
	Groundwater/ Boreholes	National Groundwater data base has been obtained and is being updated by the HRU from various sources Uthongulu Regional Council
Geographically referenced	Soil type information	Maps and profiles have been acquired from the Institute of Soils and Irrigation
	Land use information	WR90 GIS data set incudes general hydrological information for the entire country
	Satellite images	LANDSAT TM (March 1997) image has been acquired from local sources
	Groundwater Resources	Surveys and Land Information
	Digital elevation Model	Contours are being digitized from 1:50 000 topographical maps
Reports	White papers	G-61: Nkwaleni Irrigation Board Q-73 & Q-79: Mhlatuze Government Water Scheme, Goedertrouw Dam Heatonville irrigation scheme Environmental Legislation Water Legislation

HYDROLOGICAL MODELLING SYSTEM

Select a suitable catchment hydrologic model. The model must be PC-based with networking capabilities and have the capability of determining the groundwater and transmission losses

14

that are major elements of the Mhlatuze system.

A major task in hydrology, and in hydrologic modelling, is to explain the relationship between precipitation and streamflow (More, 1967). In the hydrologic cycle, precipitation is the "input" and streamflow is the "output". The components of the hydrologic cycle include evaporation, transpiration, precipitation, runoff, infiltration, interflow, percolation into groundwater storage, and surface storage in wetlands, ponds, lakes and oceans. A catchment is the topographic area that contributes water to a stream, the routes and rates of which are controlled by catchment characteristics such as soil type, land-cover and topography (Wolock & McCabe, 1995). Hydrological models are designed to simulate hydrologic responses and are used to simplify and generalize a complex reality (More, 1967), to predict hydrological events, and to predict availability for water resource planning. For example, models are needed for flood estimation and assessing the hydrological impacts of land use change (Grayson, Moore & McMahon, 1992). Floods are typically modelled as single events, while continuous simulations over long time periods are used to assess the impact of land use change.

Mathematical models may be empirical, stochastic or deterministic (Ward & Elliot, 1995). Empirical models are developed by identifying the relationship between inputs and outputs of a set of observations collected in the field or the laboratory. Stochastic models identify and predict the probability of the occurrence or the magnitude of a hydrologic event such as a rainstorm or a flood and incorporate elements of uncertainty into their structure. Deterministic models are based on classic mathematical descriptions of the cause and effect relationships among all the processes that impact catchment response including infiltration, percolation and interflow. Most catchment hydrologic models are deterministic.

Deterministic catchment hydrologic models can be classified as either conceptual or physically based on the basis of their treatment of physical processes within the catchment (Refsgaard, 1997). The parameters of conceptual models are often aggregates of physical processes that are largely empirically-based (Bergstrom, 1991) and values are model-specific coefficients with no physical meaning (Abbott *et. al.*, 1986). In contrast, physically-based models have a theoretical basis and parameters and variables are measurable in the field (Beven, 1989). Deterministic hydrologic models are also classified according to their description of spatial catchment processes as lumped, distributed (Refsgaard,

1997) or semi-distributed (Hughes & Sami, 1994). Deterministic hydrologic models therefore are either lumped conceptual models or physically-based distributed or semi distributed models.

A lumped model treats the catchment as a single spatial unit (Fleming, 1976) and parameters consist of an average value over the catchment. Several processes and their variability are often integrated into one representative value (Fleming, 1976; Bergstrom, 1991). The lumped model approach attempts to achieve a full simulation of catchment behaviour by treating components in a composite manner and simulating the behaviour of processes by largely empirical relationships (More, 1967; Fleming, 1976; Bergstrom, 1991; Seyfried & Wilcox, 1995). A major limitation of the lumped approach is that the entire catchment is treated as a homogenous unit as there is no mechanism to address catchment heterogeneity. Distributed models were developed to capture this heterogeneity (Hughes, 1993) and were made possible by high speed computer technology. Distributed models differ fundamentally from lumped models in that spatial heterogeneity is represented by providing data for a number of points within the catchment. These models place a grid over the catchment and parameter and variable data is input for each intersection point in the grid (Refsgaard, 1997). Semi-distributed models allow the user to divide the catchment into sub-areas, each with its own parameter set (Hughes, 1994). Sub-areas are characterized by homogeneity of several parameters, and each sub-area requires a single well-defined channel section draining into an adjacent sub-area (Hughes, 1989).

The number of parameters and data requirements differ greatly among these three model types. Lumped models require the least amount of data and typically have 5-10 parameters (Refsgaard & Knudsen, 1996). Distributed models are highly data intensive because parameters must be input for each grid element. The variable nature of earth materials coupled with the temporal and spatial variation of meteorological variables results in an enormous number of required measurements for distributed models (Jensen & Mantogiou, 1992). Beven (1989) found that around 2400 parameter values were required for the application of the SHE model in the Wye catchment. Semi-distributed models have fewer parameter values than distributed models, partly because the number of sub-areas is far less than the number of grid elements. However, any physically-based model has more parameters than a lumped model.

Computing power required by a model is dependent on the size of the program and the calculations required. Lumped models have low computing requirements, while physically-based models require much more computing power. If a GIS is used as either a database or coupled to the model, the computing power required increases dramatically. It is important to note that even the most rigorous mathematical models describing catchment response are crude representations of reality and while theoretical rigour of some models is impressive, it implies a degree of accuracy that may not exist (Grayson *et. al.*, 1996).

The HYMAS (Hydrological Model Application System) semi-distributed catchment hydrologic model (Hughes & Sami, 1994) was chosen for this project for several reasons. The model has moderate data requirements, can run on a PC and was developed at the Institute of Water Research Institute (IWR) at Rhodes University in South Africa for southern African conditions. HYMAS is modular and capable of including other models as part of a hydrological suite of programmes. The system provides basic parameterization of catchment features for several hydrological rainfall-runoff models including the Variable Time Interval Model (VTI), the PITMAN monthly runoff model and a reservoir simulation model (RESSIM). The model is also being applied locally in another project in the Richards Bay area as a tool for estimating spatially-derived groundwater recharge.

The VTI and RESSIM models have been examined and applied to the Mhlatuze catchment. Flow in the Mhlatuze River is driven by rainstorm events, so the DSS requires short time interval simulations rather than monthly simulations. HYMAS has its own proprietary data base which needs to be incorporated into the DSS. The model developers at Rhodes University are revising sections of the model to be compatible with Windows Operating Systems and to provide functions for displaying time series in suitable hydrological formats. These alterations and additions will be incorporated as they become available.

MODEL APPLICATION

Validate the discharge and water quality simulations for the estimated Mhlatuze parameter set during normal and extreme hydrological conditions. The severe floods of 1984 and 1987 together with the present drought should provide a full range of conditions for model validation.

The Mhlatuze catchment has been subdivided into several "homogeneous" sub-areas on the basis of physical features such as geology, landforms, soils and stream networks. Our intention is to use HYMAS in the DSS to investigate management scenarios which include changing land use, so land use will be a minor criteria in this catchment division. Since water abstraction can be simulated from anywhere within the sub-area, this is not considered a factor in delineating the sub-area boundaries.

Table 2.2 Mhlatuze hydrological project regions

#	Description	Code Name
1	Catchment of the Goedertrouw Dam	Goedertrouw
2	Catchment of the Mfuli River	Mfuli
3	Catchment of Lake Nsezi (Nseleni River)	Nsezi
4	Nkwaleni catchment of the Mhlatuze River (from Nkwaleni Valley to the DWAF weir W1H009)	Nkwaleni
5	Richard Bay catchment, covering the Mhlatuze River catchment downstream from the weir W1H009 to the outlet into the Mhlatuze lagoon at Richards Bay	Richards Bay

The Mhlatuze catchment has been subdivided into five simulation sub-projects (Table 2.2 and Figure 2.2) that have been assigned on the basis of hydrologic expertise. This allows an assessment of the transferability of the system to other regions in southern Africa. Seven undergraduate students at the University of Zululand (with a major in hydrology) are applying the VTI model to individual sub-areas in the Richards Bay project. These students are assumed to represent a "typical" researcher with a minimum level of academic training in the southern African region. Laura Brown (BSc Honours) is modelling the Mfuli project catchment as part of a MSc degree and represents a typical researcher in southern Africa with an expected academic level of training. Nina Snyman (BSc Honours) has undergone several weeks of training on the VTI model with the developers at Rhodes University and is considered to be capable of modifying model code and facilitating its transfer. Sonja Busch (MSc student) is evaluating the application of the model to a catchment in Richards Bay in a separate project but her evaluation is also considered here.

The seven undergraduates were given a very brief introduction to numerical modelling, the HYMAS parameter description, and then required to apply the VTI model to their sub-areas within the constraints of their normal academic programme. The postgraduate researchers are modelling the Mfuli project area

(Laura Brown) and the entire catchment (Nina Snyman). They have conducted field measurements and are presently undertaking the application of the model independently.

Figure 2.2 Mhlatuze catchment sub-division for HYMAS distributed modelling application

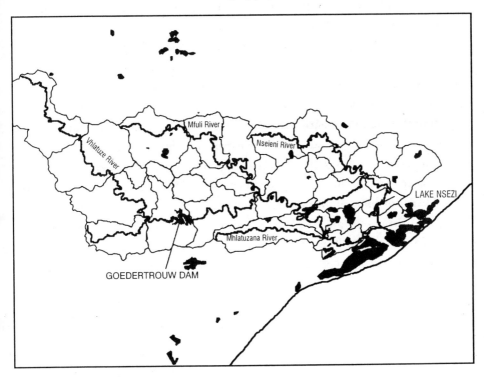

The VTI and RESSIM models have been set up with an initial set of parameter estimates derived from various sources (Table 2.1). All sub-project participants (graduates and undergraduates) had difficulty in estimating many of the parameters, primarily because of the brevity of the online instruction manual.

Calibration of the VTI Model

The preliminary results of the initial calibration presented here represent the first part of an iterative procedure for model application. The calibration period and the sub-areas used in the preliminary calibration are determined by the available observations.

▶ **1962 to 1992 period**: The simulated flow was compared with observations at the W1H009 weir in the Nkwaleni project area. The simulated flow included the simulated outflow from the Goedertrouw Dam and the Mfuli area. The observed daily flow at W1H009 and the simulated discharge series are shown in Figure 2.3. There is good agreement between observed and simulated flows in both the accumulated runoff and the individual hydrographs. Hydrograph peaks generally agree, but the simulations have a steeper recessional limb than actual flows.

1982 to 1986 period: This period covers a severe drought followed by two tropical cyclones which caused flooding in the region. The model underestimated the discharge during the drought periods and overestimated the discharge for a considerable length of time after the severe storm events.

WR90 Simulated Monthly Data: Simulations of the daily runoff model over the ten year period after the construction of the Goedertrouw Dam were compared to the simulated flows using the PITMAN model in the WR90 project. The Mean Annual Precipitation (MAP) and Mean Annual Runoff (MAR) for both simulations are shown in Table 2.3. The simulations for the post-dam period (82 to 92) have a lower MAP than the pre-dam period (62 to 78) but the MAR in several sub-catchments is higher for the corresponding period. Similar discrepancies occur for some of the other sub-catchments.

Figure 2.3 Daily rainfall (A) and simulated flows (B) for the Mfuli catchment,
January 1 – December 31, 1990

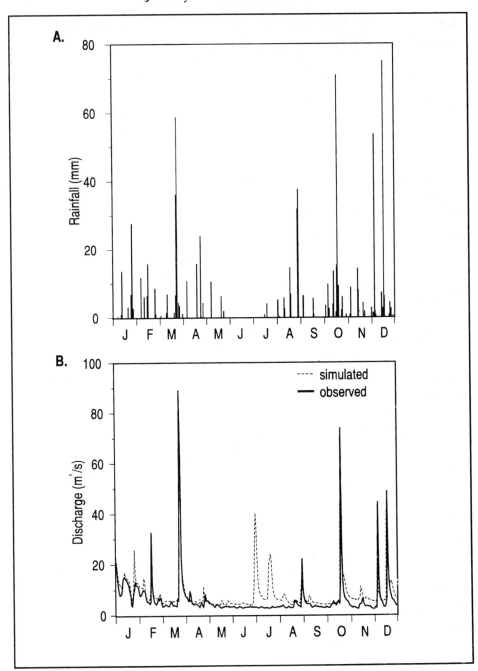

Table 2.3 MAP (mm) and MAR (* 10^6 m^3) for the Goedertrouw project before and after dam construction

| Sub Catchment | HYMAS Simulation results | | | | WR90 (60 years) | |
| | 82 to 92 (10 years) | | 62 to 78 (16 years) | | | |
	MAP	MAR	MAP	MAR	MAP	MAR
W12A	1080	266	1112	187	932	133
W12B	850	87	934	71	876	56
W12C	780	75	750	92	848	50
W12D	920	362	836	346	848	236
W12E	962	77	813	48	1041	40
W12G	1219	94	1004	55	835	30

Calibration of the RESSIM Model

The calibration of the RESSIM model requires an observed or simulated inflow to the dam. It also requires the operating management rules of the dam which apply to demand rather than compensation releases. Compensation releases are in addition to the spillway discharge and are not easily included in the RESSIM simulations, but the model developers are investigating changes to the software to include compensation releases. This is an important issue, as the new South African water law recognizes the environmental reserve of the system as an essential component of the water resources of a catchment, which must be sustained before any further use of the water resources is allocated.

TRANSFERABILITY OF THE MODELLING SYSTEM

Assess the problems of data intensity and field data collection imposed by the model. For countries in the region who have a much weaker data base the usefulness of the model will depend to a large extent on how easy it is to supply data inputs. From this analysis it would be possible to derive conclusions concerning the value of the model as a planning and decision tool for developing countries in the southern Africa region.

An important practical element of this project is to assess the problems of data intensity and field data collection imposed by the hydrological model. For countries in southern Africa with a much weaker data base, the usefulness of the model will depend to a large extent on how easy it is to supply data inputs.

    Our work to date has indicated several problems with the application of the

HYMAS model. The documentation is insufficient for a first-time user to apply the model in a complex situation like the Mhlatuze catchment. Many of the parameters are linked to others and it is not always clear which parameters are calculated from other information and which have to be specified individually. There are also several parameters which are difficult to estimate from the on-line manual because of a lack of understanding of their conceptual role in the model. It was necessary to consult with the model developers at Rhodes on a regular basis to overcome these two difficulties. This could be a serious transferability problem which may be encountered in some regions of southern Africa.

Operation of HYMAS requires a basic personal computer with a 386 or faster processor and a recent DOS operating system. However, hardware requirements increase substantially in both sophistication and cost if GIS and satellite imagery are utilized to their full potential. Application of HYMAS will generally require the use of satellite images since the regional data base is not likely to be extensive, especially in remote areas outside of South Africa. LANDSAT can provide data on land-use, vegetation cover, stream and lake distribution, soil moisture and many other inputs required for HYMAS parameters. SPOT multi-spectral satellite imagery can provide similar information as well as a digital elevation model (DEM), but the cost is very high. High RAM (>16 MB) and a 486 or faster processor is needed for GIS. Most satellite imagery is contained on a CD, so a CD-ROM drive is required. The LANDSAT image that we purchased contained all seven bands as a single file and there were problems down loading the file on a 486 PC with limited ROM. A Unix mainframe was required to parse the LANDSAT data in our study, which could be a major limitation for developing countries.

A basic GIS (ARCVIEW) is around CAN$700 and a LANDSAT satellite image around CAN$5,000. A suitably equipped PC with a colour printer would cost about CAN$3500. These hardware and software requirements would impose some financial constraints on the transferability of the system, but parameter estimation and model operation would be the greatest restriction in southern Africa.

SUMMARY

The project proposal for the DSS outlined a three year development plan which involved the application of the GIS, database and hydrological modelling systems. Support for the proposal by ECEP was limited to a one year period and consequently only the hydrological model component was selected for development. The project team has applied the VTI and RESSIM models to the Mhlatuze Catchment and conducted preliminary calibration studies. The calibration indicates a reasonable degree of correspondence between the model simulations and observed runoff during specific periods, but further iterative calibration is required.

The HYMAS model is not "user-friendly" and the documentation and on-line support are poor. It will be necessary for operators to consult with the developers of the model at Rhodes University, which could be a serious transferability problem in some regions of southern Africa. The model clearly requires considerable training and assistance before it can be applied effectively by a resource manager. The extensive data base required for model input is unlikely to exist in developing countries, although satellite images may be useful for remote regions. Hardware and software costs may be substantial, especially if satellite images are used.

ACKNOWLEDGMENTS

The financial support of the Environmental Capacity Enhancement Program (ECEP), Natural Sciences and Engineering Research Council of Canada and the Foundation for Research Development (FRD) IRDP program is gratefully acknowledged. We are also extremely grateful for the assistance and support in the application of the HYMAS model from the Institute of Water Resources at Rhodes University, particularly Dr. V. Smakhtin and Prof. D. Hughes. Considerable assistance has been given by staff of the CCWR, University of Natal in the development of the DSS, particularly Dr. M. Dent, Mr. M. Horn and Mr. R. de Vos. We also thank Brian Rawlins for valuable comments and the undergraduate student participants (Cele, Mkhize, Mkhiza, May, Made, Magagula and Radebe) for assessing the models and providing field assistance during the course of their studies.

REFERENCES

Abbott, M.B., Bathurst, J.C., Cunge, J.A., O'Connell, P.E. and Rasmussen, J. 1986: An Introduction to the European Hydrological System-Systeme Hydrologique Européen: SHE, 1, History and philosophy of a physically-based, distributed modelling system. *Journal of Hydrology* 87, 45-59.

Beven, K. L. 1989: Changing ideas in hydrology - The case of physically-based models. *Journal of Hydrology* 105, 157-172.

Bergstrom, S. 1991: Principles and confidence in hydrological modelling. *Nordic Hydrology* 22, 123-136.

Department of Water Affairs and Forestry of South Africa. 1997: *Hydrological data: rainfall, evaporation, details of Goedertrouw Dam.*

Department of Water Affairs and Forestry. 1990: *Mhlatuze River Basin Study: Operational Analysis of the Extension Mhlatuze Water Resources System.* Report PW 120/00/0490.

Department of Water Affairs and Forestry. 1993: *Mhlatuze Basin Augmentation Feasibility Study.* Report PW 120/00/1093.

Director General, Water Affairs and Forestry. 1994-1995: *Report on the Proposed Tugela-Mhlatuze River Government Water Scheme.* White Paper E-94. Republic of South Africa.

Everson, C. 1997: *The Water Balance of a First Order Catchment in the Montane Grasslands of South Africa.* Eighth South African National Hydrology Symposium.

Fleming, G. 1976: *Deterministic models in hydrology.* FAO Irrigation and Drainage Paper 32. Rome: Food and Agriculture Organization of the United Nations.

Grayson, R.B., Moore, I.E. and McMahon, T.A. 1992: Physically based hydrologic modelling 2. Is the concept realistic? *Water Resources Research* 26, 2659-2666.

Hughes, D.A. 1989: Estimation of the parameters of an isolated event conceptual model from physical catchment characteristics. *Hydrologic Sciences Journal* 34, 539-557.

Hughes, D.A. 1993: Variable time intervals in deterministic hydrological models. *Journal of Hydrology* 143, 217-232.

Hughes, D.A. 1994: Soil moisture and runoff simulations using four catchment rainfall-runoff models. *Journal of Hydrology* 158, 381-404.

Hughes, D.A. and Sami, K. 1994: A semi-distributed, variable time interval model of catchment hydrology - structure and parameter estimation procedures. *Journal of Hydrology* 155, 265- 291.

Hughes, D.A. 1994: *HYMAS VI.0 Guide to the system and user manual.* Addendum to WRC Report N 235/1/93.

Jensen, K.H. and Mantoglou, A. 1992: Future of distributed modelling. *Hydrological Processes* 6, 255-264.

Kovar, K. and Nachtnebel, H.P. 1993: Applications of Geographic Information Systems in Hydrology and Water Resources Management. *IAHS AISH, Proceedings of the Vienna Conference, April 1993.* IAHS Publ. No. 211.

Lillis and, T.M. and Kiefer, R.W. 1994: *Remote Sensing and Image Interpretation, Third Edition.* John Wiley & Sons, Inc.

Linsley and Franzini. 1979: *Water Resources Engineering, National Student Edition.* McGraw-Hill International Book Company.

Macvicar, C.N. *et al.* 1977: *Soil Classification. A Binominal System for South Africa.* The Soil and Irrigation Research Institute, Department of Agricultural Technical Services.

Martini, E. and Associates. 1994: *Characterization and Mapping of the Groundwater Resources, KwaZulu-Natal Province.* Undertaken on behalf of the Project Steering Committee. KwaZulu-Natal: Hydrogeological Mapping Unit.

McDonnell, R.A. and Macmillan, W.D. 1993: A GIS based hierarchical simulation model for assessing the impacts of large dam projects. In *Application of Geographical Information Systems in Hydrology and Waer Resources Management.* Oxfordshire: IAHS Press.

Meijerink, A.M.J., de Brouwer, H.A.M., Mannaerts, C.M. and Valenzuela, C.R. 1994: *Introduction to the Use of Geographic Information Systems for Practical Hydrology.* The International Institute for Aerospace Survey and Earth Sciences (ITC).

Meyer, R. 1997: *ISCOR Heavy Minerals Project. Environmental Impact Assessment, Special Study-Water Supply.*

Midgley, D.C., Pitman, W.V. and Middleton, B.J. 1994: *Surface Water Resources of South Africa 1990, Volume VI, First Edition 1994.* Water Research Commission Report No. 298/6.1/94.

More, R.J. 1967: Hydrologic models and geography. In R.J. Chorley and P. Haggett (eds), *Models in Geography.* London: Methuen & Co.

Nyerges, T.L. 1991: Analytical map use. *Cartography and Geographic Information Systems* 18, 11-22.

Refsgaard, J.C. 1997: Parameterization, calibration and validation of distributed hydrological models. *Journal of Hydrology* 198, 69-97.

Refsgaard, J.C. and Knudsen, J. 1996: Operational validation and intercomparison of different hydrologic models. *Water Resources Research* 32, 2189-2202.

Seyfried, M. S. and Wilcox, B.P. 1995: Scale and the nature of spatial variability: field examples having implications for hydrologic modelling. *Water Resources Research* 31, 173-184.

Streeter, V.L. 1962: *Fundamentals of Fluid Mechanics.* McGraw-Hill Book Company, Inc.

Ven te Chow, *et al.* 1988: *Applied Hydrology.* McGraw-Hill Book Company, Inc.

Ward, A.D. and Elliot, W.J. 1995: *Environmental Hydrology.* Florida: CRC Press LLC.

Wolock, D.M. and McCabe Jr., G.J. 1995: Comparison of single and multiple flow direction algorithms for computing topographic parameters in TOPMODEL. *Water Resources Research* 31, 1315-1324.

Chapter 3

A Landscape Ecological Approach to Sustainability: Application of the Communicative Catchment Approach to Lake Chilwa, Malawi

by Robert Brown and Meya Kalindekafe

Introduction

Human land use has led to world-wide degradation of the ecological environment. There is an urgent need to adopt sustainable land use practices. Landscape management and landscape ecology have provided valuable information to assist towards this goal, but the input and cooperation of local residents is absolutely necessary. "Communicative catchment" is an approach that allows both experts and residents to be involved in land use decisions, as well as in evaluating the long-term effectiveness of their action. When coupled with principles of landscape ecology (e.g. Forman, 1995), this method has potential for application in the Malawian context. The community, as participants, manages the catchment, while the resource managers have a role in action research, facilitating and coordinating community involvement and action.

Theoretical Background

The "Community Catchment" approach is described by Martin (1991) as action-based research (experts taking theory-based participatory action with communities) and systematic thinking (including the interrelationship between social and natural environments). Martin (1991) has suggested that lack of sustainable action in land use seems to be based on individuals' perceptions of what the problems are. It is often very difficult for individuals to be aware of slow, incremental processes, such as increased salinity, soil degradation or forest fragmentation. Part of the challenge of the environmental care of catchments is sensitizing individuals to these larger patterns in their environment.

Martin (1991) has also provided descriptions of four types of catchment management: reduced, mechanical, complex, and communicative.

Our approach has incorporated characteristics of the first three types of catchments along with principles of landscape ecology, into the fourth type, communicative catchment. From the reduced catchment approach, we included mapping and evaluation of each of the biophysical resources in isolation. From the mechanical catchment, we considered the integration of these biophysical resources and recognized the dynamic characteristics and connections within the catchment. From the complex evolving catchment, we utilized the concept that everything is always changing and evolving in both structure and process, and the recognition of the complexity of the human – community – environment interaction. Finally, from landscape ecology (e.g. Forman, 1995), we have utilized the concepts of mapped landscape units.

These components have been integrated into the communicative catchment (Martin, 1991), which emphasizes community responsibility and dialogue and involves working collaboratively with residents to facilitate problem identification and action strategies.

STUDY SITE

The study was undertaken in Malawi's Lake Chilwa catchment. Malawi is a landlocked country in central eastern Africa, with surface waters covering more than 20% of its area. Lake Chilwa is a shallow, closed, saline lake which lies in the south of the country and in the centre of the low-lying Chilwa-Phalombe plain. Although the lake is almost completely within Malawi, the catchment is shared with Mozambique. Throughout Africa, there are many large, shallow lakes with small volume and extensive littoral zones. Lake Chilwa, therefore, provides a valuable case study.

Lake Chilwa is surrounded by dense swamps and marshes, up to 25 km wide in some areas. The seasonally inundated grassland floodplain forms a belt around the marshes of the lake. The lake has a number of islands, two of which are permanently inhabited. The lake measures 40 km by 30 km, and is at approximately 622 metres above sea level, with a maximum depth of less than five metres. Seven main perennial rivers drain into the lake, and both perennial and seasonal influent rivers carry a high suspended load during the rainy season. The lake catchment is an almost treeless plain of approximately four times the area of the lake (8349 km^2).

The lake water fluctuates seasonally, but in years of drought the lake will dry out completely, as it did in 1968 and again in 1995. The immediate consequences of the 1968 drought were devastating to both the environment and the fishing communities (Kalk, McLachlan & Williams, 1979), but fish populations recovered completely within approximately four years.

Lake Chilwa, which has been chosen as a Ramsar Site (a convention recognizing wetlands of international significance with the goal of sustainable development), supports 153 species of resident waterbirds and 50 species of migratory waterbirds. Socio-economically, the Lake Chilwa wetlands are important because of fishing (29 species of fish), agriculture (wetland rice cultivation, dimba cultivation, irrigated rice cultivation, and livestock) and human settlement. The principal economic use of the lake is fishing, with estimated annual catches ranging from about 25 to 30% of the total fish production in Malawi. Recurrent droughts and conflicts in land use have caused a substantial decline in the production of Lake Chilwa. This means less protein in the population's diet, and less income for the fishers. It is important that the Lake Chilwa watershed environment be managed in a sustainable manner. The fishery is conducted by over 6,000 people, which is an increase of 250% over the last 10 years, largely due to immigration from Lake Malombe where the fishery collapsed (Kabwazi & Wilson, 1996). Together with fish processors and traders and other supporting services, the total number of people dependent on Lake Chilwa is estimated at 36,000 (Kabwazi & Wilson, 1996). The total population within the watershed is somewhat dependent on the fishery as well; this effect decreases with distance from the lake.

Despite the importance of the lake, no management plan exists and very little research has been conducted. From 1966 to 1972, the University of Malawi investigated the changes in the Chilwa ecosystem during the dry and recovery phases of the lake. Effects on flora, fauna, and the people were monitored and evaluated. Results showed that a lot of ecological change had resulted. The only other study was conducted in 1989 (University of Bristol, 1989) and it was only after the 1995 drying that a management plan was proposed (Chiotha, Kabwazi & Njaya, 1996). This work, however, was based on a two-day workshop and a short visit to the dry lake bed. It was not comprehensive and did not involve local residents. Chancellor's College, University of Malawi, conducted a study to have the lake accepted as a Ramsar site, and this provided baseline information that was previously unavailable.

As Lake Chilwa is a closed system with no outflow, anything introduced into the local environment stays in the local environment. This has important implications for the use of chemicals in farming. Traditional land use includes cutting trees to provide fuel for cooking. As a result, the violent rainstorms typical of the rainy season erode the bare soil into the lake. The loss of habitat and high human population density have resulted in the near extirpation of many species of plants and animals. The area is also susceptible to the invasion of introduced exotic plants. Overall, human impact on the land has created very unstable conditions.

METHODOLOGY

The steps taken in this study, within the context of the communicative catchment approach, were:

- identification of landscape units
- participatory rural appraisal with residents in each landscape unit
- interviews with extension coordinators in relevant government ministries
- collaborative action research with residents in selected landscape units
- evaluation of effectiveness of actions taken.

Identification of landscape units

The biological and physical resources of the site were first mapped based on published reports and maps. This was done at two scales: a general characterization of the whole watershed and detailed studies of two transects – one west and one south of the lake. The east side of the lake is in Mozambique and was outside the bounds of this study. Each transect was run from the lakeshore to the edge of the watershed, following parallel to a road or passable trail. The two transects were located so as to sample as many of the different biophysical and social environments in the catchment as possible. Data were collected along each transect and used to validate and upgrade information interpreted from the maps and reports. The study team consisted of five individuals (four Malawians and one Canadian) with expertise in areas of biology, ecology, plant identification, landscape ecology, geography, soils, and landscape architecture. As the team moved away from the lake, each different landscape unit (identified either from published maps or due to noticeable differences in the environment) was sampled. At each site, soil samples were taken for laboratory analysis and vegetation surveys were completed. In this way, a detailed inventory was completed for the two transects. This information was utilized for determination of landscape units.

Participatory rural appraisal

The biophysical transects were also used as a basis for collecting local knowledge. A process of Participatory Rural Appraisal (e.g. The National Environment Secretariat, Government of Kenya, circa 1990) was used to gather spatial and temporal data on land use, as well as information on social and cultural systems. Through a series of meetings with residents of local villages, differences in land use and socio-cultural characteristics throughout the catchment were identified. The categories of information that the local residents provided information on included:

- current land use and management
- existing cultivated and natural vegetation
- social systems
- economic situation
- cultural information
- habitation and settlement patterns
- land ownership and responsibility
- local wild and domestic animals
- problems
- opportunities
- information on different crops and activities in various seasons

Typically, the process involved meeting with the local headman and gaining permission to talk with the whole village. The villagers were then invited and the headman made a formal introduction. The study team then engaged the community in conversation to gather information on each category. In many situations, the villagers were asked to draw resource maps on the ground and to provide information on their seasonal activities.

This local knowledge was used, through matrix evaluation, to evaluate the sustainability of the land use activities in each village, and to categorize the problems and opportunities in each village.

Interviews with extension coordinators

Extension coordinators in Malawi's Departments of Forestry, Agriculture, Fisheries, and the Tree Seed Office were interviewed. They were asked to comment on any land use problems that they were aware of, and how the department was attempting to resolve them. These government practices were compared with perceptions of the local residents.

Collaborative action research

Once the data were collected and analyzed, landscape units with particularly degraded environments were identified. A village in one of these areas was selected and offered the opportunity to engage in action research. Further meetings were held, in which the researchers facilitated discussion among the residents, leading to a prioritization of their problems and actions that they would like to take.

Evaluating effectiveness of actions

Measures of sustainability have been identified and will be monitored over time to determine the effectiveness of various actions taken.

RESULTS

Landscape units

A total of eight landscape units were identified along transect A and 12 along transect B. There was considerable variation in such key biophysical characteristics as land slope, diversity and abundance of vegetation and mammal species, and land use activities.

Some notable situations were recorded:

▶ Throughout the catchment there were graveyards that were completely covered with native *brachystegia* woodland. The people will not disturb these areas for cultural reasons, so they remain as a sample of almost untouched native ecosystems.

▶ The shore at the southern end of the lake has been invaded by an exotic shrub (*prosopis*) that is, according to the local residents, spreading at a rate of one km per year. It is displacing native vegetation along the lake edge.

Local knowledge

Land ownership and responsibility were found to be based on traditional practices, passed down through a hierarchical system which ultimately distributes small parcels of land to individuals who then live on and farm the land.

Information collected from individuals in different villages and transects, regarding seasonal land use activities, showed considerable similarities. This indicates a strong climatic effect throughout the catchment area.

One of the most important components of the local knowledge was the perception of problems and opportunities. The people generally had difficulty identifying opportunities, but had no difficulty identifying problems. These could be categorized into problems related to:

- transportation
- health facilities
- need for advice from government extension workers
- schools
- water
- deforestation
- soil erosion and soil fertility loss
- access to loans.

Government practices

In general, it was found that the extension departments provided information to groups of people rather than to individuals. In almost every community where people were interviewed, there were citizens who felt marginalized and unable to gain information available to others because they were not part of a committee. Committees are comprised of villagers and function as liaisons between extension workers and villagers. This situation provides a serious break in communication.

The mixed success in extension workers' efforts to promote reforestation, for example, point to the variety of problems. The Department of Agriculture identified the limited availability of tree seeds. Other situations described included:

- local residents removing reforestation projects along river edges for vegetable plantings
- the perception that trees are "god-given" and don't require cultivation or conservation

33

- the difficulty of caring for seedlings planted close to a water source (for irrigation), but far from the villagers' homes
- the lack of brochures or take-away information for cultivation of seedlings.

Action taken

The village of Kachoka on transect A was selected for action research based on its severely degraded environment, large number of problems, accessibility by vehicle, and the fact that the local population was agreeable to being involved in action research.

The first activity was the prioritization of problems facing the community. After considerable discussion, which was facilitated by the research team, the community arrived at a consensus. Their problems, in order of priority, were:
- limited availability of water
- deforestation and soil degradation
- lack of loans
- lack of advice
- lack of transportation, schools, and health facilities.

The community agreed that their biggest limitation was the inability to control their water supply. They concluded that if they could regulate their water supply, particularly during seasonal extremes, all the other problems facing the community could be resolved.

The community's second priority to replant trees, improve soil fertility, and reduce soil erosion, is closely linked to the water issue.

Information on the topics of water management, reforestation and soil improvement has been gleaned from the scientific literature, magazines, experiences in other similar environments, and from government extension offices. This information will be communicated with the local residents through a series of meetings and workshops.

Measures of sustainability

The research team will monitor the changes in land use through both satellite images and field study. The environment in and around Kachoka Village will be monitored in terms of tree cover, soil fertility, and socio-economic factors as reported by the village residents.

DISCUSSION

A substantial amount of new information about all aspects of the catchment was revealed through this study. It provided insight into local society and culture, and how these characteristics affected land use and management. Problems were identified, but the local residents were largely unable to suggest long-term, sustainable solutions.

The people in the study site have a relatively short, hard life. Most have had little, if any, formal schooling. Stories shared by villagers suggest a very low level of awareness of basic science and no traditional ecological knowledge. Any information provided must be presented in a manner that is understandable within the villagers' specific context. This was underscored by one Forestry Department extension worker's description of a Western aid program for local tree planting. Seedlings were purchased through foreign donations and provided free to local residents, who were trained and hired to initially plant, irrigate and transplant seedlings in return for food. However, residents stopped taking care of the trees once aid workers left and their food "payment" ceased. Two characteristics of this program led to problems. First, the local people felt that the trees belonged to the aid agency and did not take "ownership" unless they were being paid to do the work. Second, by providing free seedlings to the people, an expectation was created that trees do not cost anything and should be provided for free. People are not prepared to pay for seeds or for seedlings because of the perception that they have no value.

From these stories, it is clear that land use decisions must be made with great care, and the residents of the Lake Chilwa catchment must be involved in every aspect.

SUMMARY AND CONCLUSIONS

The concept of the communicative catchment (Martin, 1991) was found to be an appropriate basis for the approach to this study. However, due to considerable differences in the social, cultural, and environmental settings from Martin's original study in Australia (1991), the framework was modified for this study. The limited amount and coarse detail of published biophysical, social, cultural, and economic information on the Lake Chilwa catchment necessitated considerable emphasis on the collection of field data, through both environmental transects and participatory rural appraisal. Also, due to low literacy levels of the Lake Chilwa catchment population, transfer of information became a very important factor. The local residents wanted information and assistance from the government, but the government extension coordinators said that this information was already being provided to the people. The researchers became facilitators of information through listening to what the local residents said that they wanted to do, finding the appropriate information, and communicating it to them.

The "expert knowledge", gained through collection of biophysical data, indicated that few "natural areas" remained in the catchment. Most of the land had been significantly altered for human use, and vegetation, wildlife, soils, and water were all significantly degraded. This knowledge assisted in identifying the problems. However, while technical solutions exist for each of these problems, it was not clear which would be successful.

The "local knowledge", gained through participatory rural appraisal, helped explain why there are few "natural areas" and why the land has been utilized so intensively. It also directed researchers to what the local residents see as problems, which ones they are most interested in resolving, and what types of technical solutions might by appropriate.

The village that was engaged in action research decided that their first priority was water management. They wanted more control over the amount and timing of water availability.

Their second priority was reforestation and care of the soil. They identified some problems as being beyond their control (e.g. improved health facilities), while water, reforestation, and soil management were all activities that local farmers could act on as individuals and as communities.

The results of the study include:

▸ acquisition of biophysical data that was previously unavailable
▸ social, cultural, economic, and land use information about local population that was previously unavailable
▸ insight into what local residents consider to be major problems
▸ agreement among residents and researchers on actions to be taken to rectify the environmental degradation
▸ a positive relationship between residents and researchers, in which both realize they learn from the other – and optimism that problems can be resolved.

RECOMMENDATIONS FOR FURTHER STUDY

Future work should continue the process that has been started in this study. The action research should be monitored to measure its success in making land use changes and increasing the sustainability of the environment. Also, the work should be extended to other communities within the catchment. Approaches for sharing information should be explored, including communication of information among farmers through wind-up radios.

The limited availability of biophysical data and the ready availability of satellite images offer the opportunity for a geographic information system (GIS) approach to studying and monitoring the environment. This approach would also allow modeling of environmental changes based on land use activities. Measurements of ecological integrity of the landscape would be made and monitored.

The local graveyards are a key resource as, in many cases, they provide the only natural environment in the catchment. However, due to local customs, people will not touch them or allow them to be used in any way. One possibility would be to establish regeneration areas immediately adjacent to the graveyards and let the native vegetation invade. Seeds and seedlings in the regeneration area could then be used to reforest other areas.

Overall, the process was successful in gathering relevant data and providing a forum for local people and experts to communicate and make decisions about future land use activities that might lead to a more sustainable environment.

REFERENCES

Chiotha, S.S., Kabwazi, H.H. and Njaya, F.J. 1996: Management Plan for Lake Chilwa and its Catchment. *Proceedings of a workshop jointly organized by the Department of Fisheries and the University of Malawi.* January 11-12, 1996.

Forman, R.T.T. 1995: *Land Mosaics. The Ecology of Landscapes and Regions.* Cambridge: Cambridge University Press.

Hardin, G.J. 1968: The tragedy of the commons. *Science*, 162, 1243-1248.

Kabwazi, H.H. and Wilson, J.G. 1996: The Fishes and Fishery of Lake Chilwa. In *Lake Chilwa Ramsar Site Study Report.* Zomba: University of Malawi Press.

Kalk, M., McLachlan, A.J. and Williams, J. 1979: Lake Chilwa. Studies of Change in a Tropical Ecosystem. J. Illies (ed.), *Monographiae Biologicae.* (35).

Martin, P. 1991: Environmental care in agricultural catchments: toward the communicative catchment. *Environmental Management*, 6 (15), 773-783.

National Extension Secretariat, Government of Kenya, 1990: *Participatory Rural Appraisal Handbook: Conducting PRAs in Kenya.* Washington, D.C.: World Resource Institute.

University of Bristol. 1989: *The University of Bristol Lake Chilwa Expedition.* Bristol: University of Bristol Press.

University of Malawi. 1996: *Lake Chilwa Ramsar Site Study Report.* Zomba: University of Malawi Press.

Chapter 4

A Rapid Hydrologic Wetland Evaluation Technique for South Africa

by Stephen Chapman and Reid Kreutzwiser

Introduction

Background

The Reconstruction and Development Programme (RDP) enacted by the South African Government of National Unity is a major initiative to improve the quality of life for the majority of South Africans (Ministry of Water Affairs and Forestry, 1995). Under the RDP, the Department of Water Affairs and Forestry aims to ensure that all South Africans can have access to basic water supply services while maintaining the integrity of the environment (Ministry of Water Affairs and Forestry, 1996).

Many wetland regulatory agencies around the world have recognized that wetlands play an important role in maintaining the quality, quantity and flow of surface and groundwater. By applying a wetlands evaluation system which incorporates the hydrological function of wetlands, resource managers in South Africa have the opportunity to reduce some of the problems that may arise from the implementation of the water and sanitation policy (Figure 4.1).

This paper reports upon the results of research done in designing a rapid wetland evaluation technique for hydrological functions in South Africa. The first stage of this research focused on the designing of an evaluation scheme, while the second stage was the implementation of this scheme in the South African context. This was done in the summer of 1996 on the Noordhoek wetlands, located approximately 35 km south of Cape Town.

Figure 4.1 Potential impacts of the water and sanitation policy on wetlands

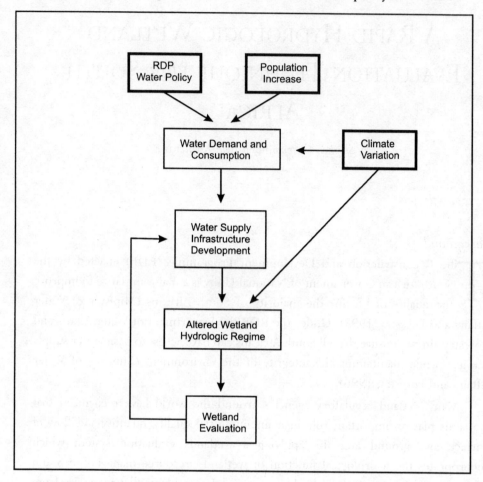

Wetland functions and values

Wetland functions are physical, chemical, and biological processes or attributes that are vital to the integrity of a wetland system, and operate whether or not they are viewed as important to society. Values, on the other hand, are wetland attributes that are not necessarily important to the integrity of a wetland system itself, but are perceived as being valuable to society (Table 4.1).

Table 4.1 Functions of wetlands and their value

Functions of Wetlands	Value of the Functions of Wetlands
Store and/or convey floodwater	Reduce flood-related damage
Buffer storm surges	Reduce flood-related damage
Recharge groundwater	Maintain groundwater aquifers
Discharge groundwater	Maintain base flow for aquatic species
Stabilize shorelines	Minimize erosion damage
Stabilize stream banks	Minimize erosion damage
Detain/remove contaminants	Maintain water quality
Detain/remove sediments	Maintain water quality
Maintain ecosystem integrity	• Maintain plant and animal populations • Preserve endangered species • Maintain biodiversity • Provide renewable food and fiber products
Setting for cultural activities	• Provide recreational opportunities • Provide education/research opportunities • Provide aesthetic enjoyment • Provide archeological and historical sites

Wetland functions, as physical or biological processes or conditions, are not always of direct relevance to human interests. Often the effects of a function (e.g., retention of sediment) can be viewed as either favourable or unfavourable (Table 4.2). Moreover, land development has social significance too. Thus, the choice is not merely whether a wetland should be allowed to continue to provide a service, but whether a proposed development offers a greater long-term, maintenance-free service than a wetland.

Table 4.2 Conflicting uses of wetland functions

Function	Beneficial	Negative
Floodflow Alteration	• Flood control	• Less flushing (more dredging required)
Groundwater Recharge	• Increased water supplies • dilution of contamination	• Surface flow reduction
Erosion Control	• Shoreline protection	• Less flushing (more dredging required)
Water Quality Improvement	• Improved downslope environment	• Degraded wetland environment

Wetland hydrologic functions

There has been, and still is, much debate over the hydrological functions of wetlands (Carter, Bedlinger, Novitzky & Wilen, 1978). However, much of the debate is a result of trying to attribute hydrologic generalities across all wetlands. It has been recognized that different wetland types have different hydrologic regimes. For example bogs receive all input of water from the atmosphere (Bay, 1969), while fens (Siegal & Glasser, 1987) and some swamps (Roulet, 1990) receive considerable groundwater inputs.

Bogs, fens, swamps and marshes have very different combinations of peat and mineral soils which affect the water table/storage-storage capacity relationships differently (Verry, 1988). Research has shown that hydrology and the dynamic nature of water affect its vegetation (composition, structure and diversity), influence its primary productivity, control its organic accumulation and transport, and drive its nutrient cycling (Gosselink & Turner, 1978). Hydrology influences the homogeneity or heterogeneity of the wetlands, from varied topographic relief and vegetative cover to broad monotypically-vegetated flats (Bedlinger, 1979).

Mitsch and Gosselink (1986) state that "hydrology is probably the single most important determinant for the establishment and maintenance of specific types of wetlands and wetland processes," and Nestler and Long (1994) state that most significant wetland functions can be described completely or in part by hydrologic factors.

Development of the evaluation technique

The development of the evaluation technique involved reviewing, testing, and modifying existing wetland evaluation schemes commonly employed by various national and international wetland management agencies. Both a theoretical and empirical approach was employed for the review, testing, and modification of wetland evaluation schemes. A theoretical approach evaluated the scheme based on commonly identified criteria outlined in the literature while an empirical approach compared the evaluation scheme to observations of site-specific conditions. The research consisted of three methodological components.

Existing wetland evaluation schemes commonly used by national and international wetland management agencies were identified from the literature. These schemes were evaluated on the basis of their consideration of the hydrological functions of wetlands and the value assigned to these functions. In addition to the review of this hydrological component, the schemes were also evaluated as to their applicability to wetland evaluation in a South African context. Of particular importance to the RDP is the need for an evaluation scheme to be rapid. The outcome of this literature review was the selection of wetland evaluation schemes that in turn were applied to a sample of wetlands in South Africa (June - August, 1996). From this application of wetland evaluation schemes, a preliminary modified scheme was developed for use in South Africa.

Finally, this modified scheme was submitted to stakeholders for review. Opinions derived from responses to the preliminary modified evaluation scheme were considered in the development of a final evaluation scheme.

CASE STUDY: NOORDHOEK

The study area is situated on the South Western Cape coastline (34' 07 S; 18' 22 E), approximately 35 km south of Cape Town. The area consists of a low-lying flat-bottomed valley, flanked by parallel sandstone ridges to the east and the Atlantic Ocean to the west (Heineken, 1985). The central area of the basin forms an almost level floodplain with depressions, which includes the Noordhoek wetland complex. The entire catchment area is approximately 1769 hectares (measured from a 1:10000 orthophoto). The highest elevation found within the catchment area is Noordhoek Piek, at 754 m above sea level; the lowest elevation is found near the mouth of the catchment area at sea level.

Noordhoek wetland

The Noordhoek wetland complex can be found at the southern edge of the catchment area. This highly modified wetland is approximately 56 hectares in area and receives the majority of its water from an upland area of 384 hectares. Originally a salt pan, the wetland has now become a shallow lake. The salt pan was a seasonal water body until it was dredged in 1974 as part of the scheme for the waterside housing development. In 1989 the housing development resumed, and the pan has since been artificially maintained as a permanent water body. All surface water entering and leaving the wetland is artificially controlled. The water that leaves the Noordhoek wetland flows slowly over fairly level terrain to the Papkuil wetland and eventually enters the tidal lagoon at Noordhoek Beach.

Geology and geomorphology

The mountains surrounding the catchment area consist of the Peninsula Formation quartzitic sandstone of the Table Mountain Group, which rests on a base of the Graafwater Shale Formation, which in turn overlies the Cape Granites. The lower slopes of the mountains surrounding the basin are made up of thick talus deposits of sand and Table Mountain sandstone scree. Tertiary to Recent sand deposits make up the basin floor (Heinecken, 1985).

▶ **Soils:** The soils found within the Noordhoek catchment are varied and reflect some of the dynamic forces acting within the catchment area. Some of the soils with a high interflow potential are of the Mispah, Darling and Longlands series, while the rest of the soils in the catchment area are considered to have a low interflow potential.

▶ **Land Use:** There are a variety of land uses found within the catchment area, with urban and agricultural activities being the most dominant. The communities of Chapman's Peak Estates are found in the northern areas of the catchment while the communities of Sun Valley and The Lakes are found at the southern edge of the catchment divide.

▶ **Surface Water:** Apart from the *voor* which drains the Noordhoek wetland, there are no well-defined water courses. The runoff from the remainder of the catchment seeps into the porous basin floor, forming two aquifers (Taylor *et. al.*, 1994). Although the Noordhoek wetland and the Wildevoevleis now contain water permanently through artificial means, they are interconnected via the high water table which exists throughout the entire basin floor (Heinecken, 1985).

▶ **Groundwater:** Based on its geology, the Noordhoek basin can be divided into two potential aquifer types. In the Table Mountain sandstones and granite, groundwater is stored in zones of faulting and fracturing. In the overlying Tertiary deposits, groundwater is stored in the original pore spaces between the constituent grains. The present rates of urbanization are putting a strain on existing water resources.

▶ **Climate:** Climatic processes are fundamental in determining and understanding the ecological and geomorphological processes of any region. No climatic data are available specifically for the Noordhoek basin. However, the climate can be considered a Mediterranean climate with hot dry summers and cool wet winters. The mean annual temperature is estimated at 17 C

(Gasson, 1983). Rainfall over the basin is both cyclonic and orographic with a pronounced winter peak, topography playing an important role in the distribution of rainfall which is highest up against the south-facing mountain slopes (Gasson, 1984).

▶ **Vegetation:** Four major plant communities have been recognized in the area by Cowling (1985). These include the dune pioneer community which occupies the hummocked dune zone adjacent to Noordhoek Beach. The community is heavily invaded in the northern section by *Acacia cyclops*, which dominates most of the study area. Dune fynbos is confined to the younger, alkaline, shelly sands. Dune thickets are confined to the old fore dunes. A total of six dominant wetland plant species were identified - *Junkus krausii, Sarcornnia dactylon, Cynodon dactylon, Carpha glomerata, Typha latifolia,* and *Phragmites australis.* Most plant species tend to be emergents that are bordered by *Acacia.*

FLOODFLOW ALTERATION

Definition

The reduction of flood peaks in areas downstream of wetlands is an important ecological function, as well as a human value. The ecological benefits include the protection of downstream riparian areas from erosion and sedimentation and from washout or siltation of spawning beds.

Wetlands can reduce floodflows by temporarily restraining water that would otherwise run downstream and, over the longer term, by allowing water to seep into groundwater or be taken up and released by plants through evapotranspiration. The ability of wetlands to provide short-term, temporary storage of water is important for reducing flood peaks. Wetlands have significant micro-relief which allows temporary storage of water in depressions and increases surface resistance to overland flow. When riverine wetlands and lakes make up between 5% and 20% of the watershed area, they can reduce flood peak rates by up to 75% (Verry, 1988).

Headwater wetlands in areas of groundwater discharge are somewhat different from other wetlands. These wetlands have developed in areas where the mineral soil is always saturated. Although the organic soil of the wetland provides only limited storage capacity, it is still significant (Roulet, 1989). If the wetland were not present, all the rain falling on the entire area of groundwater discharge would immediately runoff because the mineral soil is already saturated. Isolated wetlands, because they have no surface outflow, are 100% efficient for attenuating flood crests. The removal of such detention areas would aggravate flooding downstream.

Floodflow alteration is the process by which peak flows from runoff, surface flow, groundwater interflow and discharge, and precipitation enter a wetland and are stored or delayed in their downslope journey. Flood-flow alteration also includes floodflow desynchronization, which is the process by which flood waters are stored in numerous wetlands within a watershed, and then gradually released in a staggered manner.

Processes

▶ **Wetland Attenuation:** Wetland attenuation is used to assess the efficiency of a wetland in attenuating flood peaks. Adamus and Stockwell (1983) note that the incremental gain in terms of flood storage attenuation is minimal when the wetland area exceeds 10 percent of the area of the watershed. Wetlands comprising 10% or more (based on area) of the total storage within the basin thus receive the maximum score. Smaller wetlands are pro-rated in a linear manner based on their size relative to the total detention area in the watershed.

▶ **Upstream Detention:** Upstream detention is used to consider the net benefit derived from the wetland being evaluated relative to other detention areas in the watershed upstream of the wetland. The rationale for evaluating upstream detention is that if a significant amount of detention is already available upstream, the net benefit of the wetland for flood attenuation would be reduced. If a wetland represents 50% of total storage or more in its basin (based on area), it will provide maximum detention benefits.

▶ **Magnitude and Duration of Storms:** The intensity and duration of storm events directly influence the amount of runoff from a wetland. Wetlands in watersheds characterized by high-intensity, short-duration storm events (often termed flashy watersheds) are more likely to receive flood waters than wetlands in watersheds characterized by more attenuated runoff (e.g., extensive rainfall of long duration).

▶ **Runoff from Upslope Areas:** Flood waters enter the wetland as runoff and groundwater discharge. Runoff is most likely to reach wetlands in substantial quantities when drainage areas are large and have steep slopes, shallow or impervious soils (e.g., clay), sparse vegetative cover (less opportunity for evapotranspirative loss), channelized tributaries and land use practices that do not incorporate conservation practices. Wetlands can store peak flows most effectively if the flows enter gradually and if the drainage area is small relative to the size of the wetland.

▶ **Above-Ground Storage Capacity:** Storage (as surface water) of flood waters depends primarily on type of morphology of the wetland. The volume of water that can be stored depends on the type and location of any outlets. Of course, wetlands without outlets must store all incoming water, often resulting in considerable surface expansion.

▶ **Frictional Resistance:** Desynchronization of peak flows depends on their being slowed not only by channel constrictions but also by frictional resistance from the bottom. Frictional drag and the potential for desynchronization will be greatest where:

  ▶ the wetland is wide enough to intercept most of the flow
  ▶ the density of wetland vegetation or other obstructions (e.g., boulders, logs) is great
  ▶ the rigidity of obstructions is adequate to resist flood velocity
  ▶ vegetation or obstructions are not deeply submerged by flood waters.

Desynchronization of runoff, as partly determined by frictional resistance of wetland vegetation, may be most capable of moderating downstream floodflows when it occurs in headwater wetlands (Flores, Bedient & Mays, 1981), whereas in downstream wetlands the storage process may be more important than any desynchronization effect (Ogawa & Male, 1983).

▶ **Below-Ground Storage Capacity**: Sediments underlying wetlands normally are saturated or impervious and therefore have little capacity to store floodwaters. However if large areas are exposed to frequent water-level fluctuations (e.g., due to artificial manipulation or flashy runoff events), sediments may be unsaturated when floodwaters rise and some below-ground storage capacity may exist. Under such conditions and especially if water-retentive vegetation predominates (e.g., unsaturated moss wetlands) the wetland may act for short periods like a sponge. In most situations below-ground storage capacity is less than above-ground capacity.

▶ **Position of Wetland in the Watershed**: If wetlands high in the watershed have been drained, detention of floodwaters by wetlands along the main stem low in the watershed might at least theoretically aggravate flooding by helping synchronize local runoff with surface flows arriving from higher in the watershed.

Indicators

In the rapid evaluation technique designed for and used in this study, a number of indicators were used to rank the influence and importance of a wetland with regards to floodflow alteration. These are based upon the major processes and characteristics that affect floodflow alteration.

Table 4.3 is a summary of the rankings used. The Wetland Attenuation Factor (WAF) is a function of the ratio of the area of the wetland to the area of the catchment basin upstream of the wetland under study. The Upstream Detention ratio is the ratio of the wetland area to the total area of the upstream detention areas. The bolded values in the table represent the results when the Noordhoek wetland was examined with this method. Where no value is bolded, there was no data available.

Table 4.3 Potential for floodflow alteration

Wetland Characteristic	Low	Medium	High
Wetland Attenuation Factor (WAF)	>5%	5-9%	**10% or greater**
Upstream Detention	>30%	30-49%	**50% or greater**
Outlets Present	Yes	**Yes, but insignificant**	No
Constricted Outlet	No	No	**Yes**
Dominant Vegetation	Submergent	**Emergent**	Scrub-Shrub
Vegetation/Water Interspersion	**Wetland vegetation is completely separated from open water in wetland**	Wetland vegetation is partially interspersed with water in wetland	Wetland vegetation is completely interspersed with water in wetland
Water/Vegetation Proportions	Little standing vegetation exists within the wetland area	**Wetland area is partially vegetated**	Wetland area is completely vegetated
Channel/Sheet Flow	**Main water input is through channel flow**	Although some channel flow exists, sheet flow dominates during storm events	Sheet flow is the dominant form of water input
Catchment Landuse Factor (CLU)	Over 50% natural vegetation	Between 30 and 50% agricultural and/or urban	**Over 50% agricultural and/or urban**
Channelization	Wetlands have been channelized to drain excess water	**Although some modification has taken place, channels are somewhat ineffective**	Wetlands have not been channelized
Soils	Soils are permeable	**Soils are somewhat permeable**	Soils are impermeable
Surface area expansion	>15% expansion for at least 20 days of the year	15-20% expansion for at least 20 days of the year	**<25% expansion for at least 20 days of the year**
Discharge Differential	No evidence that flood peaks are flood peaks are higher at inlet compared to that of the outlet.	Although data suggests that flood peaks are higher at the inlet compared to the outlet, the relationship is not clear.	Strong evidence to suggest that flood peaks are higher at the inlet compared to those of the outlet.

Floodflow alteration in the Noordhoek wetland

▶ **Wetland Area:** The Wetland Attenuation Factor (WAF) was calculated to be about 15% for the Noordhoek wetlands. The wetland area was calculated by examining the maximum extent to which flooding occurs in the wet season during the field visits, and translating this area to 1:10000 air photographs. The upstream area was calculated by examining the topography upstream of the wetland on 1:10000 air photographs.

▶ **Wetland/Watershed Area Ratio:** The Upstream detention factor was found to be 97%. Although some upstream detention areas could be seen on 1:10000 air photographs, it was necessary to survey the entire catchment area during the field visits to get a better estimate of the detention areas upstream of the wetland. Once these detention areas were identified, their surface area was estimated visually.

▶ **Inlets, Outlets:** Although not readily apparent on air photographs and topographic maps, there are two outlets which drain the Noordhoek wetland, both of which constrict the flow of water leaving the wetland. It is likely that the first outlet discovered (Outlet 1) drains water from the wetland at all times of the year, given the depth of the channel and the placement of the culvert. The second outlet (Outlet 2) consists of a small dam and culvert, which significantly contribute to the control of the water level in the wetland. It is likely that water flows over this dam at periods of higher rainfall. There is one discernible inlet that allows water to enter the wetland. This mostly collects runoff from the local urban surroundings.

▶ **Constrictions:** The hydrologic regime of the Noordhoek wetland is controlled by the dam at Outlet 2. This maintains the water level in the wetland to a maximum depth of 1.6 metres during the wet season. Outlet 1 is also constricted, but only plays a minor role in the outflow of water from the wetland.

▶ **Dominant Vegetation:** The area surrounding the Noordhoek wetland is dominated by *Acacia sp.* This scrub-shrub vegetation forms dense thickets and crowds out all other vegetation. There is an exception, however. The inlet area of the wetland is dominated by *Typha latifolia* and *Phragmites australis*. This emergent vegetation is extremely dense and dominates the entire south eastern edge of the wetland area. Because the *Typha/Phragmites* dominates the inlet area of the Noordhoek wetland, it is rated as being predominantly emergent.

▶ **Vegetation/Water Interspersion:** There is no interspersion of water and vegetation with the wetland complex at Noordhoek. Water levels are kept artificially high during most of the year and the berm and concrete barrier that is along 80% of the perimeter of the wetland does not permit a gradient from lowland to upland that normally exists in wetland environments.

- **Water/Vegetation Proportions:** Approximately 25 ha of the total wetland area of 56 ha is dominated by a very dense stand of *Typha/Phragmites*.
- **Channel, Sheet Flow:** The earth and concrete berm that surrounds the wetland would impede any sheet flow that would normally enter the wetland. In addition, the entire wetland complex is surrounded by roads which would serve to channelize water. Therefore, the inflow of surface water in the Noordhoek wetland is predominantly channel flow.
- **Land Cover of the Watershed:** In examining 1:10000 air photographs a grid overlay system was used to estimate the dominant land uses within the Noordhoek catchment. The entire western portion of the catchment has been urbanized, while new developments are being built in the northern area. It is estimated that 60% of the land uses within the catchment are urban/agricultural, while the remaining 40% is dominated by *Acacia/fynbos* vegetation.
- **Channelization:** Both the inflow and outflow area of the Noordhoek wetland have been channelized.
- **Soils:** Although the soils in the immediate area of the Noordhoek wetland are slightly impermeable, the entire catchment area is dominated by well-drained sandy soils (less than 6% clay).
- **Flood Extent and Duration:** In the past, the water level in the Noordhoek wetland would have been much lower than it is at present. Data shows that there is, on average, a one-metre fluctuation in wetland water levels. This represents approximately a 30 to 40% fluctuation in the areal extent of flooding within the wetland. On average, the wetland water level stays at 1.6 metres for at least 5 months of the year.
- **Discharge Differential:** No data

GROUNDWATER FLOW

Discharge and recharge

- **Recharge:** A wetland can be considered a groundwater recharge area if a component of groundwater flow is downward from the wetland to underlying soils

(Siegal, 1988). Many wetlands can act as recharge areas in the spring, and as discharge areas in the summer and autumn (Whiteley & Irwin, 1986). For those wetlands that have impermeable soils at the base, significant recharge can occur only at the perimeter of the wetland when it floods. For a wetland to provide a significant groundwater recharge function, it requires a reasonably constant source of water, such as from a stream (Woo & Valverde, 1981), or surrounding slopes situated on permeable soils.

The recharge of groundwater supplies and aquifers is considered to be one of the most important function of certain kinds of wetlands. Through recharge, consumers of water may be served by the provision of higher water tables downhill from the wetland. This evaluation will recognize that because certain headwater wetlands do not discharge through outlet drains or streams they function to reduce the amount of erosion as well as to reduce the downstream velocity of flow (Roulet, 1989).

▶ **Discharge:** A wetland can be considered a groundwater discharge area if the groundwater moves upwards from the underlying material or emerges from surrounding uplands (Roulet, 1990). Discharge wetlands have a high value, both for ecological reasons and because of their utility in erosion control and water quality improvement.

Groundwater discharging in a wetland is usually nutrient and mineral rich, allowing the development of locally unique ecosystems. These wetlands may also have local seepage habitats that are essential habitats for rare species. With respect to the hydrological function of groundwater discharge, it is the water quality improvement that is being evaluated.

Seldom, if ever, do wetlands themselves provide "low flow augmentation" (Carter, 1986). Stream flow augmentation derives mostly from discharging groundwater emerging from upland areas adjacent to streams (Roulet, 1990). However, as the "ecosystem of last contact" (Johnson & Naiman, 1987) the wetland does serve a water quality function. The wetland is the last ecosystem to receive all the material (nutrients, contaminants, sediments, etc.) from upstream environments (via both surface and groundwater flow) before it reaches a water body such as a stream, river or lake. Because many wetlands occupy the zone adjacent to stream and lakes – i.e. riverine, palustrine, and lacustrine settings – upstream materials funnel through these wetlands which can play a disproportionate role in biogeochemical exchanges between terrestrial and aquatic ecosystems. It is assumed that the groundwater which emerges in a wetland will be of a higher quality than it would if the wetland were not present to filter the water (Hill, 1990; Peterjohn & Correll, 1984; Pinay & Decamps, 1988), as it has been acted upon by microorganisms and soil particles.

While hydrological characteristics are difficult to measure, certain observations can suggest a wetland's groundwater function. These involve understanding the wetland in the context of the basin, both surface and subsurface. While surface hydrology can be evaluated by general map analyses, subsurface flow components cannot because of the lack of specific local and regional information on the hydrological setting of the wetland. Suitable data for making an assessment of groundwater effect would usually require considerable expenditure of time by professional hydrologists.

Processes

▶ **Groundwater Flow Rates And Storage Capacity:** The movement of groundwater to or from a wetland depends primarily upon the elevation of the wetland relative to the groundwater (elevation head), the mass and pressure of the water (pressure head), and the physical characteristics and frictional resistance of the sediments and underlying strata (hydraulic conductivity).

Pressure head is influenced in a downward direction by the mass of water and in an upward direction by confined groundwater flow caused by underlying strata (e.g., springs). Larger wetlands (i.e., greater water volume) have a greater pressure head, other factors being equal.

The physical aspects of the sediments such as porosity, transmissivity, permeability, and storage capacity can influence hydraulic conductivity. Groundwater best moves through coarse sands and gravels and is successively slower through peats and clays (Mitsch & Gosselink, 1986). Although rooted wetland vegetation may enhance permeability of compacted bottom sediments (Eisenlohr, 1966), the more usual effect is that as vegetation dies, it accumulates and forms an organic layer that is less permeable to groundwater exchange. Sediments of high clay content are usually more effective seals. In such situations, most groundwater exchange may be along wave exposed shorelines where less clay is present.

▶ **Direction and Location of Groundwater Movement:** The water in a wetland represents the component inflows of heavy precipitation, upland runoff, flowing surface water, and groundwater discharge, balanced against outflows or groundwater recharge, evapotranspiration, surface water, and possibly consumption.

The role groundwater plays in the hydrologic budget depends upon the physical position of the wetland with respect to the water table. Both groundwater discharge and groundwater recharge occur when the water table intersects the surface water of a wetland. When the wetland is perched above the water table, only groundwater recharge is possible. Perched wetlands tend to be only seasonally wet (Novitzki, 1979).

Groundwater may leave or enter a wetland at any point, but in wetlands that are wider than the thickness of the underlying porous sediments, most significant movement (usually discharge) occurs where vegetation is absent, usually along wave scoured, unstable sandy shorelines (McBride & Pfannkuch, 1975). Locations of recharge and discharge within the basin, as well as the overall magnitude of the recharge and discharge, frequently vary by the season and from year to year.

▶ **Evapotranspiration:** Evapotranspiration refers to the combined processes of evaporation and plant transpiration. The role of transpiration becomes obvious as wetland water levels increase as watersheds are developed and as they fluctuate under normal circumstances on a diurnal basis (Wharton, 1970). Transpiration is greatest during the growing season and during daylight hours. Densely vegetated wetlands are thought to lose water faster than sparsely vegetated wetlands and, consequently, have less water available to augment low flows or recharge groundwater.

Indicators

In the rapid evaluation technique designed for and used in this study, a number of indicators were used to rank the influence and importance of a wetland with regards to groundwater recharge and groundwater discharge. These are based upon the major processes and characteristics that affect groundwater flow.

Tables 4.4.1 and 4.4.2· demonstrate the rankings used for groundwater discharge and recharge respectively. The bolded values represent the results for the Noordhoek wetland. Where no value is bolded, there was no data available.

Table 4.4.1 Potential for groundwater recharge

Wetland Characteristic	Low	Medium	High
Water table slopes away from wetland	**No**	Gradient within the catchment area is insignificant	Yes
Inlets, Outlets	**Has both an inlet and an outlet**	Wetland has no inlet or outlet	Wetland has a permanent inlet but no outlet
Catchment Landuse Factor (CLU)	Over 50% natural vegetation	Between 30 and 50% agricultural and/or urban	**Over 50% agricultural and/or urban**
Channelization	**Presence of ditches or channels that drain wetland**	Ditches or channels are present, but only drain wetland during the wet season	No channels or ditches are present
Soils	Impermeable	**Slightly Permeable**	Permeable
Wetland is permanently flooded	No	No	**Yes**
Wetland is upslope of a dam or dyke	No	**Yes, but permit some water flow**	Yes
Flooding Extent	**Extremely variable water levels**	Variable Flow	Stable Flow
Direct evidence of recharge from well or piezometer data	**No**	Conflicting Evidence	Yes
Water Quality Anomalies	Yes	No	No
Water Temperature Anomalies	Yes	No	No
Underlying Strata	Underlying strata is stratified, non-porous sediment	**Underlying strata is partially permeable**	Underlying strata is thick and unsaturated porous material (e.g., sand)
Discharge Differential	Outflow exceeds inflow	Inflow slightly exceeds outflow	Inflow is much greater than outflow

Table 4.4.2 Potential for groundwater discharge

Wetland Characteristic	Low	Medium	High
Wetland Attenuation Factor (WAF)	>5%	5-9%	**10% or greater**
Topography	Flat/Rolling	Hilly	**Steep**
Permanant Outlet, No Inlet	No	**No**	Yes
Water Budget	Data suggests that precipitation inputs are consistent with discharge measurements	Discharge from wetland is slightly more than precipitation inputs	Data suggests that discharge exceeds precipitation inputs for the wetland
Catchment Landuse Factor (CLU)	Over 50% natural vegetation	Between 30 and 50% agricultural and/or urban	**Over 50% agricultural and/or urban**
Wetland Area: Upslope Area	>50%	6-50%	<5%
Channelization	Presence of ditches or channels that drain wetland	**Ditches or channels are present, but only drain wetland during the wet season**	No channels or ditches are present
Wetland is immediately below a dam	**No**	No	Yes
Surface area expansion	>15% expansion for at least 20 days per year	15-20% expansion for at least 20 days of the year	**<25% expansion for at least 20 days of the year**
Located within 1km of a major aquifer	No	No	**Yes**
Water Quality Anomalies	No	No	Yes
Water Temperature Anomalies	No	No	Yes
Discharge Differential	Inflow exceeds outflow	Outflow slightly exceeds inflow	Outflow clearly exceeds inflow

Groundwater recharge and discharge in the Noordhoek wetland

▶ **Topography (relevant to both recharge and discharge):** The Noordhoek wetland is situated in a depressional area surrounded by a low-lying, flat-bottomed valley. Geological data and field observations indicate that the wetland complex is in a discharge area for groundwater. There is a significant elevation change from the northern areas of the watershed to the valley floor where the Noordhoek wetland is situated, ie., 750 metres above sea level to 10 metres above sea level. This change represents an opportunity for groundwater discharge to take place given the porous nature of the soils in the middleslopes.

- **Wetland/Watershed Area Ratio (discharge):** As noted earlier, the Wetland Attenuation Factor (WAF) equals 97%.
- **Inlets, Outlets (recharge & discharge):** The Noordhoek wetland has both inlets and outlets.
- **Land Cover of the Watershed (recharge & discharge):** In examining 1:10000 air photographs a grid overlay system was used to estimate the dominate land uses within the Noordhoek catchment. The entire western portion of the catchment has been urbanized, while new developments are being built in the northern area. It is estimated that 60% of the land within the catchment are in urban/agricultural uses, while the remaining 40% is dominated by *Acacia/fynbos* vegetation.
- **Channelization (recharge & discharge):** Both the inflow and outflow area of the Noordhoek wetland have been channelized.
- **Water Budget (discharge):** No data
- **Soils (recharge):** Over 40% of the soils found in the valley bottom can be considered sandy loams, which have a low potential for runoff. The remaining soils in the valley bottom are considered to be loamy sands and sandy clay loams, also with a low potential for runoff.
- **Hydroperiod (recharge):** This wetland complex is seasonally flooded. There is at least a 100 cm difference between the high water and low water marks at the gauging station. In addition, the open water area expands by at least 30% during the wet season.
- **Water Level Control (recharge & discharge):** There is an impoundment located at Outlet 2 that maintains the water depth. The maximum height that the water attains before spilling over the impoundment is 1.6 metres.
- **Flooding Extent and Duration (recharge):** On average, the water level fluctuates by 100 cm between the dry and wet seasons.
- **Groundwater Measurements (recharge & discharge):** The reports by Rosewarne (1991) and Taylor *et. al.* (1994) suggest that the Noordhoek wetland complex is acting as a discharge area for groundwater.
- **Water Quality Anomalies (recharge & discharge):** No data

- **Water Temperature Anomalies (recharge & discharge):** No data
- **Underlying Strata (recharge):** The underlying strata within the vicinity of the wetland is partially permeable sandstone and consolidated sand deposits.
- **Discharge Differential (recharge & discharge):** No data

EROSION CONTROL

Definition

Shoreline wetlands, i.e. riverine and lacustrine types, provide a measure of protection from shoreline erosion caused by flowing water or waves. The erosion problem occurs principally when water levels are high. Wetland vegetation ameliorates the effects of flowing water and wave action and thus reduces or eliminates soil erosion. There is substantial evidence that native plants bind soil both under and above the water, reduce current and wave energy by friction, increase sediment deposition by slowing the current, and stabilize banks (Carter *et. al.*, 1978).

Processes

- **Energy Associated with Erosive Forces:** Incoming waves, currents, water level fluctuations, and groundwater discharge are capable of creating erosive conditions. In general, the potential ability of water to displace and transport soil particles increases with increasing flow velocity. The major factors that influences the energy of incoming waves or currents are wind velocity, wetland gradient and bottom roughness, presence of protective structures, and runoff. Erosiveness depends on the frequency, period, amplitude, and seasonal timing of water level fluctuations.

  Erosive energy also depends on the suspended solids concentration in the water. Relatively sediment free waters are more erosive than those with heavy sediment loads because suspended sediment tend to reduce turbulence, which is responsible for transporting sediment. Relatively sediment free waters are likely to occur in some wetlands with substantial groundwater input, below dams, or when upstream wetlands significantly alter the sediment load equilibrium.

- **Frictional Resistance offered by the Wetland:** The frictional drag on incoming waves or currents increases with the width of the wetland, the density of its vegetation (or other obstructions), the rigidity of the vegetation, and the degree to which the vegetation extends above the incoming waves or currents. Wetlands with perennial vegetation are more effective on a net annual basis than are wetlands with non-persistent vegetation or those dominated by annuals.

- **Position of the Wetland:** Wetlands that project into open water, due to accretion and expansive anchoring by rooted vegetation, are better able to intercept and deflect waves that otherwise might erode adjacent shorelines. However, these wetlands usually exist because their environment is basically depositional, and seldom exposed to such waves.

- **Ability of Wetland Plants to Anchor the Soil:** The depth and degree of root branching influence the ability of wetland plants to anchor the soil. Sod-forming ability is species specific. Even if plants are not particularly effective at producing frictional drag for incoming waters because they are not rigid or they are fully submersed, some may still help to anchor the sediment and prevent scour.

- **Erodibility of Uplands being Protected:** The intrinsic erodibility of shorelines is greater with increased sand and silt content of the soil, bank slope, groundwater seepage, runoff from farther upslope, and nearness of heavy objects to the top of the bank slope. Often, much of the erosion along channel banks occurs as bank failure following a rapid decrease in water level.

Indicators

In the rapid evaluation technique designed for and used in this study, a number of indicators were used to rank the influence and importance of a wetland with regards to erosion control.

Table 4.5 demonstrates the rankings used and displays where the Noordhoek wetland placed when submitted to evaluation (bolded values). Further explanation of the evaluation of the Noordhoek wetland is given below the table.

Table 4.5 Potential for erosion control

Wetland Characteristic	Low	Medium	High
Topography	Flat/Rolling	Hilly	**Steep**
Wetland is riverine or lacustrine and has one of the following vegetation categories dominating 10 metres from the shoreline	No vegetation	**Submergent and Emergent vegetation**	Trees and shrubs
Vegetation/Water Interspersion	**Wetland vegetation is completely separated from open water in wetland**	Wetland vegetation is partially interspersed with water in wetland	Wetland vegetation is completely interspersed with water in wetland
Water/Vegetation Proportions	Little standing vegetation exists within the wetland area	**Wetland area is partially vegetated**	Wetland area is completely vegetated
Vegetated Width	Banks of wetland are not vegetated	Sparse vegetation exists along the banks of the wetlands	**Persistent, robust vegetation is found all along the banks of the wetland**
Channel/Sheet Flow	**Main water input is through channel flow**	Although some channel flow exists, sheet flow dominates during storm events	Sheet flow is the dominant form of water input
Flow	No flowing water present	**Water only flows during storm events**	Permanent flowing water present
Channel Modifications	No modified channels present	Some channelization has taken place, but only at the outflow	**Inflow of the wetland has been channelized**
Sediment Sources	No potential inputs of sediment upstream of wetland	**Some opportunity for sediment input upstream of wetland**	Several significant sources for sediment input upstream of wetland
Water Level Control	Yes	Yes	**No**

Erosion control in the Noordhoek wetland

▶ **Gradient:** The gradient upstream of the wetland is sufficient that severe erosion can take place. The average gradient of the middleslope areas in the catchment range from 5 to 30 degrees.

- **Dominant Vegetation:** The dominant vegetation of the catchment can be considered scrub-shrub (*Acacia/fynbos*). However, the presence of the berm and road that surround the wetland negates any effect the vegetation may have in controlling erosion. *Phragmites* and *Typha* dominate at the inlet of the wetland, where some erosion control may be taking place.
- **Vegetation/Water Interspersion:** There is no interspersion of water and vegetation with the wetland complex at Noordhoek. Water levels are kept artificially high during most of the year and the berm and concrete barrier that is along 80% of the perimeter of the wetland does not permit a gradient from lowland to upland that normally exists in wetland environments.
- **Water/Vegetation Proportions:** Approximately 25 ha of the total wetland area of 56 ha is dominated by a very dense stand of *Typha/Phragmites*.
- **Vegetated Width:** Although there are some patches of *Junkus krausii, Sarcornnia dactylon, Cynodon dactylon,* and *Carpha glomerat* along the western and northern edges of the wetland, *Acacia* is the dominant vegetation form in the 10-metre periphery of the wetland.
- **Sheet/Channel Flow:** As noted in previous sections, due to the presence of berms and roadways, the inflow of surface water in the Noordhoek wetland is predominantly channel flow.
- **Flow:** It was difficult to check for scour lines or other indications of the erosive capacity of the water because of dredging activities taking place near the inlet of the wetland. In addition, the inlet channel had recently been modified, erasing any potential evidence.
- **Channelization:** Both the inflow and outflow area of the Noordhoek wetland have been channelized.
- **Sediment Sources:** Given the erosive capacity of the wind within the Fishhoek gap, the steep slopes of the catchment area, and the composition of the soils of the middleslope, there are many potential sources of sediment upstream of the wetland. In addition, sediment buildup was found in the area where the inlet intersects the *Typha/Phragmites* area, east of the open water.
- **Water Level Control:** There is an impoundment located at Outlet 2 that maintains the water depth. The maximum height that the water attains before spilling over the impoundment is 1.6 metres.

WATER QUALITY IMPROVEMENT

Definition

The quality of water discharged from a wetland reflects the quality of the water entering the wetland and the chemical transformations that occur in the wetland (Carter *et. al.*, 1978). Wetlands temporarily store some nutrients such as phosphorus and nitrogen, but they do not normally retain them (Devito, Dillon & Lazerte, 1989). Even when nutrients are removed permanently through the accumulation of organic soils, the removal rate is relatively small due to the net exchange through the wetland (Urban & Eisenreich, 1988; Whigham & Bayley, 1978).

The ability of wetlands to improve water quality depends on the rate of the water flow through the wetland and its position in the drainage basin. Johnston, Detenbeck and Niemi (1990) found that wetlands were more effective at removing suspended solids, total phosphorus, and ammonia during high flow periods, but were more effective at removing nitrates at low flows. Hill and Warick (1987) showed that wetlands can also transform the chemical characteristics of emerging groundwater.

The ability of a wetland to improve water quality is based primarily on the location of the wetland in the watershed, rather than on the size of the wetland. There is little evidence that wetlands that represent less than 5% of the watershed can have significant benefit (Hill, 1990). However, for wetlands to be important in water quality improvement, they must be located between contributing areas and receiving areas. In particular, the water quality improvement value of lacustrine wetlands varies with their location. Wetlands on large lakes provide no downstream benefits and receive no score.

The benefits that a wetland provides for water quality improvement downstream must consider what inputs it must treat. Wetlands provide an important and immediate benefit to water quality when land use practices immediately upstream and adjacent to the wetland provide organic or metal wastes which enter the wetland. Municipal, industrial and agricultural wastes are altered by biochemical and oxidative processes. Aquatic bacteria can mineralize dissolved organic molecules including toxins.

More sediments and chemicals are added to the surface waters in those areas where urban and agricultural uses have replaced natural ecosystems. Hence, any wetland within a drainage basin where agriculture or urban areas predominate will have more eutrophic and polluted waters than those in forested and/or naturally vegetated areas (Kadlec, 1983).

Sediment/toxicant retention is the process by which suspended sediments and chemical contaminants such as pesticides and heavy metals adsorbed to them are retained and deposited within a wetland. Deposition of sediments can ultimately lead to removal of toxicants through burial, chemical breakdown, or temporary assimilation into plant tissues.

The length of time sediments and toxicants are retained depends on the hydrologic and chemical characteristics of the specific wetland. Moderate frequency floods, occurring at periods of one to several years, are responsible for most erosion of riverine wetland sediments. Contaminated sediments can be re-suspended over decades, posing a chronic threat to aquatic life (Marron, 1987).

Some wetland vegetation forms are more important in the short-term removal of nutrients from water than others. The efficiency of removal is proportional to the vegetation forms present (Adamus & Stockwell, 1983). Plants that are annuals and have a high primary productivity will provide the maximum rate of nutrient uptake, but most of the nutrients will subsequently be released as the annual biomass decomposes. However, as maximum uptake occurs during the spring and early summer, annuals have the potential to remove nutrients during the period when downstream ecosystems are most biologically active.

Wetland vegetation can help trap sediment and retain suspended sediments by anchoring the shoreline, reducing the re-suspension of bottom muds by wind mixing, increasing the length of the flow path, contributing organic matter, and slowing water velocities. Even aquatic bed vegetation, which typically provides less resistance to water flow than emergent or woody vegetation, may reduce wave or current energies sufficiently to induce sediment settling.

The sediment trapping ability of wetlands will decline if they fill in or if flooding kills their vegetation, especially in dynamic environments. Physical processes and characteristics (e.g., gradient) in some cases may be more important for trapping sediment than the actual presence of wetland plants.

Compared with other landscape components, wetlands can be disproportionately important for sediment retention. Sediment retention in wetlands averages about 30 percent of the total entering, with a maximum retention of 95 percent (Streigal, 1987; Wolaver & Spurrier, 1988). Trees and shrubs are more long lived than emergents or submergents; therefore they tie up a fraction of their annual biomass growth as litter fall. However, the cycle of nutrient retention and release is not as seasonally dependent as in the case of annual plants.

In the long term (several years) the vegetation type of a wetland should be insignificant to nutrient retention. It is the soil condition which determines the rate of decomposition and, therefore, determines the nutrient pool that is buried and undecomposed organic material. The evaluation by vegetation type presented below addresses only the short-term, or seasonal, water quality benefits.

Long-term improvement of water quality refers to the capacity of inorganic sediments and organic soils to more or less permanently "lock up" nutrients and other chemicals from the water in a wetland. Major delta marshes (Whigham & Bailey, 1978) and peat forming wetlands that are still actively accumulating peat (Urban & Eisenriech, 1988) would be places where wetlands perform this function.

Any wetland with a retentive capacity for nutrients (e.g., those with organic soils), provides protection for recharging groundwater.

To a large degree, the physiographic circumstances of a wetland in the landscape will determine the extent to which it can act as a net receiver of nutrients and other compounds. Thus, wetlands located in places where rivers enter large lakes or reservoirs and deposit some of their sediment load are ones that would act as long-term nutrient sinks.

Processes

▶ **Amount of Incoming Sediment:** Sediment delivery usually increases with increased drainage area size, acreage of cleared land, precipitation, and lack of soil management measures. Important soil characteristics that relate to erodibility include soil particle size, aggregate stability, permeability, water holding capacity, and infiltration rate.

▶ **Particle Size and Density of Suspended Sediment:** Heavier particles naturally settle faster than lighter particles of the same size. It is for this reason that inorganic particles settle faster than organic particles.

▶ **Difference in Energy Levels:** Sediment deposition occurs where water velocity slows, usually as a result of increased cross-sectional area or bottom roughness. Sediment deposition is also enhanced by channel obstructions and other factors, such as wetland vegetation, which reduce wave or current velocity or extend the overland flow path. Sediment retention in wetlands without outlets approaches 100 percent because flow is totally stopped.

- **Vertical Layering Caused by Salinity and/or Temperature:** Intense stratification associated with salinity or temperature causes differences in water density and may counteract the natural settling tendencies of sediment by restricting vertical mixing across the layers.

- **Bioturbation and Mobilization:** Sediments and/or their associated toxicants can be re-suspended as the result of bottom-feeding fishes, aquatic invertebrates, and birds. This is termed bioturbation. Contaminants associated with deposited sediment can be reintroduced into the water column either by this process or by uptake by aquatic plants and subsequent release during decay. Bioturbation may also significantly alter the substrate such that soil drainage characteristics and plant growth are altered.

- **Storage Capacity of the Wetland:** A wetland's sediment trapping efficiency depends on its depth, volume and surface area. Where sediment deposition occurs, some wetlands gradually fill in. As the wetland surface is built up by sediment deposition, flooding frequency decreases, resulting in decreased sediment input. However, many wetlands may become filled over periods of hundreds of years. Others may be periodically flushed of stored sediment by large storms, or by herbivore activity and long-term precipitation cycles (Mitsch & Gosselink, 1986).

Indicators

In the rapid evaluation technique designed for and used in this study, a number of indicators were used to rank the influence and importance of a wetland for water quality improvement.

Table 4.6 demonstrates the rankings used and displays where the Noordhoek wetland placed when submitted to evaluation regarding the potential for water quality improvement (bolded values). Further explanation of the evaluation of the Noordhoek wetland is given below the table.

Table 4.6 Potential for water quality improvement

Wetland Characteristic	Low	Medium	High
Wetland Attenuation Factor (WAF)	>5%	5-9%	**10% or greater**
Prevailing current velocities are greater than the suspension thresholds of the prevailing sediment types	Yes	**Sometimes**	No
Wetland has a constricted outlet	No	Constricted at certain times of the year	**Always constricted**
Dominant Vegetation	Scrub-Shrub	**Emergent**	Submergent
Vegetation/Water Interspersion	**Wetland vegetation is completely separated from open water in wetland**	Wetland vegetation is partially interspersed with water in wetland	Wetland vegetation is completely interspersed with water in wetland
Width of vegetation adjacent to wetland	Less than 5 metres	5-10 meters	Greater than 10 metres
Catchment Landuse Factor (CLU)	Over 50% natural vegetation	Between 30 and 50% agricultural and/or urban	**Over 50% agricultural and/or urban**
Potential erosive forces present upstream of wetland	No	Found in some isolated parts	**Yes**
Sediment Sources	No potential inputs of sediment upstream of wetland	**Some opportunity for sediment input upstream of wetland**	Several significant sources for sediment input upstream of wetland
Contaminant Sources	No urban/ agricultural/ industrial areas upstream of wetland	Some urban/ agricultural/industrial areas upstream of wetland	**Urban/agricultural/ industrial areas upstream of wetland**
Wetland is channelized	Yes	**Partly**	No
Wetland is immediately downstream of an impoundment	Yes	N/A	**No**
Evidence of long term erosion/deposition of sediment	No	Some	**Yes**
Water Depth	Water depth is consistent throughout the year	Some fluctuation in water level	Extreme variation in water depth
Substrate Type	Gravel/Rubble	**Sandy**	Muddy/Organic

Water quality improvement in the Noordhoek wetland

▶ **Wetland/Watershed Ratio:** As noted earlier, the Wetland Attenuation Factor (WAF) equals 97%.

▶ **Gradient, Velocity:** The gradient upstream of the wetland is sufficient that severe erosion can take place. The average gradient of the middleslope areas in the catchment range from 5 to 30 degrees. Moreover, the urbanized areas upstream of the wetland would tend to "flush" sediments during storm events.

▶ **Inlets, Outlets:** One inlet and two outlets are present in the wetland complex.

▶ **Constrictions:** As noted earlier there are two outlets and one dam relevant to the wetland.

▶ **Vegetation Type:** The dominant vegetation of the catchment can be considered scrub-shrub (*Acacia/fynbos*). However, the presence of the berm and road that surround the wetland negates any effect the vegetation may have in controlling erosion. *Phragmites* and *Typha* dominate at the inlet of the wetland, where some erosion control may be taking place.

▶ **Vegetation/Water Interspersion:** There is no interspersion of water and vegetation with the wetland complex at Noordhoek. Water levels are kept artificially high during most of the year and the berm and concrete barrier that is along 80% of the perimeter of the wetland does not permit a gradient from lowland to upland that normally exists in wetland environments.

▶ **Vegetated Width:** Although there are some patches of *Junkus krausii, Sarcornnia dactylon, Cynodon dactylon,* and *Carpha glomerat* along the western and northern edges of the wetland, *Acacia* is the dominant vegetation form in the 10-metre periphery of the wetland.

▶ **Land Cover of the Watershed:** In examining 1:10000 air photographs, a grid overlay system was used to estimate the dominate land uses within the Noordhoek catchment. The entire western portion of the catchment has been urbanized, while new developments are being built in the northern area. It is estimated that 60% of the land within the catchment are in urban/agricultural uses, while the remaining 40% is dominated by *Acacia/fynbos* vegetation.

▶ **Sediment Sources:** Given the erosive capacity of the wind within the Fishhoek gap, the steep slopes of the catchment area, and the composition of the soils of the middleslope, there are many potential sources of sediment upstream of the wetland. In addition, sediment buildup was found in the area where the inlet intersects the *Typha/Phragmites* area, east of the open water.

▶ **Contaminant Sources:** The land use upstream of the wetland is predominantly urban. Although no industrial activities are taking place, septic systems and sanitary storm sewers can act as potential contaminant sources.

▶ **Direct Alteration:** Both outlets and the inlet to the Noordhoek wetland are constantly being altered. In addition, dredging operations take place periodically within the open water area of the wetland.

▶ **Water Level Control:** The Noordhoek wetland complex is upstream from a small impoundment found at Outlet 2.

▶ **Flooding Extent and Duration:** As noted earlier there is an approximately 1 m variance in the water level of the wetland resulting in approximately 30 to 40% fluctuation in the areal extent of flooding.

▶ **Water Depth:** On average, the wetland water level stays at 1.6 metres for at least 5 months of the year.

▶ **Substrate Type:** Core samples were taken at various locations around the wetland margin, and the samples were classified as being sandy with a small amount of organic material and mud at the top of the cores.

CONCLUSIONS

Assumptions/limitations of the evaluation scheme

The evaluation technique functioned rather successfully within the limits it was intended to. Out of the evaluation scheme has arisen the creation of the manual (Chapman & Kreutzwiser, 1997) "A Rapid Wetland Evaluation Technique forHydrological Functions in South Africa." The evaluation scheme functions as a broad-brush approach to evaluating the hydrologic functions of wetlands, and is based on information about correlative predictors that can be gathered quickly. It is primarily intended for use by persons who do not have access to an interdisciplinary team of technical experts on a daily basis.

This evaluation scheme is designed to alert resource managers, planners, and others to the probability that a particular wetland performs a specific hydrologic function, and also provides insight as to the local, regional, and national significance of those functions. This evaluation scheme should not be used where questions regarding wetland hydrologic functions must be answered definitively.

This evaluation scheme can also be used to compare ratings of a wetland under various future management or impact scenarios with its present ratings. However, evaluators must understand three limitations of such use. First, predictions of future physical and biological conditions must be accurate in order for the scheme to make accurate predictions about hydrologic conditions in the future. Second, because the scheme uses correlative variables rather than causative ones, post-impact ratings should be screened carefully. Last, this scheme cannot anticipate the cumulative impacts of various combined activities over time.

Hydrological significance of the Noordhoek wetland

In using the evaluation scheme to better understand the hydrological functions of the Noordhoek wetland, much was learned. Although it has been highly modified over the past decades, the hydrologic functions that the wetland performs cannot be underestimated. In some cases the modifications have actually provided more of an opportunity for the wetland to perform certain functions. However, the further modification of the wetland and the development of upstream areas may overload the wetland and diminish its ability to perform many of the important hydrologic functions.

The wetland has been rated as medium to high for floodflow alteration because of the following factors: the size of the wetland relative to the upstream area; the wetland has been dammed and all flood waters are confined; the urban and agricultural activities upstream of the wetland and; the ability of the wetland to expand during the wet season. The role of vegetation with respect to floodflow alteration is minimal, principally because of the channelization of the inlet and outlet and the presence of the berm surrounding the wetland.

Although the studies have shown that the Noordhoek wetland is situated in a groundwater discharge area, there is some possibility that the wetland may also be acting as a periodic recharge area. This is partially due to the fact that most of the upstream area does not allow for recharge and also because of the hydraulic head created by the damming of the receiving waters. The recharge capabilities of the wetland, however, are most like insignificant compared to those of other recharge areas found within the catchment area.

Previous studies have shown that the Noordhoek wetland is found within a groundwater discharge area. In addition to this direct information, a number of indicators also strongly suggest that the wetland is acting as a groundwater discharge area: the size of the wetland relative to the upstream area; the steep slopes of the catchment area surrounding the wetland and; the expansion of the wetland area during the wet season.

The Noordhoek wetland not only serves to protect downstream areas from erosion; the immediate area around the wetland also benefits from the presence of the wetland. The wetland ranks medium to high for the probability that it performs an erosion control function. One of the difficulties in rating the wetland for erosion control stems from the fact that the open water area is surrounded by a berm which artificially confines floodwaters. Although these berms are heavily vegetated with *Acacia*, there is very little submergent or emergent vegetation in the periphery of the open water area. The dense thickets of *Phragmites* and *Typha* more than likely provide the most benefit for erosion control within the immediate area of the wetland.

Many of the indicators used to assess the wetland for its erosion control capability are also used to assess the water quality improvement function. Again, the presence of the *Phragmites* and *Typha* at the inlet serves to decrease the velocity of the water and also to cause some sediment to accumulate. The dam found at the main outlet of the wetland serves to keep water levels artificially high and aids in the deposition of sediments. In addition to the effect of the vegetation and the dam, activities upstream of the wetland provide the opportunity for the wetland to improve the quality of the incoming water. Activities upstream of the wetland have the potential to be sources of contaminants and sediments and also serve to provide more surface runoff compared to "naturally" vegetated areas.

The direct links to the hydrologic functions that the wetland performs and the increasing pressures caused by developing water supply infrastructure can already be seen in the Noordhoek area. Although drawdown has not become a serious problem in the basin, the local aquifers are already seen as a potential water source for the rapidly developing urban area surrounding the wetland.

In the face of urban development and the need for clean water, the Noordhoek wetland not only serves to trap sediments, but it also acts to improve the water quality for downstream users. In some cases, the wetland may act to recharge localized aquifers during the dry season because of the impounded water.

Although the potential of the wetland to be a surface water source in the future is minimal, many of the secondary effects of developing water supply infrastructure may impinge on many of the important functions the wetland performs. Sanitary sewers upstream of the wetland can cause more frequent flooding, overload the wetland with nutrients and toxicants, and decrease the amount of groundwater that would normally discharge in the wetland. Removal of vegetation upstream of the wetland for development and further channelizing the incoming waters could possibly negate much of the function that the wetland performs with respect to water quality improvement, erosion control, and floodflow alteration.

REFERENCES

Adamus, P.R. and Stockwell, L.T. 1983: *A Method for Wetland Functional Assessment. Vol. 1 and 2*. Report FWHA-1P-82-23. (US Federal Administration).

Bay, R.R. 1969: Runoff from Small Peatland Watersheds. *J. Hydrology*, 9, 90-102.

Bedlinger, M.S. 1979: Relation Between Forest Species and Flooding. In P.E. Greeson, J.R. Clark, and J.E. Clark (eds), *Wetland Functions and Values: The State of Our Understanding*, pp. 427-435. Minneapolis: American Water Resources Association.

Born, S.M., Smith, S.A. and Stephenson, D.A. 1979: Hydrogeology of Glacial-Terrain Lakes, With Management and Planning Applications. *J. Hydrology*, 43, 7-43.

Carter, V., Bedlinger, M.S., Novitzki, R.P. and Wilen, W.O. 1978: Water Resources and Wetlands. In P.E. Greeson, J.R. Clark, and J.E. Clark (eds), *Wetland Functions and Values: The State of Our Understanding*, pp. 344-376. Minneapolis: American Water Resources Association.

Carter, V. 1986: An Overview of the Hydrologic Concerns Related to Wetlands in the United States. *Can. J. Bot.*, 64, 364-374.

Cowling, R.M. 1985: *Vegetation of the Noordhoek Basin*. Cape Town: Kirstenbosch Institute of Botanical Research.

Devito, K.J., Dillon, P.J. and Lazerte, B.D. 1989: Phosphorous and Nitrogen Retention in Five Precambrian Shield Wetlands. *Biogeochemistry*, 8, 185-204.

Eisenlohr, W.S., Jr. 1966: Water Loss from a Natural Pond Through Transpiration by Hydrophytes. *Water Resources. Res.*, 2, 443-453.

Flores, A.C., Bedient, P.B. and Mays, L.W. 1981: Method for Optimizing Size and Location of Urban Detention Storage. In *Proceedings of the International Symposium on Urban Hydrology, Hydraulics and Sediment Control*, pp. 357-365. New York: ASCE.

Gasson, B. 1983: *Planning Implications for the Noordhoek/Kommetjie Environment: Development Options in the Noordhoek Valley. Volume 1: Sun Valley.* Noordhoek and District Civic Association.

Gasson, B. 1984: *Planning Implications for the Noordhoek/Kommetjie Environment: Development Options in the Noordhoek Valley. Volume II: Kommetjie.* Noordhoek and District Civic Association.

Gosselink, J.C. and Turner, R.E. 1978: The Role of Hydrology in Freshwater Wetland Ecosystems. In R.E. Good, D.F. Whigman and R.L. Simpson (eds), *Freshwater Wetlands: Ecological Processes and Management Potential*, pp. 63-78. New York: Academic Press.

Heinecken, T.J. 1985: *Estuaries of the Cape Part II. Synopsis of the available information on individual systems. Wildevoelvlei/Noordhoek (cw 28)*. Research Report No. 27. Stellenbosch: CSIR.

Hendrickson, G.E., Knutilla, R.L. and Doonan, C.J. 1973: *Hydrology and Recreation on Selected Coldwater Rivers of the St. Lawrence River Basin in Michigan, New York, and Wisconsin.* Rep. USGS-WRD-73009. Reston: US Geological Survey.

Hill, A.R. 1990: Groundwater Flow Paths in Relation to Nitrogen Chemistry in Near-Stream Zone. *Hydrobiologia*, 206, 39-52.

Hill, A. and Warick, J. 1987: Ammonium Transformation in Springwater Within the Riparian Zone of a Small Woodland Stream. *Canadian Journal of Fisheries and Aquatic Sciences*, 44, 1938-1956.

Johnson, C.A. and Naiman, R.J. 1987: Boundary Dynamics at Aquatic-terrestrial Interface: The Influence of Beaver and Geomorphology. *Landscape Ecology*, 1, 47-57.

Johnson, C.A., Detenbeck, N.E. and Niemi, G.J. 1990: The Cumulative Effect of Wetlands on Stream Water Quality and Quantity. A Landscape Approach. *Biogeochemistry* 10, 105-141.

Kadlec, R.H. 1983: The Bellaire Wetland Wastewater Alteration and Recovery. *Soc. Wetland Sci.*, 3, 44-63.

Marron, D.C. 1987: Floodplain Storage of Metal-Contaminated Sediments Downstream of a Gold Mine at Lead, South Dakota. In R.C. Averett and D.M. McKnight (eds), *Chemical Quality of Water and the Hydrologic Cycle*, pp. 193-209. Clesea: Lewis Publishers.

McBride, M.S. and Pfannkuch, H.O. 1975: The distribution of seepage within lakebeds. *J. Res. US Geol. Surv.*, 3, 505-512.

Ministry of Water Affairs and Forestry. 1995: *Water Supply and Sanitation White Paper.* URL http://www.polity.org.za/govdocs/white_papers/water.html.

Ministry of Water Affairs and Forestry. 1996: *Fundamental Principles and Objectives for a New Water Law in South Africa: Report to the Minister of Water Affairs and Forestry of the Water Law Review Panel.* URL http://www.polity.org.za/water/lawreview.html.

Mitsch, W.J. and Gosselink, J.G. 1986: *Wetlands.* New York: Van Nostrand Reinhold.

Nestler, J.M and Long, K.S. 1994: *Cumulative Impact Analysis of Wetlands Using Hydrologic Indices.* Technical Report WRP-SM-3. Vicksberg: U.S. Army Corps of Engineers, Waterways Experiment Station.

Novitzki, R.P. 1979: The hydrologic characteristics of Wisconsin wetlands and their influence on floods, streamflow, and sediment. In P.E. Greeson, J.R. Clark, and J.E. Clark (eds), *Wetland Functions and Values: The State of Our Understanding,* pp. 377-388. Minneapolis: American Water Resources Association.

Ogawa, H. and Male, J.W. 1983: *The Flood Mitigation Potential of Inland Wetlands.* Amherst: University of Massachusetts Water Resources Centre.

Peterjohn, W.T. and Correll, D.L. 1984: Nutrient Dynamics in an Agricultural Watershed: Observations on the Role of a Riparian Forest. *Ecology,* 65, 1466-1475.

Pinay, G. and Decamps, H. 1988: The Role of Riparian Woods in Regulation Nitrogen Fluxes between the Alluvial Aquifer and Surface Water: A Conceptual Model. *Regulated Rivers: Research and Management,* 2, 507-516.

Rosewarne, P. 1991: *Proposed Noordhoek Kaolin Mine - Report on Ground Water Investigation.* Report 173078/6. Cape Town: Steffan, Robertson and Kirsten Consulting Engineers.

Roulet, N.T. 1989: Groundwater Flux in a Headwater Wetland in Southern Ontario. In M.J. Bardecki and N. Patterson (eds), *Ontario Wetlands: Inertia or Momentum,* pp. 301-308. Don Mills: Federation of Ontario Naturalists.

Roulet, N.T. 1990: Hydrology of a Headwater Basin Wetland. Groundwater Discharge and Wetland Maintenance. *Hydrological Processes,* 4, 387-400.

Siegal, D.I. and Glasser, P.H. 1987: Groundwater Flow in a Bog-Fen Complex, Lost River Peatland, Northern Minnesota. *J. Ecol.,* 75, 743-754.

Siegel, D.I. 1988: A Review of Recharge-Discharge Functions of Wetlands. In Hook *et. al.* (ed.), *Ecology and Management of Wetlands,* pp. 61-69. Croom Helm Ltd.

Streigal, R.G. 1987: Suspended sediment and metals removal from urban runoff by a small lake. *Water Resources. Bull.* 23(6), 985-996.

Taylor, Van Rensurg, Van der Spuy and Visser. 1994: *Noordhoek Wetlands: Planning and Management Guidelines for the Proposed Nature Conservation Area.* Cape Town: Western Cape Regional Services Council.

Urban, N.R. and Eisenriech, S.J. 1988: Nitrogen Cycling in a Forested Minnesota Bog. *Can. J. Bot.*, 66, 435-449.

Verry, E.S. 1988: The Hydrology of Wetlands and Man's Influence on Them. *Proceedings of the International Symposium of the Hydrology of Wetlands in the Temperate and Cold Regions. The Academy of Finland, Helsinki*, 1, 41-61.

Verry, E.S., Brooks, K.N. and Barten, P.K. 1988: Streamflow Response from an Ombrotrophic Mire. *Proceedings of the International Symposium of the Hydrology of Wetlands in the Temperate and Cold Regions. The Academy of Finland, Helsinki*, 1, 52-59.

Wharton, C.H. 1970: *The Southern River Swamp: A Multiple Use Environment.* Atlanta: Georgia State University, Bureau of Business Economics Research.

Whigham, D.F. and Bayley, S.E. 1978: Nutrient Dynamics in Freshwater Wetlands. In P.E. Greeson, J.R. Clark, and J.E. Clark (eds), *Wetlands Functions and Values: The State of Our Understanding*, pp. 478-488. Minneapolis: American Water Resources Association.

Whiteley, H.R. and Irwin, R.W. 1986: The Hydrological Response of Wetlands in Southern Ontario, Canada. *Water Res. J.*, 11, 124-147.

Wolaver, T.G. and Spurrier, J.D. 1988: The exchange of phosphorous between a euhaline vegetated marsh and the adjacent tidal creek. *Esturaine Coastal Shelf Sci.*, 26, 203-214.

Woo, M.K. and Valverde, J. 1981: Summer Streamflow and Water Level in a Mid-Latitude Swamp. *Forest Sci.*, 27, 177-189.

Chapter 5

LUSAKA'S GROUNDWATER RESOURCES AT RISK

by Chimwang'a Maseka and Imasiku Nyambe

INTRODUCTION

The city of Lusaka, capital of the Republic of Zambia, lies on a plateau with an elevation of about 1300 metres above sea level. It is a growing urban centre, with a rapidly rising population of about 1.5 million people. Underlying Lusaka is a dolomite and karstic aquifer which supplies 90,000 cubic metres of water daily, representing 42% of the city's urban water supply. The remainder of the water supply is obtained via pipeline from the Kafue River, located 60 kilometres south of the city. Groundwater use to supply the city has changed drastically over the latter half of this century. Between 1950 and 1965, an average of 40,000 cubic metres of water per day were pumped from this aquifer for the urban water supply. From 1978, the pumpage from the aquifer was increased to 110,000 cubic metres per day of water. By 1996, the pumpage was reduced to 80,000 cubic metres per day.

Groundwater extractions for the city's urban supply and other purposes, such as farming and industry, have been going on without control. Various private users indiscriminately drill wells and extract groundwater. Human activities accompanying urbanization go on without regard to aquifer protection. The Lusaka South Forest is considered to be the recharge area for the aquifer supplying the city's water. The area was degazetted in 1985. As a result, most of the current and future industrial development will be on this karst aquifer. The aquifer already suffers from over-pumping, indiscriminate drilling, pollution from industrial effluents, and domestic pollution. The future of Lusaka's groundwater resources is indeed at risk.

This study addresses a number of issues relevant to that risk, including:

▶ the hydrological and environmental impacts of uncontrolled groundwater extraction from the dolomite aquifer around Lusaka

- available groundwater supplies
- groundwater pollution resulting from industrial and human activity directly associated with a sensitive aquifer
- an assessment of possible pollution sources such as industrial effluents, garbage disposal sites, and septic tanks
- the effect of poor land practices around the aquifer recharge zone on the groundwater resources of the Lusaka area

STUDY AREA

Lusaka is situated on a flat plateau at an elevation of about 1300 m, occupying an area approximately 70 km long and 10 km wide. The main business district is centrally located, with light and heavy industries situated to the northwest. The area under examination is located approximately between latitudes 15E°10' and 15E°50' S and longitudes 27E°45' and 28E°30' E.

The study area was selected to include borehole data available at the Lusaka Water and Sewerage Company. The private water supply company was established in 1985 and is wholly owned by the Lusaka City Council. The company is the sole supplier of water to the people of Lusaka. The city uses about 190,000 cubic metres per day of water, of which 53% is derived from surface sources and 47% from the underground aquifer (groundwater). The groundwater is extracted through a network of about 40 active boreholes scattered across the city. Surface water is pumped via pipeline from the Kafue River. As this study hinges on the sustainable development of the aquifer, the Lusaka Water and Sewerage Company took an interest in it and allowed the monitoring of 52 of their wells, of which 40 are production wells and 12 are observation wells.

The research base was the Department of Water Affairs located near the city centre. The research base is about 30 kilometres from the four observation wells, which are located to the southeast of Lusaka, along an unmaintained gravel road. It takes five to six hours to travel from the research base to these wells, including time to walk on bush trails to reach the well sites. Eight observation wells are situated in Lusaka West, scattered over an area about 45 kilometres long by 10 kilometres wide. It takes about eight hours of driving on partly tarred road, gravel road, bush, and farm tracks to reach these wells from the research base. The 40 production wells scattered throughout the urban region of Lusaka, over an area of about 20 square kilometres, are reasonably accessible.

Geomorphology and drainage

The morphology of the area is the result of weathering of schist and quartzite, resulting in hills intersected by many valleys. The plateau forms part of the Central African Plateau, which has an average elevation of 1200 m, and is part of extensive erosion known as the Gondwana and African Surfaces (King, 1948, 1967; Dixey, 1945).

The study area ranges from an elevation of just over 1300 m on the Lusaka plateau on the southwestern section to just below 1100 m near Chongwe in the northeast. Schist and quartzite underlie the northeastern section, which consists of hills intersected by valleys. Surface drainage in this area is well developed, with streams beginning at the intersection between limestone/dolomite and schist (Figure 5.1). The central area is underlain mostly by dolomite and limestone and is generally flat, with a notable absence of surface drainage. Subsurface drainage, however, is well developed in the highly permeable karstic dolomite and limestone. In this area, streams emerge where sub-surface drainage meets a hydraulic barrier such as impermeable schist, and then flow on the surface schist terrain, only to again disappear underground, where they intersect another dolomite and limestone area.

Rainwater drains into fissures and sinkholes in areas where the rock outcrops, and infiltrates through the laterite cover in areas with thick overburden, hence joining the underground water. The Lusaka dolomite plateau forms the watershed among the Chunga flowing westwards to join the Mwembeshi (a tributary of the Kafue), the Ngwerere and Chalimbana flowing northeastwards to join the Chongwe (a tributary of the Zambezi), and the smaller streams heading south and dewatering directly into the Kafue.

Figure 5.1 Drainage map of Lusaka area

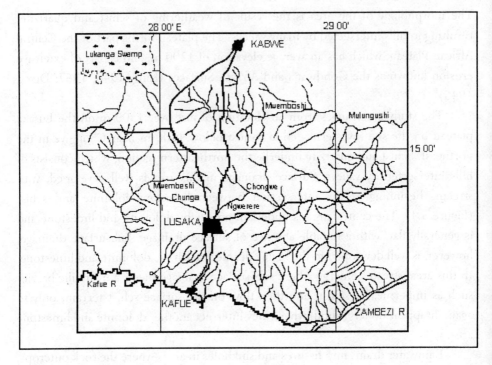

Climate

Zambia is located near the centre of the high plateau of central and southern Africa. The climate is largely dependent on latitude, elevation, and position on the continent. The plateau has a temperate climate. There are three distinct seasons in Zambia: a dry, cool season or winter from mid April to August, a hot season from September to October, and a rainy season from November to April. The average annual rainfall is about 820 mm. The mean minimum and maximum temperatures are 17°C and 32°C. Most of the Zambian rainfall is controlled by convection, with local effects due to relief.

Vegetation

Savannah-type woodlands cover Zambia. The vegetation types relate closely to soil types, such that in areas of poor rock exposure, the vegetation generally can be a reliable indicator of underlying lithology. Miombo woodland is the predominant vegetation on the plateau.

Soils

The soils are derived from underlying rock types and fall into two main types:

- **soils derived from the Basement complex and the Kantangan schist:** These are light yellowish brown and sandy soils, 1.5 m thick. The National Council for Scientific Research's 1971 research results over similar soils at Luano catchment indicate an infiltration rate of about 76 mm/hr, effective porosity of 417 mm/m, field capacity of 250-328 mm/m and wilting point of 164-209 mm/m.

- **soils overlying the karstic dolomite:** Residue dark brown clays and pellet laterites cover the karst surface to depths up to 30 m. Infiltration tests on the Lusaka dolomite by M. Tague (quoted in Jones, 1971) gave infiltration capacity of 76 mm/hr. The shallow depressions liable to seasonal waterlogging are floored by impervious clays. The soils have very high potential for groundwater recharge and a correspondingly high potential for contamination.

Hydrogeology

The study area comprises Cambrian to Pre-Cambrian rocks of the Katanga Supergroup namely, limestone, dolomite, schist and quartzite, lying on the basement complex which consists of crystalline rocks such as gneiss, quartzite and amphibolite. Overlying the Katangan rocks are Quaternary to Recent alluvium and colluvium deposits.

Previous researchers have evaluated the hydrogeology of the Lusaka area and their findings were summarized in Maseka (1994). Briefly, these findings were:

- The Lusaka dolomite aquifer has the best groundwater potential to support the city water supply and for large-scale exploitation.
- There are no hydraulic differences between the Lusaka dolomite and the Cheta Formation carbonate rocks as suggested by previous reports. Groundwater availability is therefore not limited to the Lusaka dolomite only.
- The other lithologies such as schist and quartzite have poor groundwater potential (poor aquifers) and hence cannot be used for large-scale water supply (FIGNR, 1978; Jones, 1971).
- Monthly climate data analysis showed that the annual recharge to the aquifer was 162-200 mm, depending upon vegetation cover, and represents 20-40% of the total rainfall.

In other Karstic areas (Hadwen, 1972; Wimpey Laboratories Limited, 1983) such as the Kabwe Carbonates (Jones, 1971) about 200 km north of Lusaka, 30-45% of the annual rainfall infiltrates to recharge the aquifer.

Recent studies with similar findings as above are those of Yachiyo Engineering (1995). The Yachiyo Engineering study covers the entire country with a focus on the National Water Resources Master Plan for Zambia. The study indicates that Karstic aquifers, such as the Lusaka Dolomite, are the best sources of groundwater in Zambia, with an average aquifer thickness of 18 m and average specific capacity of 50.2 m^2/day.

Groundwater circulation, and subsequently karstification, is controlled by the water base level given by less pervious schist surrounding the carbonate rocks. The main flow in the Lusaka Dolomite is directed to the northwest (FIGNR, 1978). Natural discharge occurs in certain areas along the schist-dolomite intersect as small intermittent springs and seepage.

GROUNDWATER RESOURCE ANALYSIS

Rainfall

The climate in Zambia is characterized by an annual alternation between the wet and the dry season. In Lusaka the wet season lasts for about six months from November to April. An average of about 820 mm of rainfall is received during this time. The dry season lasts from May to October, during which there is little or no rain.

Table 5.1 Showing monthly rainfall figures for Lusaka International Airport, 1995 to 1997 rain seasons

	Sep	Oct	Nov	Dec	Jan	Feb	Mar	Apr	May	Jun	Jul	Aug	Total
1995/96 (mm)			29.9	20.1	164.4	216.9	91.2		6.9				529.4
1996/97 (mm)			77.8	148.7	296.9	169.1	21.5						714

Stream gauging

Reconnaissance surveys were carried out between December 26, 1997 and January 1, 1998 to identify stations within the project area where stream flows could be carried out. At each of the sites visited the following features were considered:

- site accessibility
- geological and geomorphological features
- hydraulic conditions necessary for maintaining a permanent relationship between stage and discharge

A total of ten sites were visited and assessed during the reconnaissance survey. Of these, only three (Chalimbana River at Romor Farm, Ngwerere River at Malima Village, and Mungu River at Mungu Village) were found to be perennial and therefore suitable sites. Due to limited time and logistics, further stream gauging activities could not be carried out.

Static and dynamic groundwater levels

Groundwater levels from 11 observation wells located on the outskirts of Lusaka and 40 production wells used for the Lusaka Urban water supply were observed beginning July, 1997. Water levels from the 11 observation wells show an annual drop in water levels of 6.2 m.

The annual variation of water levels in the production wells is 10.6 m. The average dynamic water level within urban Lusaka in July 1997 (three months into the dry season) was found to be 12.2 m. There are, however, areas of concern regarding dynamic water levels far below the average (Table 5.2).

Table 5.2 Showing dynamic water levels of areas of concern in Lusaka Urban

	July	Feb	Nov
Chelstone	30.80 m	25.30 m	35.55 m
Freedom (Chilanga area)	20.85 m	16.00 m	22.10 m
Mulungushi	25.50 m	25.60 m	22.00 m
Show grounds	23.20 m	24.50 m	26.20 m
Shaft 5	22.98 m	17.70 m	24.63 m

Groundwater abstraction versus water demand

The water supply for urban Lusaka has at least 50 production wells. An average of about 40 wells are used daily to pump about 90,000 m³/day. This figure is only 47% of the total 190,000 m³/day of surface and groundwater utilized for the urban water supply. Of the 40 production wells, about 80% are pumped continuously for 24 hours per day. The population of Lusaka for 1998 as projected from the

National Water Master Plan Study stands at 1,122,500 people. Using 180 litres/capital/day, this gives a domestic water demand of 202,050 m³/day. The industrial water demand for 1998 as projected from the same study is 86,580 cm³/day. The total water demand (domestic and industry) for Lusaka is therefore 288,630 m³/day. Compared with the total water pumped per day of 190,000 m³/day, the demand far outstrips the supply. Consequently, between 3,000 and 4,000 private boreholes have been indiscriminately drilled throughout Lusaka to meet the shortfall. The situation is worsened by the absence of a control mechanism in the form of groundwater legislation.

Groundwater potential

Fractured schist and dolomite/limestone underlie the city of Lusaka. In rock formations, groundwater occurs in weathered zones, fractures, joints, faults, and solution channels. It follows then, that the aquifers in these fractured rocks are heterogeneous and anisotropic, often isolated from one another.

The Lusaka Schist: The Chunga and Cheta Formation schist are lithologically similar. Because of this they have been grouped into one hydrogeological unit. The occurrence of groundwater in schist depends upon tectonic fracturing, quartz veining, and chemical weathering. The schist have only fracture and intergranular porosity of tectonic origin, as primary porosity has been destroyed by metamorphism. Highly fractured quartz veins produce localized zones of high porosity and permeability. Jones (1971) has given a detailed description of weathering in the Kabwe schist that is quite similar to the Lusaka schist. Progressive chemical weathering of the schist destroys the fracture porosity and produces clays. Thus the top-most zones of the schist profile are characterized by high intergranular porosity, low specific yield and low permeability. A decomposed zone and an active weathering front exist below this clay layer. The base of the active weathering front is marked by unaltered schist. Porosity, specific yield and permeability are highest at the bottom of the decomposed zone.

The Lusaka schist generally has low yields ranging from 0.4 m³/hr to 18 m³/hr. Boreholes are drilled up to a depth of about 60 m, depending on the extent of the weathered zones. Groundwater occurs under confined and semi-confined conditions. Specific capacities range from 0.01 to 10.0 m³/hr/m (FIGNR, 1978). The schist has low infiltration rates and high runoff, due to the existence of clays which result from weathering. It therefore makes a poor aquifer with localized groundwater occurrences.

The Lusaka Karstic Dolomite Aquifer: A number of reports describe the limestone and dolomite of the Cheta Formation as having poorer groundwater potential than the Lusaka Dolomite. Simpson, Drysdall and Lambert (1963) pointed out that the availability of water from the Cheta Formation was poor and the probability of boreholes suitable for large-scale abstraction was low. The Lusaka Dolomite, on the other hand, is described by most reports as the most suitable for large-scale groundwater extraction. However, it must be pointed out that there are no hydraulic differences between the Lusaka Dolomite and the Cheta Formation carbonate rocks, as both have strong karstic features resulting from the dissolution of carbonate rocks.

Dolomite and limestone aquifers generally are partly tectonically deformed metamorphosed rocks. Groundwater flow occurs through fractures and joints, which have been enlarged by dissolution of carbonate rocks. The flow of groundwater is controlled by conduit location. Groundwater flow occurs as a result of tube location in cave passages or by diffuse flow paths in karst areas. This structure is formed by the topographic relationship between the aquifer recharge zone and discharge zones.

Karst areas have a flat topography and surface runoff is rare. Recharge areas occur on elevated locations such as hilly areas and may be characterised by thin soils, rock outcrops, a zone of collapse features, and sinkholes. Discharge zones are controlled by altitude and occur in low-lying swampy areas or *dambos*, which overflow to perennial watercourses. Springs are common along discharge zones. A network of enlarged fissures following joint planes and cavitation in the form of sheet fissures occur at various depths cutting the limestone and dolomite aquifer.

The zone of greatest circulation and karstification is between 0-25 m. Solution cavities, with some laterite infilling, occur at depths of 65-80 m and 125-150 m. This suggests a vertical link with the higher aquifer base. The epikarst zone is at 25 m and the general aquifer base at 150 m.

Simpson *et. al.* (1963) observed that where collapsed breccia occurs in soluble bands of dolomite, there is often extensive cavitation which acts as an interconnected reservoir. Such occurrences are often favourable sites for high-yield boreholes.

The karstic dolomite and limestone aquifer has very high permeability and porosity varying with depth. Average borehole yields are between 15-30 m3/hr.

Exploration drilling for the Lusaka water supply encountered borehole yields of 126-360 m3/hr. Specific capacities vary between 0-03 - 100 m3. Pumping tests were conducted on these exploration boreholes, but cannot be used for the analysis of aquifer characteristic, as karst aquifers have localized transmissivity and aquifer characteristics cannot be evaluated with standard pumping test analysis. Based on a flow net analysis, Jones (1972) obtained a transmissivity of 372 m2/day for the Kabwe dolomite, which is similar to that of the Lusaka area. Evaluation of the unconfined storage, based upon annual variations in the groundwater table, returned a storage ratio of 3%. This is comparable to values of 3% from Mpongwe Mission (Wimpey Laboratories, 1983), and values of 3 to 5% (Maseka, 1994), which were based on daily rainfall of a one dimensional catchment water balance model.

The main groundwater flow direction over the aquifer is from the southeast to the northwest, with branches to the northeast and southwest. The highest potentiometric levels are around 1300 m over the Lusaka Forest Reserve; this appears to be the principle recharge area. Groundwater flow in this part of the aquifer is confined and the water table follows the topography. The discharge areas are in low lying swamps or *dambos* located amongst the areas of Kalingalinga to University of Zambia, the Natural Resources Development College to Avondale, the Chamba Valley to Ngwerere, and Chunga to Barlaston Park. The discharge zones are associated with the dolomite-limestone/schist contact and are characterized by perennial springs.

Ground water recharge

Measurements of the groundwater level in a well or borehole plotted against time result in a groundwater hydrograph. Changes in the level of the hydrograph during the year reflect gross changes in the flow of water to the aquifer in the area. The groundwater hydrograph provides a way of assessing aquifer response to recharge and to losses by seepage and evapotranspiration. The change in groundwater storage may be expressed as follows:

$$\sum \Delta S = \Delta GWL \times \text{storage coefficient} \times \text{area}$$
$$\sum \Delta S = \Delta GWL \times t \times A$$

ΔS = Change in groundwater storage

ΔGWL = Annual variation in groundwater level

t = storage coefficient

A = Area

Groundwater recharge, on the other hand, may be calculated from the balance between input from rainfall and output in the form of losses to runoff, seepage and evapotranspiration. This may be expressed by the equation:

$\Delta S = P - E_{ta} - R$

where P = precipitation (mm)

E_{ta} = actual evapotranspiration (mm)

R = runoff, expressed as depth over catchment (mm)

ΔS = increase in stored water (mm)

The present well field for Lusaka's urban water supply exists over an area of 16 km by 12 km, giving a total area of 192 km^2. Using an annual variation in groundwater levels of 6.2 m and a storage coefficient of 0.03, the change in groundwater storage is therefore:

$\sum \Delta S$ = 6.2m x 0.03 x 192,000,000 m^2

= 35,712,000 m^3/year

= 97,841 m^3/day

The change in groundwater storage of 97,841 m^3/day is comparable to 90,000 m^3/day of groundwater pumped from the Lusaka Urban supply well field. From an annual variation of 6.2 m observed in the Lusaka aquifer and from an annual rainfall of 714 mm, a recharge of 186 mm of rainfall was obtained. This represents about 27% of the annual rainfall. This indicates an annual supply of 35,712,000 m^3/year in the urban Lusaka water supply well field.

Urbanization of Lusaka has resulted in the degazetting of the Lusaka South Forest no. 26 in 1985. This area forms the headwaters of the Chalimbana River and many other smaller streams. Above all, it is considered to be the principal recharge area for the Lusaka karstic dolomite-limestone aquifer. Following the degazetting of the forest, the area was sub-divided into smaller farms (smallholdings). In 1995, part of the forest was regazetted due to pressures from environmentalists, community-based organizations, water resources experts and the Ministry of the Environment. Nonetheless, human settlement in the area has led to the cutting down of trees, the cultivation of crops, and construction. Such development pressures will continue. Urbanization in this area has introduced many changes to the aquifer. The natural recharge mechanism has been modified, resulting in reduced stream discharge over the Chalimbana catchment and reduced well yields throughout the aquifer. Other poor land use practices in Lusaka include industrial pollution, the pit latrines commonly used in the informal settlements surrounding the city, leaking sewer lines, and considerable effluent discharge into the Ngwerere River.

GROUNDWATER QUALITY

Electrical conductivity

For most groundwater, electrical conductivity (EC) is a good measure of the relative mineral concentration. Waters containing dissolved inorganic salts and the resulting ions are relatively good conductors and therefore have high electrical conductivity values. Electrical conductivity measurements are generally quick and reliable indicators for relative differences in water quality between different aquifers. Water high in dissolved salts, and therefore high in conductivity, may not be suitable for use. EC values were taken from 33 boreholes and these indicate values between 324-820 μs/cm, with the exception of four areas that have values between 1040-1400 μs/cm. The water quality in these areas is deteriorating, but is still acceptable for water supply purposes.

Groundwater pollution

The Lusaka aquifer is becoming increasingly polluted as a result of human activity. Three major sources of pollution threatening the aquifer are urbanization, industrial activity and agricultural practices.

Impact of urbanization on groundwater

The city suffers from an inadequate sewerage system. Only about 32% of the city is served by sewer line. Approximately 43% is serviced by septic tanks and 25% by pit latrines. Ironically, the areas serviced by pit latrines, though smallest in size, have higher population densities than those served by septic tanks and sewer lines. Pollutants from leaking sewer lines, septic tanks and pit latrines easily penetrate into the groundwater. Lusaka has many shallow, privately owned boreholes providing drinking water. Most of these are inadequately protected from pollutants and may produce microbiologically contaminated water. The level of nitrate in Chainda, Mumbwa Road (Roadside), Freedom, Chawama, and Chunga boreholes, as observed from chemical analysis of raw water, is higher than the World Health Organization (WHO) accepted limit of 10 mg/l. The source of the nitrate is decomposing organic matter associated with pit latrines and septic tanks.

About 400,000 tonnes/year of domestic and industrial garbage is generated in the city and less than 20% of this is collected by city employees. Uncontrolled dumping is common within the boundaries of Lusaka Urban and no records are kept of the nature of wastes disposed even at the controlled disposal sites. Rainwater leaches chemicals from the garbage and infiltrates into the aquifers, resulting in serious groundwater pollution. A good example of this is the Libala dumpsite, located in the groundwater recharge zone.

Pollution from Industrial Activity: The heavy industrial area in Lusaka is located directly on the karstic aquifer. Industries include meat processing, vegetable oil, paper, breweries, metals, various materials, and engineering workshops. Service industries such as metal workshops, dry cleaners, photo processing, and printers use considerable quantities of potentially toxic contaminants. These are usually poorly disposed of by dumping into trenches and drains along the side of the roads.

Groundwater contamination can also be caused by spills and leaks of toxic hazardous chemicals. There is little or no information regarding the life-span of underground fuel tanks situated on this aquifer. It is highly probable that many of them have slow leaks.

Throughout Lusaka, there are many industrial quarries from which rock is obtained for various uses such as construction and the supply of marble. Most of these quarries, upon intersecting the water table, are abandoned and used as refuse dumps. Surface water from these sites is a pollution source which eventually finds its way into boreholes. Of great concern are the relatively small pits dug close to roads throughout Lusaka to extract dolomite boulders which are manually crushed for building materials.

Pollution from Agricultural Practices: A number of commercial farms are located on the outskirts of Lusaka, directly over the aquifer. The intensive use of nitrogen-rich fertilizers and of pesticides is a threat to water resources. A high level of nitrate and, in some areas, pesticides in groundwater is attributed to intensive agriculture. Groundwater pollution is generally worse where soil is very permeable, allowing agricultural chemicals to quickly percolate to underlying aquifers. The extent of pollution from fertilizers and pesticides in the area has not been accurately and thoroughly studied.

DISCUSSION AND CONCLUSION

Groundwater levels observed over the period of this research have been used as a basis for evaluating groundwater recharge. Annual variations in water levels averaged 6.2 m in observation wells and 10.2 in production wells. The groundwater recharge to the aquifer is estimated to be 186 mm. This is a direct result of an annual rainfall of 714 mm. This gives annual groundwater supply of 35,712,000 m^3/year in the Lusaka water supply well field, which is comparable to the 32,850,000 m^3/year abstracted for the urban water supply. When abstractions from private boreholes are considered, the groundwater supply is obviously endangered. Areas within the well field around Show grounds, Chelstone, and Shaft 5 show signs of over-pumping as seen from the dynamic water levels. Analyses of water samples indicate high conductivity levels, in the range of 1000-1400 μs/cm, coupled with high nitrate levels (15-40 mg/l) in some suburbs. Human activity in the Forest Reserve, considered to be the principle recharge zone, has modified the recharge mechanism, resulting in reduced stream discharges in the Chalimbana catchment and reduced well yields over the karstic aquifer.

Effects of pollution

The population increase in Lusaka Urban over the last 30 years, from below 500,000 to approximately 1.2 million people in 1998, has meant an increase in the rate of pollution from landfills, rubbish pits, septic tanks and pit latrines. This has led to increased costs of water treatment for the Lusaka City Council and the Lusaka Water and Sewerage Company. There has been a greater cost on public health resulting from the need to control water-borne diseases arising from polluted groundwater.

Groundwater pollution is expensive. Once an aquifer has been polluted, groundwater from it may never be restored to drinking water standard, as pollution is often an irreversible process.

City water table

Urbanization and the heavy demand of water accompanying it have resulted in a falling water table leading to reduced yields. In addition, low to non-existent service levels for urban water in some areas of Lusaka have resulted in indiscriminate drilling of private boreholes in and around the city. Whereas only 52 boreholes, all located in an area of roughly 20 km^2, are used for the urban water supply, the aquifer which stretches for over 45 km has between 3000 to 4000 privately owned boreholes.

Policy implications

Although groundwater is a very important resource for Lusaka, it is improperly exploited and generally unprotected. At present, groundwater use is not controlled and the resource is becoming polluted. There is an urgent need for better aquifer protection. Three basic steps are required for protecting the groundwater resources of Lusaka:

- **Controlling groundwater abstraction:** This is particularly important in areas where large-scale abstractions are occurring (e.g. Chelstone Compound area) and indications of over-pumping are becoming obvious. The Lusaka area has between 3000 to 4000 indiscriminately drilled wells, and this drilling is still going on. It is recommended that the Department of Water Affairs take up this task and submit proposals to the authorities to introduce the groundwater controls in the Water Act, which currently relates only to surface water.

- **Controlling groundwater pollution:** This would include evaluating aquifer pollution vulnerability, assessing potential contamination loads, and implementing land-use plans specifically designed to protect groundwater resources. Monitoring programmes are recommended which should include the installation of monitoring wells within the aquifer to ascertain the extent of the pollution. Recharge areas need to be zoned and activities within these areas restricted. There is a need for a protection zone of 50-60 m around a borehole, within which human activities should be restricted.

- **Expansion of groundwater resource base for Lusaka Urban Water Supply:** Abstraction of groundwater in the well field cannot be increased, as the resource is limited. Expansion of the abstraction area for urban water supply is strongly recommended.

Without the implementation of such actions, the city of Lusaka faces a water supply crisis. Its groundwater supply for both the public system and private usage is bound to become both polluted and over exploited.

REFERENCES

Dixey, F. 1945: The Geomorphology of Northern Rhodesia. *Transactions of Geological Society of South Africa*, 47 (1944), 9-45.

FIGNR. 1978: *Groundwater and Management Studies for Lusaka Water Supply*. Hannover.

Hadwen, P. 1972: *The Groundwater Resources of the Greater Ndola Area.* Groundwater

Resources Paper 1. Lusaka: Department of Water Affairs.

Jones, M.J. 1971: *The Old Pump Station. Lusaka - a Hydrogeological Study.* Department of Water Affairs Hydrogeological Report No. L24.

King, L.C. 1948: *The Geology of Pietermaritzburg and Environs.* Special Publication Geological Survey of South Africa, 13.

King, L.C. 1967: *Morphology of the Earth.* Edinburgh: Oliver and Boyd.

Maseka, C. 1994: *A Groundwater Resource Evaluation of Fractured Rock Aquifers.* Lusaka: UNSW Unpublished M. App. Sc. Thesis.

Simpson, J.G., Drysdall, A.R. and Lambert, H.H.J. 1963: *Geology and Groundwater Resources of Lusaka Area.* Report No. 16 Northern Rhodesia Geological Survey.

Tague, M. 1965: *The Groundwater Reserves of the City of Lusaka, Zambia.* Hydrogeological Report No. 50.

Yachiyo Engineering Company Ltd. 1995: *The Study on National Water Resources Master Plan in Zambia.*

Wimpey Laboratories Limited. 1983: *Review of the Groundwater Development Potential - Mpongwe Development Project.*

UNEP 1996: *Groundwater: a Threatened Resource.* UNEP Environmental Library No. 15. Nairobi: UNEP.

Chapter 6

NAMIBIAN APPLICATION OF FOG-COLLECTING SYSTEMS

by Joh Henschel, Vilho Mtuleni, Nina Gruntkowski, Mary K. Seely and Elias Shanyengana

INTRODUCTION

Fog transports water into the hyperarid Namib Desert. Working together, the Desert Research Foundation of Namibia (DRFN) and the residents of five Topnaar villages along the lower Kuiseb River in the Central Namib Desert evaluated the potential of collecting this water for domestic purposes, following a model case in Chile. The evaluation entailed studying climatological, temporal and spatial parameters of Namib fog, while determining the local water needs and ensuring participation and awareness by potential consumers of fog water.

The primary objective of the project was to recommend whether, how and where fog water could be collected to help alleviate the water shortage along the lower Kuiseb Valley in the Namib Desert. Phase 1 consisted of twelve objectives concerning the quantity and quality of fog water, the collecting equipment, the local water needs, information transfer, the identification of socio-economic and environmental consequences, the design of a fog water supply scheme, the production of a report and publications, and finally, the dissemination of information and plans for phases 2 and 3. Fieldwork was conducted between October 1996 and December 1997. Although monitoring continues at some sites, most of the data used for analysis was gathered between October 1996 and September 1997.

It was found that the quantity and quality of Namib fog is sufficient for a fog water supply scheme. At a potential site for fog-harvesting near a Topnaar village, the daily average of fog water collected in the course of a year exceeded 1 litre/m^2 of collector/day. Although fog occurs throughout the year, the variations of season, location, and time of day affect the design of a water supply scheme. The costs of a fog-water supply scheme are similar to that of the more commonly used wind pump, but it is a more sustainable and environmentally sound water source.

A partnership is being formed with the rural community for the joint development of fog harvesting schemes based on this evaluation. Fog water as a resource needs to go hand in hand with an integrated awareness of all natural resources and the need to manage them in a sustainable manner.

BACKGROUND

Namibia is a desert country with a decreasing gradient of rainfall from NE to SW. The west coast is the hyper-arid Namib Desert with no perennial rivers. The extreme dryness can be ascribed to its proximity to the low sea surface temperatures of the Benguela upwelling system and Namibia's latitudinal position within the subtropical high pressure zone. These factors are, amongst others, essential for the formation of coastal fog (Olivier, 1992).

Fog is important in the Namib. It affects the climatic pattern of the western part of the desert (Schulze, 1969; Seely & Stuart, 1976; Lancaster, Lancaster & Seely, 1984). Its precipitation is five times greater than that of rain (less than 22 mm of rain compared to 30-180 mm of fog annually). Fog occurs on 60-200 days per year, making it a predictable source of water with a coefficient of variation of 44% compared to 116% for rain (Pietruszka & Seely, 1985; Seely & Henschel, 1998).

It is therefore not surprising that fog is used by animals and plants (Seely, 1979; Seely, Henschel & Robertson, 1998), and can be used by humans. Approximately 100,000 people live in the cities of Swakopmund, Walvis Bay and the surrounding coastal towns and villages. The latter include small communities of indigenous people, the Topnaar villages and the research and training centre at Gobabeb, situated in the desert interior. Potable water is obtained from groundwater via manually maintained wells, boreholes and the Central Namib Water Scheme based on aquifers in the ephemeral rivers, Kuiseb and Omaruru (Dausab et al., 1994; Jacobson, Jacobson & Seely, 1995).

Groundwater reserves depend on input from rainfalls in the distant interior of Namibia's highlands (>200 km from the coast). In recent years, water abstraction has exceeded input and the groundwater is being depleted. Alternative water supplies will be required. Fog water may have the potential to supplement small-scale users and can thereby contribute to alleviating the water deficiency along the Namibian coast (Nagel, 1959; Nieman, Heyns & Seely, 1978). A model case, developed in Chile, has demonstrated that this is possible (Cereceda,

Schemenauer, Suit, 1992; Schemenauer & Cereceda, 1994a), and the Chilean experience has since been applied in Peru, Ecuador and Oman. Fog as an alternative water resource is presently gaining attention in many developing countries, including South Africa (Struthers, 1995, 1997; Olivier, pers. comm.[1]) and Namibia.

The NAMFOG project is a study of the potential fog water harvesting along the lower Kuiseb River. A number of Standard Fog Collectors were erected at various locations downriver from Gobabeb in order to measure the frequency of fog events and the amount of water collected. If data collected showed that the yields were sufficient, fog water could provide the Kuiseb residents with a supplementary water source to the existing supply from boreholes and wells. This would not only supply the people with fresh water, but it would also reduce the current pressure on receding groundwater resources.

Phase 1 of the project entails evaluating the potential for the rural Topnaar community to collect and use potable fog water. The occurrence, water content and climatological parameters of fog were investigated. From this information, the yield and quality of fog water was determined along with the suitability and durability of the potential fog-collecting equipment. Water needs, along with social, environmental and economic considerations were taken into account in the preliminary design of a fog-water supply scheme for a Topnaar village to serve as a model for others. The experience gained in the pilot schemes will facilitate the further application of this technology in Namibia.

FOG WATER COLLECTION TECHNOLOGY

The Standard Fog Collector (SFC; Schemenauer & Cereceda, 1994b) comprises a double layer of Rashel-type polypropylene shade netting spanned over a $1m^2$ frame, with the base fixed at a height of 2m above the ground. This mesh covers roughly 60% of the collector's surface and leaves around 40% of the area free for the wind carrying the water drops to pass through. The vertical zig-zag weave of the Rashel mesh is important as this structure does not hold the collected water, but allows it to run downwards and the double-layer increases the yield. A gutter below the frame collects the water and channels it through a hose to a water storage container, which is monitored manually by emptying into graduated cylinders. The hose may be interrupted by a small Rain-O-Matic analog water gauge connected to an Adtron data logger to record the quantity of water collected ($\pm 0.5ml$). An anemometer with a wind direction sensor is fitted 0.5m next to the screen. The data logger recorded the quantity of fog (ml/m/h) and the average wind speed (m/s) and direction ($\pm$ 45°) for each hour.

All the SFCs were oriented towards NW, based on an initial supposition that most fog comes from that direction. This was the agreed-upon orientation for all SFCs used in the Namib by the DRFN and the DWA since the middle of 1996. It should be pointed out that this assumption was not correct and modifications have been suggested.

Manual measurements were also carried out on a daily basis. At Gobabeb different possibilities of fog collecting were observed and this information was linked to the data from the First Order Weather Station. At other sites the manual results served as an addition to the information from the data logger, or a supplement to test the micro-variation between the sites in an area. They also served as a backup in case of instrument failure of data loggers. Manual monitoring consistently measured (83.1 $\pm$6.8%) less fog water than the loggers and consequently this figure (multiply manual results by 1.203 for actual volume) was used to compensate for the losses by evaporation, spilling and the retention of water in containers.

Fog Climatology

Seven to ten million years ago, the cold water upwelling system of the Benguela current was established on the east side of the Atlantic Ocean and heralded the approach of the current Namib Desert phase. The Central Namib is essentially a flat plain with a gradual slope of 5-8 m per km up to the foot of the Great Escarpment. Despite a few isolated Inselbergs and dunes, there are few major landscape features that would influence the macro-climate. These physical characteristics make the Namib unique among deserts of the world (Taljaard, 1979).

Between 1962 and 1996, the weather station at Gobabeb used a cylindrical wire mesh screen, 10 cm in diameter and 22 cm high, above a rain gauge to collect fog and data. The autographic weather station also had an anemometer and thermohygrograph. Similar weather stations were situated at nine places (Lancaster et al., 1984), of which four are still maintained, namely, Gobabeb, Kleinberg, Vogelfederberg and Ganab. In 1990-1993 they were furnished with electronic data loggers. During 1997, the stations were fitted with Standard Fog Collectors (Schemenauer & Cereceda, 1994) which correlate with the cylindrical collectors.

Spatial and seasonal variation of fog

Olivier (1992) showed how stratus clouds penetrate from the Atlantic up to 100 km into the Central Namib. There are indications that these clouds are associated with the upwelling cell off Walvis Bay (Shannon, 1972; Shannon, Seely & Ward, 1989; Olivier, 1995) from where they drift inland. The frequency of stratus cloud cover declines from more than 100 days at the coast to less than 10 days at 100 km inland. Lancaster et al. (1984) indicated how fog precipitation changes from the coast to the inland. There was an increase in the fog day frequency and in fog precipitation from the coast to 20-60 km inland beyond which the fog declined. Highest precipitation was at two stations situated at altitudes of 340 and 500m amsl (altitude above mean sea level) at distances of 33 and 60 km from the coast. The monthly distribution of fog differs between the coastal and inland areas (Nieman et al., 1978; Lancaster et al., 1984). At the coast, the peak months are May - September, while inland the peak months are around August - October with a secondary peak around March.

Surface winds

There are many complex factors influencing the wind direction and consequently the fog transport with respect to season, time of day and topography. There are also differences in the wind regimes between the coastal and inland areas. Winds at the coast are predominantly SSE–SSW throughout the year, while N and E winds occur for 8-10% of the time. Four winds predominate in the interior of the Central Namib (Tyson & Seely, 1980; Lancaster et al., 1984; Lindesay & Tyson, 1990). A SW sea-breeze (5-10 m/s) occurs throughout the year with peaks in September and March. It begins at the coast during the late morning and can penetrate inland across the entire Namib by evening, typically ceasing at nightfall. The strength of the sea-breeze declines with distance from the coast. A fairly strong NW plain-mountain wind (10-15 m/s) begins in the late afternoon and continues until around midnight. This wind is driven by a thermal gradient between the cool western part of the desert and the hot eastern part. This wind dominates in summer and often undercuts the sea-breeze. The counterpart of the plain-mountain wind is the moderate SE mountain-plain wind (5-10 m.s^{-1}) that begins at night and peaks at sunrise. This wind is driven by a reversal of the thermal gradient caused by the eastern part of the Namib, cooling more rapidly under a clear sky than the coastal region and ocean. Mountain-plain wind strengthens in winter. Occasionally during winter, very strong, dry easterly berg winds interrupt the pattern of the other three winds.

Types of fog

It has been recognized for some time that the Namib has several kinds of fog (Taljaard, 1979; Lancaster et al., 1984; Vendrig, 1990; Olivier, 1995) including advective fog, the less frequent radiation and frontal fogs, as well as intercepted clouds or high fog. Although the advective fog occurs frequently, its precipitation of water is only moderate and SW wind speeds are mild. By contrast, the high fog involves the dynamic interaction of two air masses, causing an oscillation of wind directions from NW to E, and then to NNE when the fog arrives. High fog results from a low stratus cloud of 100-600m high that moves from the Atlantic Ocean across the Namib in a NW direction until it intercepts the easterly mountain-plain wind, mixes with it and precipitates as fog.

The NNE fog direction is preceded by northwesterly wind, often with a SE wind between the NW and NNE. This is interpreted as an easterly mountain-plain wind that rises during the late hours of the night and hugs the land on its way to the coast. The stratus cloud, coming from the northwest, penetrates this air mass coming from the east, while the stable inversion may prevent the cloud from rising above this layer. Mixing occurs and the resultant wind direction is NNE. This direction is oblique to the isobar from the interception point with only a slight decline in altitude as the fog progresses. The fog thus has a different direction on the ground than the higher winds that transport the cloud that feeds it.

The seasonal distribution of peak periods of high fog, September and March, is consistent with the association of these fog events with both plain-mountain (NW) and mountain-plain (SE) winds. Plain-mountain winds are weak in mid-winter (May-July), and mountain-plain winds weaken in mid-summer (December-February) (Lindesay & Tyson, 1990), and both wind types are well developed during the peak fog period.

The importance and the nature of the high fog have often been overlooked. For instance, this study mistakenly oriented a network of SFCs towards NW based on the general belief that inland fog comes from this direction (Mtuleni, Henschel & Seely, 1998). It is now suggested that an orientation of the SFCs to NNE (or N) would substantially increase the yield. This would increase the viability of potential fog water supply schemes at Topnaar villages. Furthermore, the knowledge that the coastal fog may differ fundamentally from the inland fog studied by Mtuleni *et al.* (1998) supports the need for a separate evaluation of the potential of harvesting the coastal fog. Some previous authors may not have distinguished between the coastal and the inland fog types.

The climatology of Namib fog may not have enjoyed the attention it warrants because of the depth of understanding that has been gained in detailed studies of fog in the cross-continental South American counterpart (Schemenauer, Fuenzalida & Cereceda, 1988; Cereceda & Schemenauer, 1991). The indications are, however, that there are important differences, and that the Namib fog may be more complex than previously believed. The high fog of the Namib warrants much more detailed study than it has received to date, especially if there are intentions to tap this water source more extensively.

SITE SELECTION

For this survey, small rural settlements along the Kuiseb River in the interior of the Namib Desert were selected, all located 20-60 km from the coast. Criteria for selecting the sites included altitude and exposure to fog-bearing winds, topography, residents' general knowledge of fog, as well as occurrence of biotic indicators such as lichen or fog-utilizing plants like Arthraerua leubnitziae. In Namibia, Topnaar residents in rural villages walk, bicycle or use donkey carts as transport. As it is necessary for the people to take care of their own fog collectors, it was highly desirable to find the closest possible site with enough fog.

Study sites

Gobabeb: To collect detailed data of fog and the related conditions in the Namib, daily observations and detailed recordings at the Gobabeb Desert Research Station were necessary. Gobabeb (23° 34'S; 15° 03'E) is located at an altitude of 408m above mean sea level (amsl) and 56 km from the coast. Because of this distance it is not the best location to study fog, but there are permanent staff to do the detailed observations and to conduct experiments.

Soutrivier: This village is approximately 5 km west of Gobabeb (23° 32'S; 15° 02'E). Because of its distance from the sea and proximity to Gobabeb, there is only one manual SFC placed on a hill above the settlement.

Klipneus: This village is 36 km downriver of Gobabeb (23° 23'55.9"S; 14° 54'07.0"E). It is located 46 km from the coast at an altitude of 352 m amsl.

There are two sites with SFCs at Klipneus. One is situated alongside the river and the other is on a hill, at an altitude of 360m amsl.

Swartbank: Located 45 km downriver of Gobabeb (23° 24'S; 14° 54'E) and 38 km from the coast, this area has several topographic features. The settlement, at an altitude of 306m, is situated next to the Swartbankberg with its peak at 464m amsl. The proximity to the sea and the altitude make it an extraordinary site for collecting fog.

Utuseb: In order to inform school children, one manually-monitored SFC was placed next to the J.P. Brand School at Utuseb. This school receives water from the municipal water supply of Walvis Bay.

Rooibank: One SFC equipped with a data logger is situated next to the waterworks at Rooibank. There is no settlement in the immediate area, but this site was chosen because of its proximity to the sea and the presence of staff of the Water Works of the Walvis Bay Municipality.

Fog Water Quantity

When determining the potential for using fog as a water source, it is important to find out the water yield from fog at locations close to the potential users. The quantity of fog water collected per unit area of collector and its distribution over time (days, months, seasons, years) determine the technical side of a water supply scheme. The initial technical decisions, as outlined in the landmark studies conducted by Pilar Cereceda and Bob Schemenauer in Chile (Schemenauer et al., 1988; Cereceda & Schemenauer, 1991; Cereceda et al., 1992, 1996; Schemenauer & Cereceda, 1994a, b), concern the most suitable site for a test, one that is located near a target site where the water is required. While the terrain and the macro- and micro-climatic conditions influence the location decision, the Standard Fog Collector is used to determine the quantity of fog water at that site.

Fourteen Standard Fog Collectors (SFC, Schemenauer & Cereceda, 1994b) were placed with a northwest orientation on six sites near Topnaar villages along the lower Kuiseb River in the Central Namib Desert. Based on their physical characteristics and a need for water, three sites were further selected for focused study: Swartbank, Klipneus and Soutrivier.

Results

The SFC at Klipneus Top was the most successful fog collection site of this survey.

The total volume recorded by data loggers during the one-year period from October 1996 to September 1997 differed from 32 753 ml at Klipneus, 24 137 ml at Swartbank to 2 487 ml at Gobabeb. During the period from October 1996 until February 1997, when there was an average of 10 fog events per month, there was a good correlation between the average amount of water per fog event and the average per day. During this time, the average amount of collected fog per day fluctuated between 1 674 ml in October 1996 and 872 ml in February 1997. Likewise, the results from August 1997 onwards were good, with a daily average amount of 1 121 ml in August and 2 801 ml in September. In October 1997, following the one-year survey, only five fog events were recorded, but with an extremely high average of 7 208 ml per event (Table 6.1).

Table 6.1 Fog records at three Topnaar villages in the Namib Desert

Place	Swartbank	Klipneus	Soutrivier
Locational Characteristics			
Altitude (above mean sea level)	332 m	340 m	387 m
Distance from Sea	37 km	46 km	53 km
Distance from Village	8 km	2 km	0.3 km
Number			
Record Days	321	356	273
Fog Events	108	111	60
Quantity of Water Collected (litres/m^2) per			
Fog Event	2.384	3.345	0.437
Day: Year	0.802	1.043	0.096
Day: Aug-Jan	2.720	2.122	0.704
Day: Feb-Jul	0.423	0.453	0.084

Looking at the seasonal variations, it is possible to subdivide the year into a wet foggy season and dry foggy season. The foggiest time of the year is during summer, from September until March. During this time, fog occurred on 45% of the days, and the average daily yield was greater than 2 litres/m^2 of collector/day. In contrast, from February to July, fog occurred on only 15% of the days, yielding less than 0.5 litres/m^2 of collector/day. The monthly distribution of fog also differed between the coastal and inland areas (Nieman et al., 1978; Lancaster et al., 1984). At the coast, the peak months are May - September, while inland the peak months are around August - October with a secondary peak around March. Despite variations, fog does occur throughout the year, with mostly wet episodes. In 60%

of all 111 fog events, the amount of water exceeded 1 litre. The longest period with a steady supply of fog water exceeding 1 litre per event and occurring every day or every second day, was 10 days in October 96. The longest duration without fog which produced 1 litre or more, was for 17 days in March 97.

FOG WATER QUALITY

Water samples were collected from SFCs at Gobabeb and sent to the Department of Water Affairs for analysis. Although the fog water is relatively pure with a neutral pH (Eckardt, 1996), the SFC mesh accumulates dust and wind-blown salts that are washed off by the fog water during collection. The initial rinse off the SFC after a non-foggy period yielded turbid, brackish water that was only marginally fit for human consumption, but could be used for livestock. The subsequent water was considerably cleaner and of lower salt content.

EQUIPMENT STURDINESS

The SFCs were observed during and after dry, strong winter storm winds. On twelve occasions during 1997, there were strong winds with average hourly speeds exceeding 12-16 m/s, gusting at an estimated 24-32 m/s. Several SFCs were damaged during winter storms and were strengthened with additional supporting structures. Some of the plastic logger equipment did not withstand this weather, resulting in data loss. It was determined that the fog collectors should be designed to withstand gusts of at least 35 m/s coming from easterly to northerly directions.

TOPNAAR WATER NEEDS ASSESSMENT

The Topnaar are a Nama-speaking tribe, originally nomadic pastoralists, with a long history in the Namib Desert (Dentlinger, 1983). Besides keeping livestock (goats, cattle, and donkeys for transport), they traditionally harvest an endemic cucurbit fruit: the !Nara (*Aconthosicyos horridus*). Attempts have been made to garden on a small scale, but the water is too salty and too scarce in many settlements to allow this. The community living along the lower Kuiseb River Valley is very susceptible to water shortages, especially because the flooding of the Kuiseb River is reduced by dams, while water extraction for towns and mines is lowering the groundwater level (Dausab *et al.*, 1994, Jacobson *et al.*, 1995).

To assist with the planning of a fog water supply system, it was necessary to assess the needs of the people and the livestock during the whole year, including the increased water consumption during the holidays. A water use survey was carried out during winter (July) and summer (December) at settlements where the fog screens are located, namely, Klipneus, Soutrivier, and Swartbank. The people were asked about their water sources and requirements. Also recorded were current water management systems and the estimated volume of water from the size of the containers used to fetch or store it at the homes.

A questionnaire was prepared and only permanent residents at each settlement were interviewed. A household was defined as all the people, animals, and gardens whose water requirements are managed together. The number of inhabitants in each settlement can vary from time to time on a seasonal and weekly basis. This influences the water consumption. Therefore figures are only approximate and should be treated with caution. They do provide a guideline that should facilitate the planning of a fog water supply scheme.

The people use water for drinking, cooking, laundry, washing and livestock. The water sources are traditional, hand-dug wells of 5-15 m depth in the riverbed. In addition, there is a wind pump at Klipneus and a borehole fitted with a diesel pump at Soutrivier, both of which were installed and maintained by the government. However, the pumps become unreliable when they are a few years old. The Swartbank people fetch a considerable proportion of their water with donkey carts from the 20-km distant Utuseb school, which gets its water from the municipal supply of Walvis Bay.

People use between 11 and 68% of the total water consumed, and the rest goes to domestic animals with cattle requiring about half of that water. The consumption fluctuates least at Klipneus (47%), and most strongly at Soutrivier (137%). The total volume of water consumption is highest at Swartbank (2.3-3.8 m^3 /day), intermediate at Klipneus (1.2-1.8 m^3/day), and least at Soutrivier (0.7-1.6 m^3/day).

INFORMATION AND TRAINING

The attitude of the people towards fog as a potential water source is as important as providing the ability to access this source. In preparation for managing a fog collecting scheme, the people of Klipneus, Soutrivier, and Swartbank gained access to information, hands-on training and experience concerning this technology. A participatory relationship was developed with the Topnaar leaders addressing fog harvesting as a component of sustainable resource management. The possible formation of water committees in each village, also promoted by the Department of Water Affairs, was discussed. Residents actively involved in the project explained the process to other villagers, making the technology familiar to many Topnaars.

SOCIAL ASPECTS

People living along the lower Kuiseb River are in need of alternative water sources. However, following years of government dependency, they seem to have accepted their daily struggle with the existing systems as a way of life: walking long distances to hand-dug wells that require much maintenance, while they wait patiently for a government technician to arrive to fix a pump. Many people believe that the fog water harvesting system would be good because it is a simple technique and appears to be easier to service than the current diesel or wind pumps. However, they have limited funds and do not intend to invest in a new water scheme, a service the government always provided in the past. Therefore, the means to fund fog harvesting technology would need to be developed through a process parallel to and integrated with that of the Department of Water Affairs.

With their current problems, they will only be convinced of the usefulness of this technique when they see that it can supply them with sufficient good water. Despite this wait-and-see attitude, they said that if a fog harvesting scheme were implemented at their settlement, they would do their best to maintain it.

ENVIRONMENTAL ASPECTS

After fog has passed through the fog-water collecting screens, it bears less water than before (about 50% less in optimal conditions; Schemenauer & Cereceda, 1994b). As numerous desert organisms, plants and animals depend on fog water, it could be argued that this reduced fog moisture could have a negative impact on the environment. However, this appears to be negligible. The SFC screen is two metres off the ground so that the bottom portion of fog that animals and plants would utilize is unimpeded. Secondly, the sides of the fog cloud close around the relatively narrow SFC (12m wide) and the fog shadow soon becomes indistinct (Cereceda, Cruzat, Ossandon & Schemenauer, 1996). The SFC, and even a whole bank of SFCs, is tiny compared to other obstacles in the landscape, such as hills. The amount of water that it removes from the thick fog cloud stretching hundreds of kilometres over the Namib is negligible.

The environment can also be affected by building artificial structures on hilltops in an otherwise undeveloped area. The effects can be aesthetic as well as physical, both of which are of particular concern in the Namib Naukluft Park where the targeted Topnaar villages are located. The aesthetic effects can be minimized by using unobtrusive sites that are not visible from afar. A physical impact is expected in the placement of the necessary pipeline and a road to the site. However, the whole area within several kilometres of Topnaar settlements is already frequently traversed by people, livestock, donkey carts, bicycles and cars travelling off-road, so that the organized development of a fog water supply scheme should not be a major new interference to the landscape.

Finally, people have indicated that if they obtained more water, they would keep more goats. This could increase the impact that these animals have on the environment. However, the Department of Water Affairs has a stated objective of integrated water and range management. Careful management of any fog water harvesting schemes in conjunction with government departments may mitigate such change.

DESIGNING A FOG WATER COLLECTION SCHEME

The above points were taken into consideration in designing a pilot fog collecting scheme. The suggestion that the first experimental scheme be constructed at Klipneus has been discussed by the Topnaar community, although a final decision is awaited. The lessons from this scheme would facilitate planning for the more complex situation at Swartbank. In the meantime, the research team has made a preliminary design for the Klipneus conditions based on the model at Chungungo in Chile (Cereceda et al., 1992, 1996). The design assumes that fog water will become the only water source, though in Namibia a hybrid system may be more realistic.

The following factors were taken into account for the design:

▶ seasonal variation in fog water availability
▶ the effect of the storage capacity on water availability
▶ the consumption rate that can be sustained without running the storage tank dry
▶ the ability to vary the consumption rate.

The optimal magnitude of each factor was calculated. Most importantly, due to the intervals between fog events, the reservoir can frequently run empty unless the consumption is managed. Ideally the water will be rationed, with an adequate quantity available each day, which cannot be exceeded if a tap is inadvertently left open. The resulting design comprises the following elements:

- enough fog collecting units of 48 m2 each (modified after Cereceda et al., 1996) to supply the average daily water requirements
- pipes and sedimentation tanks
- a reservoir to sustain the consumers for up to 3 weeks without fog
- a tank to contain the daily ration of water for households as well as domestic animals other than cattle
- another tank for the daily water ration for cattle at times when the main reservoir is over half full; cattle require alternative water when the reservoir is less than half full.

COSTS

A fog water collecting scheme with 25 SFCs would cost nearly N$180,000 and require 13,400 hours of work by members of a settlement over a 10-year period. The cost would be substantially reduced if the yield was underestimated by the incorrect orientation of the SFCs during the current study, as is suspected.

Table 6.2 Estimated cost of constructing one Fog Collecting Unit (FCU) by the community. Transport costs are shared, based on the simultaneous purchase of 25 FCUs. * = the quoted price in Namibia during May 1998 was N$8.12/m².

Item	Cost N$
Screen mesh (@ N$10/m² for 100 m² per FCU) *	1,000
Other Hardware for FCU	1,500
Labour: 120 h	self
Transport (1/25th of N$3,500)	140
Total	2,640

The cost of water from various sources was compared, including fog water, borehole operating with diesel pump or wind pump and hand-dug wells. Of all the water sources, fog has the best potential for individual households to operate their own supply system. This would increase the total costs somewhat because the water management system is not shared. Assuming that a small water management system would cost N$10,000 and that one household and its domestic animals would require 5 SFCs, the construction costs would be N$23,200. The total cost in 10 years would be about N\$36,400, or N\$31.66/m^3. The possibility of households having their own water supplies increases the flexibility for the application of this technology. It may increase the potential of individual economic development within the communal setting of the settlements. SFCs would become equivalent to "estate", where the frame is the "immovable" and the mesh the "movable", similar to other parts of their homesteads. Such a system would take the onus off having to predict the future population in a settlement, which has always been variable in the Topnaar settlements. Individuals can decide for themselves, provided they can raise the money to construct their own fog water scheme. If the Topnaar community forms water committees and cooperatives that assist in this regard by reducing costs or make loans available, then this more flexible approach may have potential. This possibility should be investigated.

Table 6.3 Calculated total cost over 10 years of different types of water sources. Unit cost is calculated for Klipneus, which uses 1.5 m^3 per day, giving 547.5 m^3/yr, with an incremented 5% annual increase, totalling 5,749 m^3 in 10 years.

Type	Self-labour h	Installation & Maintenance N\$	Water Management	Total Cost N\$	Cost N\$ per m^3	Time h per m^3
25 FCUs communal	13,400	132,000	46,407	178,407	31.03	2.33
Diesel pump	3,650	174,336	46,407	220,743	38.40	0.63
Wind pump	3,650	116,367	46,407	162,774	28.31	0.63
Hand-dug well	31,220	11,200	0	11,200	1.95	5.43

Water from boreholes and wells has an inherent disadvantage compared to fog water, in that the source is limited and declining and the water quality is often poor because it is brackish (Topnaar Community[2] & Department of Water Affairs[3], pers. comm.). Fog water is not only of good quality, but it is also a sustainable resource with no more of an environmental disturbance than a building. Given that the relative cost of fog water is equivalent to that of a wind pump, which appears to be acceptable to the Topnaar community in preference to the labour-intensive, traditional hand-dug wells, and that fog is a better water source in terms of sustainability and environmental friendliness, fog has a distinct advantage over the other sources.

Conclusions and Recommendations

Fog has the potential of providing potable water to villages that are located less than 50 km from the Atlantic Ocean, where the average daily yield of fog water is greater than 1 litre/m^2 of collector/day. Given that throughout the study area there is fog year-round, albeit at different frequencies and wetness (Lancaster et al., 1984; Afrikaner, 1998), it is a good potential water source well-suited for small-scale users, such as individual households or small settlement systems. The average consumption rate needs to be carefully balanced against the average supply rate, otherwise the reservoir would frequently run empty and this water source would be seen as unreliable. This can be avoided by designing a sufficiently large fog harvesting water scheme and adding checks to prevent extreme fluctuations in consumption. One simple management aid would be transferring daily rations into a smaller tank and separating the water used for cattle from the water used for the rest.

Other uses of fog water should also be considered. For instance, if the indigenous !Nara plant is supplemented with water, it may increase the melon harvest for the Topnaars (Dausab & Henschel, 1997). People in the coastal town of Swakopmund are investigating the possibility of watering vegetables with fog water (Coetzee[4] & Mulder[5], pers. comm.). Besides the Topnaar settlements on which this project concentrates, other potential users of fog water could be isolated settlements along the Namibian Coast, household owners in coastal towns, and perhaps even the bulk water scheme. A study area near Wlotzka's Baken was the wettest of all the sites examined. This site is situated next to the Omdel Aquifer Water Scheme of Namwater and it may be possible to integrate fog water into the bulk water supply system of the West Coast.

A better understanding of the mechanisms and behaviour of fog is required in order to optimize the collection method, place and time, and to be able to increase the predictability of this source of water. In the current study, the quantity of available water may have been underestimated because the SFCs were oriented obliquely towards the dominant fog wind direction. The use of a bi-directional fog collector, the BSFC (Cereceda et al., 1996), that can be standardized against the optimal direction of a fixed SFC is suggested. When the BSFC is deployed with a weather station, it will provide accurate information on the direction of fog winds and will enable the correct orientation for the large collectors of a fog water supply scheme to be chosen.

Rural communities throughout Namibia are currently planning to improve self-sufficiency in terms of accessing and managing water sources and the associated infrastructure. For instance, this is the goal of the Cost-Recovery Programme of WASP (Water Supply and Sanitation Sector Policy) of the Ministry of Agriculture, Water and Rural Development (MAWRD, 1997). Local Water Committees composed of community members will eventually be charged with maintaining the rural water supply infrastructure and will assume legal ownership of it. In a five-year transition period, beginning in August 1998, the government is planning to train water point managers to implement financially sound systems. Communities will begin handling their own operation and maintenance activities until they assume full responsibility for the operation, maintenance and replacement of equipment in September 2003. The current investigation and future plans for water use by the Topnaars then needs to be seen in the light of this National Policy. The NAMFOG project focused on the question of how these needs can be met by fog water collection.

Phase 1 of the project should serve to introduce fog collecting technology into Namibia by adapting it to local conditions. The construction of a pilot fog water supply scheme would demonstrate the validity of the calculations while testing the acceptability of this type of water source in the community. In partnership with the Topnaar community, an experimental pilot plant should be built and managed at a village such as Klipneus.

ENDNOTES

1. Dr. Jana Olivier, University of the North, Department of Geography, Private Bag X1106, Sovenga 0727, South Africa.
2. Topnaar Community Foundation, PO Box 2017, Walvis Bay, Namibia.
3. Department of Water Affairs (DWA), Ministry of Agriculture, Water and Rural Development, Private Bag 13193, Windhoek, Namibia.
4. Mr. Martin D. Coetzee, PO Box 1599, Swakopmund, Namibia.
5. Mr. Karl-Heinz Mulder, PO Box 1127, Swakopmund, Namibia.

REFERENCES

Afrikaner, C. 1998: *The investigation of fog frequency and occurrence patterns in the Central Namib as a possible alternative source of water supply to the Topnaar Community along the Kuiseb River in the Namib Desert*. BA(hons) Thesis. Department of Geography,

University of Namibia.

Botelle, A. and Kowalski, K. 1995: Changing resource use in Namibia's lower Kuiseb River valley: perceptions from the Topnaar community. In *Institute of Southern Africa Studies at the University of Lesotho and the Social Sciences Division at the University of Namibia*, pg. 90. Windhoek: Desert Research Foundation of Namibia.

Cereceda, P. and Schemenauer, R. 1991: The occurrence of fog in Chile. *Journal of Applied Meteorology,* 30, 1097-1105.

Cereceda, P., Schemenauer, R. and Suit, M. 1992: An alternative water supply for Chilean coastal desert villages. *Water Resources Development,* 8, 53-59.

Cereceda, P., Cruzat, A., Ossandon, J. and Schemenauer, R. 1996: *Prospection, evaluation and construction of fog water collection systems: a new technology of simple application and large economic and social impact.* IDRC/CIID-GAFCS.

Dausab, R., Francis, G., Johr, G., Kambatuku, J., Molapo, M., Shanyengana, S.E. and Swartz, S. 1994: *Water Usage Patterns in the Kuiseb Catchment Area (with emphasis on sustainable use).* Occasional Report No. 1. Windhoek: Desert Research Foundation of Nambia.

Dausab, R. and Henschel, J.R. 1997: Nara workshop of the 19th November 1997 at Lauberville. Proceedings, Desert Research Foundation of Namibia and Topnaar Community.

Dentlinger, U. 1983: *Social and spatial mobility along the Kuiseb River in the Namib Desert, Namibia.* MA Thesis. Cape Town: University of Cape Town.

Eckardt, F. 1996: *The distribution and origin of gypsum in the Central Namib Desert, Namibia.* PhD Thesis. University of Oxford.

Goudie, A. 1972: Climate, weathering, crust formation, dunes, and fluvial features of the central Namib Desert, near Gobabeb, South West Africa. *Madoqua, Series II,* 1, 15-31.

Jacobson, P.J., Jacobson, K.M. and Seely, M.K. 1995: *Ephemeral rivers and their catchments: sustaining people and development in western Namibia.* Windhoek: Desert Research Foundation of Namibia.

Lancaster, J., Lancaster, N. and Seely, M.K. 1984: Climate of the Central Namib Desert. *Madoqua,* 14, 5-61.

Lindesay, J.A. and Tyson, P.D. 1990: Thermo-topographically induced boundary layer oscillations over the central Namib, southern Africa. *International Journal of Climatology,* 10, 63-77.

Loris, K. 1990: Zur Problematik der Wasserversorgung von Arthraerua leubnitziae in derAuBeren Namib, mit Daten des Nebelniederschlags. In *Symposium zum Gekenken an Prof. Dr. h.c. H. Walter.* Stuttgart-Hohenheim: University of Stuttgart-Hohenheim.

MAWRD 1997: *The implementation of the community management and cost recovery aspects of the Water Supply and Sanitation Sector Policy (WASP).* Agenda memorandum for Cabinet, Ministry of Agriculture, Water and Rural Development.

Mtuleni, V., Henschel, J.R. and Seely, M.K. 1998: Evaluation of fog-harvesting potential in Namibia. *Proceedings of the 1st International Conference on Fog and Fog Collection, Vancouver, Canada.*

Nagel, J.F. 1959: Fog precipitation at Swakopmund. *Union of South Africa Newsletter,* 125, 1- 9.

Nieman, W.A., Heyns, C. and Seely, M.K. 1978: A note on precipitation at Swakopmund. *Madoqua,* 11, 69-73.

Olivier, J. 1992: Some spatial and temporal aspects of fog in the Namib. *SA Geographer,* 19, 106-126.

Olivier, J. 1995: Spatial distribution of fog in the Namib. *Journal of Arid Environments,* 29, 129-138.

Pietruszka, R.D. and Seely, M.K. 1985: Predictability of two moisture sources in the Namib Desert. *South African Journal of Science,* 81, 682-685.

Schemenauer, R.S. and Cereceda, P. 1994a: Fog collection's role in water planning for developing countries. *Natural Resources Forum,* 18, 91-100.

Schemenauer, R.S. and Cereceda, P. 1994b: A proposed standard fog collector for use in high-elevation regions. *Journal of Applied Meteorology,* 33, 1313-1322.

Schemenauer, R.S., Fuenzalida, H. and Cereceda, P. 1988: A neglected water source: the Camanchaca of South America. *Bulletin of the American Meteorological Society,* 69, 138- 147.

Schulze, B.R. 1969: The climate of Gobabeb. In *Scientific Papers of the Namib Desert Research Station,* 4, 5-12.

Seely, M.K. 1979: Irregular fog as a water source for desert dune beetles. *Oecologia,* 42, 213- 227.

Seely, M.K. and Henschel, J.R. 1998: The climatology of Namib fog. *Proceedings of the 1st International Conference on Fog and Fog Collection, Vancouver, Canada.*

Seely, M.K., Henschel, J.R. and Robertson, M. 1998: The ecology of fog in Namib sand dunes. *Proceedings of the 1ˢᵗ International Conference on Fog and Fog Collection, Vancouver, Canada.*

Seely, M.K. and Stuart, P. 1976: The climate of Gobabeb, ten year summary 1962/72. *Namib Bulletin,* 1, 7-9.

Shannon, L.V. 1972: Circulation patterns and water mass movements along the West and South-West Coasts. *South African Journal of Science,* 68, 124-126.

Shannon, L.V., Seely, M.K. and Ward, J.D. 1989: *Proceedings of the Namib-Benguela Interactions Workshop at Gobabeb.* Foundation of Research Development, Ecosystem Programmes, Occasional Report Series.

Struthers, M.J. 1995: *Pilot fog study at Kleinzee - Progress Report: July 1995 to October 1995.* Stellenbosch: CSIR, Division of Earth, Marine and Atmospheric Science and Technology.

Struthers, M.J. 1997: *Water from fog study on the Cape West Coast progress report: December 1995 to May 1997.* Reprint No. CSIR ENV/S-I 97018. Stellenbosch: CSIR, Division of Water, Environment and Forestry Technology.

Taljaard, J.J. 1979: Low-level atmospheric circulation over the Namib. *Newsletter of the Weather Bureau of South Africa,* 361, 65-67.

Tyson, P.D. and Seely, M.K. 1980: Local winds over the central Namib. *The South African Geographical Journal,* 62, 135-150.

Vendrig, M. 1990: *Fog occurrence and measurement in Namibia.* Unpublished manuscript.

Chapter 7

LOCAL KNOWLEDGE MANAGEMENT SYSTEMS AND THE PROCUREMENT OF DOMESTIC WATER SUPPLIES IN RURAL MALAWI

by Moira Simpson

WATER: A LIFELINE TOWARD DEVELOPMENT

A provision for water

Present realities dictate that populations in most developing countries will not have access to safe water supplies upon entering the 21st century. Studies conducted over the past three decades reveal that former development endeavours have, in many cases, failed to provide a sustainable water supply for rural communities. Common characteristics have been identified among water supply projects labeled as failures. The majority of these projects broke down within years of execution primarily because the intervention initiative utilized control-management strategies that placed reliance upon technical solutions involving external agents. "Outsiders" monopolized the role of decision-making, execution and management of water supply systems. Little effort was made to understand the needs and cultural norms surrounding the practiced environmental management systems of the intended beneficiaries.

The very survival of rural populations faced with water scarcity has depended on the people developing their own solutions to securing water supplies. Community procurement of water evolves into a management system illustrated through innumerable small and large decisions and practices made by individual households and the community as a whole, on a daily basis. Over time, the foundation of an organizational structure is formed that functions within the confines of the local social, political, and economic environment. In the literature, such organizational structures are often referred to as local knowledge management systems (LKMS). Local knowledge management systems are a fluid and dynamic package of elements that change and adapt to new circumstances, and form the backbone of management decisions taken by the local people (Niamir, 1990). Practices (and/or technologies) from the outside may be adopted if it is understood as beneficial and functional within LKMS framework. The solutions to the barriers to the procurement of water are not solely found in LKMS, however, for the fact remains that rural domestic water supply is still a problem for many communities.

Addressing the challenge

Villages all over the world are faced with problems such as population increases, environmental disasters, wars, urbanization, and a growing dependency on a cash-based economy. In the context of traditional water supplies, purity of source and accessibility are becoming more and more of a problem.

In order for intervention programmes to be effective, a "common ground" must be found between a planner and community's conceptualization of "development" that can function with respect to an evolving LKMS. This is the challenge facing domestic rural water supply programmes.

BACKGROUND TO RESEARCH

The problem

Freshwater in Africa is unevenly distributed temporally and spatially. According to the water stress index, Malawi is one of nine water-scarce countries in Africa. It is also one of the poorest countries in the world with a high fertility rate (6.7%) and growth rate (3.3 % per annum). More than half the population of Malawi does not have access to potable water (UNESCO, 1995). Lack of resources, limited funding and technological breakdowns are just some of the barriers to a protected water supply. It is necessary to seek out low-cost alternative measures that may supplement or replace existing boreholes and protected shallow wells found in Malawi. Such measures may be found in traditional sources.

Three villages were targeted in this case study: one village possessing an external technological input (protected borehole with an 'Afridev' pump); a village relying on a protected shallow well; and a base village solely dependent on hand-dug wells (both in sand river beds and soil). The study sought to compare and contrast these villages in order to better understand how development interventions may be of sustainable benefit to rural people within the context of their own local knowledge management framework. It is assumed that each village is a heterogeneous entity; thus, significant distinctions between social classes as they pertain to the study were obtained through wealth-ranking exercises.

Study design

The research set out to describe and determine how existing LKMS may be integrated with "external" technical expertise to support sustainable alternative water supply initiatives. The following section will describe the goals and objectives of this study and how they provide the framework for a development dialogue.

In order to describe the context of a development dialogue, the goals of this study are as follows:

- To describe the local management systems associated with the procurement of water for domestic use during both the wet and dry seasons in selected villages; and,
- To determine how LKMS in water may be combined with external expertise (i.e. provided by the government or NGO) to create a more technically and socially reliable, sustainable water supply.

The study concentrates on the domestic utilization of water, excluding water management practices such as irrigation for agricultural production. "Domestic water" is water used for household purposes, priority being placed on water for consumption. Thus, another variable taken into consideration will be water quality. It is important to note that water quality will be discussed at two levels: as perceived by the villagers from the three study areas and as defined by developing agencies. The objectives of this study are as follows:

1. **Define and contrast the possible impacts of varying water supply sources upon the community and individual household.** Water resource options available to each village will be identified (including alternative sources), as well as patterns of source utilization. Discussion will focus on how each of the villages classifies, protects and operates each source.

2. **Describe mechanisms established for providing water to individual households.** The service of providing water from source to household is an important issue often ignored in rural areas. The villagers' association with

water is described in relation to the seasonal impact of transport mechanisms, protection of water, and use of vessels.

3. **Discuss the domestic utilization of water.** Both the community and individual household place priority on the manner in which water is utilized. Discussion will concentrate on contrasting and comparing the study villages and the three social classes identified for prioritization of domestic water utilization and storage.

4. **Examine the social organization and management structure regarding local water resources.** Water is often regarded as a "free good" until scarcity arises, placing pressure upon the social system. Attitudes towards water will be examined as they pertain to a community and an individual household. The role of traditional structures will be discussed in relationship to the management of local water resources.

5. **In light of objectives 1 to 4, to learn from villages with externally introduced water supply technologies and the impact of technologies upon domestic water resource management strategies; and to determine from villages without such technology, how technologies may be introduced and effectively managed.** All domestic water management systems consist of four basic components: a source, a transport and delivery system, a utilization pattern (community and household), and a safeguard mechanism either in the form of water quality control and/or on-site source protection. This study seeks to understand LKMS for the procurement of domestic water supply by collecting data on the functioning of water supply systems in three villages. Village water supply systems can be compared and contrasted based on the technology each possesses for attaining household water supplies. Understanding the structure behind local water supplies can lay the much needed groundwork for supporting coping mechanisms and preventing the need for emergency drought interventions.

METHODOLOGY

In the context of this study, both participant observation and participatory appraisal research methods were utilized because of their unobtrusive impact upon community life. It was also perceived as the best methodological tool to employ in unraveling the meaning behind interactions associated with water management practices. Water management consists of a series of conscious and subconscious actions that can only be understood in the context of day to day survival.

Preliminary fieldwork and research preparations

Data collected in a participatory evaluation by the researcher between July and September 1996 served as baseline information in the study design. Before fieldwork could begin, preparations were carried out that involved: obtaining approval from District authorities, locating a research site, selecting a research assistant, and most importantly, gaining acceptance into the host community.

Chikwawa District villages were targeted as the study site because:

▶ the researcher was familiar with the region owing to preliminary fieldwork,
▶ many villages had little or no access to water and sanitation facilities,
▶ high population density,
▶ distance from trading centres,
▶ semi-arid conditions,
▶ and, most importantly, vulnerability to climatic variations such as drought and floods.

The three selected villages of Therere, Chang'ambika and Dzosuma shared common characteristics with regard to environmental conditions, social and economic structure, food production and remoteness from a trading centre, but contrasted in terms of water supply sources (borehole, shallow well, and reliance on surface water supply).

The success of the study depended upon effective communication between the researcher and the involved parties, therefore a female resident with advanced language skills in both Chichewa and English was selected. Gender was important due to the perception of water procurement as a "woman's issue". Residence was taken up in the village of Dzosuma.

Data collection

Direct involvement in people's daily lives provided both a point of reference for the logic and process of participant observational inquiry as well as a strategy for gaining access to phenomena that commonly are obscured from the standpoint of a non-participant (Jorgensen, 1989). As much effort as possible was made to prevent any "intrusion" upon the village life which ultimately led to modifications in data collection methods, particularly in the use of participatory rural appraisal (PRA). Table 7.1 describes the data collection framework.

Table 7.1 Data collection framework

	Sub-Themes	Information Classification	Data Collection Method
Background information	Background reading	-NGO reports on water & sanitation -literature on Chikwawa District -history of region -general information on area & resource availability -general information on people & relationship to community	-timelines -focus group discussions -local survey (transect walks) -participation in daily tasks -social & resource mapping (PR) -participatory rural appraisal tools -attending village meetings -participating in local events
	Establishing rapport in the community		
Source	Classification	-identification of source alternatives -availability of water (seasonal impact) -water harvesting -alternative sources (natural) -ownership over source(s) -source utilization -water collection -source preservation	-participation in water collection activities -informal interviews -focus group discussions -structured interviews -observation -decision tree -causal diagram
	Protection		
Provision to household	Transport	-gender role -mechanism(s) for provision -protection in transit	-observation -participation -informal discussions -structured questionnaire
Domestic utilization	Water consumption	-utilization (wet & dry season) -prioritizing water use -storage	-as above
Social organization	Structures	-tradition & "foreign" decision-making structures -community participation -individual household decision-making	-interviews -participatory exercises -observation

The utilization of PRA in this study was designed to serve three functions:

▶ to provide background information in the local environment (social and physical) which could serve as a baseline for all future inquiries;

▶ to build the capacity of local extension workers in the study area to serve their constituencies; and to encourage villagers to consider their role in development of the village and evaluate what they can do to produce positive change within the community.

Nine extension workers were trained in participatory rural appraisal methodology. Sessions proceeded in each village with varying degrees of village participation. Table 7.2 describes the activities undertaken during PRA sessions. Information gathered through these sessions were verified through focus group sessions conducted by the researcher and assistant.

Table 7.2 Activities undertaken during PRA sessions

Tool	Information	Methods
Historical Timeline	-Settlement -Development interventions -Ethnic makeup -Major events	-Focus group discussions with elders of village -Individual interviews -Timeline drawn on paper
Wealth Ranking	-Identified social classes & their characteristics -Who in village belonged to what category	Individuals identified at random to review cards with each villager's name. Classes identified with corresponding characteristics. Cards were placed in a pile representing social class. Exercise repeated on average with ten men & women from each village. Results consolidated into one list of breakdown.
Village Mapping	-Social -Physical -General information on each household	Combined groups (male & female) using local materials drew village map. Several group members transferred information onto paper. In addition, cards were made on each household with the following information: family name, number of people in house, pit latrine, bath shelter, dishrack, rubbish pit, cattle, pigs, goats, chickens, radio, bicycle. On the physical map, resources of villages such as water, trees, graveyards, fields were indicated.
Problem Tree	-Problem tree on water	Combined group drew (on ground) problems associated with water in their village & possible solutions.
Matrix	-Prioritization of water use -Ranking	Groups were divided into men & women. Discussion on water followed by matrix which prioritized water use from most important usage to least important.

Daily Calendar	-Daily activities	Combined groups divided into youth, middle age & elder illustrated (on paper) activities for a typical day in wet & dry seasons. On separate occasions, individuals asked to gather (middle age group selected according to social status) & outline their activities for wet & dry season.
Household Income & Expenditure	-Sources of income & expenditure	Combined group outlined (on ground) seasonal impact of income & expenditure for their village. Later recorded on paper.
Problem Ranking	-General village problems	Village as a whole discussed their problems & possible solutions with an action plan (an action plan was not the final result in all villages). Problems were ranked from most important to least important.
Season Calendar	-Disease patterns -Work patterns	Separate male & female groups drew chart (on ground) recording patterns according to season. Later recorded on paper.

Note: PRA sessions were planned to be carried out over a three-day period. In each village it varied as to how many activities could be carried out owing to time constraints and/or attendance. Incomplete activities were implemented at a later date in smaller groups. In addition, the majority of activities were repeated through smaller focus group sessions.

Focus group discussions served several functions in the data collection process. They served as a means to gather data by consensus on subjects being discussed. In recollecting historical events, group dynamics ensured agreement on precision of events. Focus groups could be used to verify or expand upon data during PRA sessions. Finally, focus group sessions allowed for issues which were of importance to that particular group to be discussed.

A structured questionnaire was designed and administered to a stratified sample from three villages. The senior woman of each household was interviewed. Households were selected to gather information and compare and contrast that information between social classes and villages with different water supplies.

Participant observation, a methodology for collecting data, is based upon the experiences derived from everyday life activities. Through participating in village life, immediate experiences associated with water produced casual conversations that served as a basis for enquiry through unstructured and structured interviews. Participant observation seeks to uncover, make accessible and reveal the meanings (realities) people use to make sense of their daily lives (Jorgenson, 1989). Integrating into local life had both positive and negative aspects that placed certain limitations upon data collection. Becoming a part of village life made it possible to observe behaviours that villagers would not be able to describe simply because they take such activities for granted in their lives. Participating in day-to-day life allowed certain members of the community the freedom to approach the researcher and assistant and discuss matters that may not otherwise be shared in a participatory rural appraisal session or interview. In addition, villagers found a common ground to relate to the researchers upon observing their activities in the village (i.e. drawing water, cooking, cleaning, etc.), which allowed them a certain amount of leeway into partial integration into the community.

Why only partial integration? Although villagers accepted the researchers within the community and perhaps some even fully understood our purpose for being there, the role still had to be categorized, based upon prior experiences. It seemed that the researchers had to be placed in an unspoken social class category – the "rich" class. This association was because of ethnic background (*azungu*, meaning "European"), clothes, food, and the fact that there was an unknown income source that was not generated from a garden. It was thought that being female researchers would allow for an ease of association with woman, but this was a hasty conclusion. Men associating with an *azungu* boosted their status within the community. Women who had special ties with the *azungu* were at times shunned by social groups who designed rumours to discourage such activity. Women who felt "free" to associate with the researchers were of a respected position in their community through their marriage or they were village elders. Any association beyond these groups of individuals had to be sought by the researchers. Despite these limitations, it was found that participant observation was the most productive form of data collection.

BACKGROUND INFORMATION ON RESEARCH SITE

Within the Chikwawa District (Lower Shire) there are a total of 14 villages under the leadership of the group village headman from Therere. Therere is the largest, located approximately 25 km from the nearest trading centre. It has a primary school, several stores, churches and government posts including a health post. Chang'ambika has only a few stores, while Dzosuma contains only mud-walled houses in a dispersed settlement pattern dictated by proximity to gardens. However, in all three villages, farming is the top priority for each household. Travel in the region is primarily by foot and by bicycle or the occasional motorized vehicle during the dry season when the roads are passable.

This area experiences a wet season from November to March and a dry season from June to October. It has one of the lowest annual rainfall averages, as well as the highest potential evaporation rates in the country. The seasons are often characterized by extreme conditions of flooding and drought. Such climatic conditions set the stage for environmental degradation, when the factor of a high population density is also taken into consideration. Water scarcity problems do not simply rest upon the *quantity* of water available but also the *quality*, due to the pockets of saline water found in the Lower Shire Valley alluvium.

Historical foundation

The first village in the study area was Therere, settled about four generations ago by people of the Sena clan who migrated from Mozambique. At that time, the area was heavily forested, rich with water sources and plentiful with game. In the same year, more clan members settled along the Phwadzi River, some 5 km away, in what became Dzosuma. Chang'ambika originally came into being in 1921 as a village named Mwalawahtanda, in an area now known as Lengwe National Park. The elders report that their parents left Mozambique because of an ongoing war of independence (against the Europeans). In 1977, the entire village of Mwalawahtanda was ordered to relocate to its present location by the Malawian government because they resided in a forest reserve. When the people refused to leave due to the land's high productivity, the government sent in trucks with "cages" to assist in the relocating of the people.

Adapting to change

As original settlements, both Therere and Dzosuma were described as being surrounded by many trees, wild animals and streams. At that time, the rivers had abundant water and fish throughout the year. People were both farmers and hunters, and both men and women grew crops. Past agricultural outputs were described as sufficient enough to feed the entire family for the whole year. Traditional farming methods did not require chemicals and fertilizers. A system based on rotational bush fallow avoided soil deterioration by periodic forest destruction. These were methods practiced by both the first and second generations from Portuguese East Africa (Mozambique).

In 1903-04, the British government pushed for the growth of cash crops by means of manipulative taxation strategies and provision of cheap cash crop (cotton) seed. Subsequently, cotton production not only created a dependency relationship upon a cash-based economy, but also influenced traditional family structures.

In pre-colonial Southern Malawi, the Mang'anja household was headed by both the wife and the husband. The Sena who settled in Malawi were patrilineal (land inheritance through father's lineage) and virilocal (wife moves into the husband's village upon marriage); whereas, the Mang'anja were matrilineal (land holding through mother's lineage) and uxorilocal (husband moves to his wife's village). According to custom, when a Sena man married a Mang'anja woman, he was expected to follow the wife to cultivate her land. In contrast, if a Mang'anja man married a Sena woman he was required to pay labola (bride wealth to parents in the form of money or livestock), after which he was allowed to take the bride to his village. The village headman allocated land to families that settled in the village. Increasing pressure upon the land made it impossible to produce enough food to support the family through the entire year. The customary Mang'anja requirement that a husband settle in his wife's village was less often enforced, although not legally abolished. Husbands took principal control over cotton production, using the household as a labour base. The women, however, were responsible for both cash and subsistence crops. It was at this point that women were forced by external influences to abandon tradition, subsequently becoming marginalized in the development process.

Agricultural systems governed by tradition were transformed to land tenure practices that became subject to question, depending on the individual household involved. At the time of the study, land tenure in the Therere area seemed to be dictated by availability of land. In other words, if a male has access to land before marriage, then the wife is obliged to take residency in his village (with the encouragement of labola). If the wife inherits land, then it is more than likely to be used for the production of subsistence crops.

Monocropping, as an attempt to increase agricultural output, was an agricultural method adopted by the second generation and practiced until recently (Davison, 1993). At present, agricultural extension workers and the media are encouraging intercropping as the most effective and efficient agricultural land use. The people of Chang'ambika say that this method has improved their agricultural output, but not enough to feed their families during the dry season. Wage labour is still sought to provide food for the household for six months out of the year.

Problems observed over time

In the three study villages, the problems observed over time may be compartmentalized into three common themes: agriculture, water and social relations. Those interviewed in all three villages expressed the view that land use practices in their preseht form are not the same as those experienced by their parents or grandparents. Everyone agreed that in the past the land was more fertile and could be relied upon to produce more crops. Therere elders stated that even if you now have a big garden, it cannot produce enough to feed the whole family for the entire year. These conditions are attributed to the lack of water and population pressure upon the land. In Dzosuma, there is a demand for land and a frustration with the forestry department for not allowing agricultural land beyond designated points. It is felt that the land is no longer fertile because their parents burnt surrounding trees and shrubs, but they are unable to practice crop rotation as they had in the past. New land is wanted in order to allow the soils to "rest". In addition, the land cannot hold water because it is bare. A half kilometer away, Chang'ambika residents also feel that their soil is not productive and often express their desire to return to their former settlement site in Lengwe Forest. It was admitted that some of the poorer farmers have illegally planted gardens in these areas and are risking fines (200MK) from the government. Adopted intercropping land use methods taught by the government have assisted villagers, who do see a difference in output.

Water is expressed as a major problem concerning all three villages. Elders say that the water has disappeared and is no longer available for their crops throughout the dry season. This is attributed to the felling of trees, an opinion that can be attributed to the educational work done by agricultural extension workers and information gained from radio. Chang'ambika villagers assert that water has been a problem since they moved to the area in 1977. In all three villages, water is a cause of dispute both for agriculture and domestic use.

The final theme of problems observed over time revolves around social relations. At present, it is perceived that many children are being born and opinions differ as to whether or not this is a positive or negative point. Female elders say that in the past traditional family planning methods were practiced, which are rarely used by the present generation. As for child survival, the elders see little difference from the past – children are still dying from the same diseases. Another serious social problem is associated with beer. In the past, only old men would drink beer, which was brewed in association with certain rituals or seasonal and other celebrations. Now, everyone is drinking, which leads to many fights.

Economic environment

Malawi has an agrarian economy in which the seasons rule the rhythms of daily rural life. Climate has both a direct and indirect impact upon the social and economic welfare of the people (Chambers et. al., 1981). Therefore, it is important to examine rural activities according to the villagers' concept of time, in order to effectively implement any development initiatives.

In the study area, villagers divided the year roughly into four periods: rainy season (November-March), harvesting period (March-April), cold season (April-June) and hot/dry season (August-November).

From October to May, villagers are very busy with farming activities. Off-peak season is between May and September, a time traditionally reserved for village entertainment and rituals. The government has pressured traditional leaders to ensure that ritual ceremonies do not coincide with school days. Shifting cultivation is now impossible because of the population pressure on land and – the villagers believe – the limitations set by the forestry department. The "hungry season" runs from January to April when people are busy working in their gardens but can only eat once a day because food is in short supply. By this time, a household's maize supply is usually finished and survival is dependent on either *dimba* garden produce, gifts (cash or food) from relatives, money earned through *ganyu* (temporary labour) during the dry season, or sale of household goods (radio or bicycle).

From May to July, less time is spent in the garden, because of food preparation, which includes drying and storing seeds and leaves. October to December is considered a difficult period, when the diet consists of fruit (mango and banana) and dried vegetable leaves such as okra, beans, peas, and cassava. Some seeds, such as cucumber and watermelon, are stored within the mud walls of the house. Little relief is given during planting and harvesting – the "hungry season" when energy output is at its highest. Plans are made during the dry season to reduce food shortage through the migration of household males seeking *ganyu* in either Mozambique or local trading centres. Meat from chicken, pigeon, or goat is only eaten on special occasions. Livestock is kept as an emergency measure to sell for cash to cover costs of funerals, weddings or Western medicine.

In all villages, everyone has a garden, from those considered to be rich to the very poorest of the poor. The only variation would be the size of garden, which was not measured for this study. Businessmen or government workers in Therere had gardens that were tended by family members or *ganyu*. Poorer families with little land were forced to have gardens either close to or in Lengwe forest, despite the knowledge that this is illegal and they could be fined, and despite the nuisance of monkeys which damage crops.

Daily activities

During the wet season, all members of the household, including children and the elderly, are involved in the gardens. Young girls have the added responsibility of assisting in the care of young babies and household chores, as well as being expected to attend school. The adults spend from morning light until early afternoon in the garden. Close to the end of April, men will also build houses which the women will plaster with mud. Women also have the tasks of collecting firewood, fetching water, heating water for bathing, preparing the maize, sorghum or millet for the maize mill, and cooking (approximately two hours of cooking per meal). After lunch, everyone rests for about two hours, then the adults return to the gardens and children use the afternoon to play and perhaps take care of odd jobs.

In the dry season, the same schedule applies to all age groups except that more emphasis is given to selling goods such as cotton, grass, firewood or food. During this period, the men have more free time and leave the bulk of garden work to the women. Women spend more time fetching water and taking care of their houses, which becomes more important in the dry season due to dust and animal droppings. Animals roam free in the dry season, but are usually tethered in the wet season. Houses require smearing to prevent the presence of mites and ticks.

When comparing daily activities between the three different social classes, it was found that in the dry season, men from the poor class spent more time on income-generating activities than any other social class. In addition, at the end of the wet season, men from both the poor and middle classes spent time drinking beer (locally made by women). This indicates that after the cotton has been sold, both classes have what they consider to be expendable income. The rich class have businesses that are open all year round, with expendable income lasting into the dry season, when they spend their afternoons mixing drinking with business. Both men and women participate in the household business activities.

Preference of water source

There are four primary sources of water: surface water, precipitation, ground water and consumption alternatives. It is interesting to note the resources that the villagers do not utilize. Depressions are not dug to retain surface water in the form of ponds. Dams are not created to trap surface water, whether it be in the seasonal rivers/streams or collecting slope runoff. Rain is harvested in its most basic form during the wet season, but dew is ignored as a potential drinking water source. Consumptive alternative is a category that supplements drinking water. Elders reported that some plants, such as banana leaves, provide water in the dry season. Certain foods (sugarcane, finger millet, fruits) with high water content supplement and provide a nutritional water source. However, these foods are only available during the wet season. Milk is considered a luxury and drunk by few. Soda, though also considered a luxury is purchased because mothers from all social classes believe that drinks such as Fanta have a high nutritional value beneficial for their children. Bottled water is available in cities, but not in rural areas.

Despite the different levels of technology in the three villages, the preferred water supply source in all villages was rainwater in the wet season and ground water collected from hand-dug wells from the end of the wet season to the dry season. In Therere, the borehole was utilized as a secondary measure in the wet season when sediment load was high in the river, when no rainwater was available, and in the dry season when the ground water tables became too low for hand-dug wells. In the wet season, water is plentiful, which eases the burden upon women who work in their gardens for the entire day. In addition, food serves as a (partial) water replacement, thus would be the most suitable choice for drinking water. Supplementary water supplies were used for other domestic purposes.

Alternatives and the freedom to choose water source define the stability of local water management systems. The wet season is a time of plentiful supplies, when ground water systems are recharged. As the seasons progress, water supply diminishes and management shifts from household to community as sources are dug to support larger numbers of people. In periods of drought, villagers are forced to rely upon a single water source. A single water supply source is associated with hard times – a period of no alternatives. This perspective may partially explain why the percentage of households utilizing a borehole varies according to season.

Boreholes use seems not so much a drinking water supply preference, but rather a necessity when times are difficult.

Protection of source

Protection or conservation of water resources is an essential element to water management systems. Villagers approach water management at a micro-scale, protecting individual traditional wells and sections of water-ways. Comprehensive planning of rivers/streams is not carried out between villages. Awareness is growing, due to radio broadcasts, that cutting trees contributes to the depletion of ground water tables and attempts are being made by village headmen to discourage the cutting of trees near waterways.

A river/stream is divided into sections between household supply points in which washing areas (separate for men and women) are always downstream from drinking water supplies.

Hand-dug wells are divided according to utilization with drinking water wells located upstream and away from wells used for washing. At the beginning of each day, hand-dug wells are cleaned out, allowing fresh water recharge. Attempts are made to prevent livestock from using drinking wells by covering the site with thorn branches. Unfortunately, livestock is allowed to wander free after harvesting season and can contaminate water sources. Metaphysical beliefs also provide guidelines on how to protect wells, which at times can be a hindrance in water management. For example, water sources believed to be the site of witchcraft rituals will not be used; the researcher could find no reason or "hidden" explanation as to why certain sites were declared unusable.

Traditional water supply sources are often dismissed by external observers as inadequate and unhygienic. Observations over time led the researcher to conclude that there are management practices carried out consciously or unconsciously to protect drinking water hand-dug wells. One of the main barriers in the study area was the damaging impact of livestock (primarily goats) upon water resources. During times of water scarcity, there is much concern over livestock utilizing precious resources − more than fear of contamination. The problem is essentially one of control of resources and allocation of tasks according to gender. Women have little control over the movement of livestock, which are usually the responsibility of the male head of the household. Building barriers such as fences is deemed to be a male task.

Identifying sites for shallow wells

From wet to dry season, the use of wells progresses from household groups to wells that support an entire village. From generation to generation, with new problems such as population growth and irrigation, the search for water is becoming more difficult. A knowledge base still exists for siting locations that have ground water. In a time of unpredictable climatic conditions, however, the question remains as to how long such knowledge will be useful.

Particular trees and plants were identified as indicators of ground water. Wells in river beds were located under the shade of a particular tree because it was believed to make the water "sweet". Well locations are also based upon sitings made by past generations or upon dreams or visions considered to be messages from ancestors.

There is no tradition of water-divining among villagers, although borehole drilling teams often have practical knowledge of divining and use it to verify drilling sites. This skill has been adopted from Chinese agricultural workers.

Villagers are able to locate ground water primarily through utilizing past knowledge and supporting it with metaphysical beliefs. It is difficult to calculate if this knowledge can sustain growing populations residing in areas with limited ground water resources.

Rainwater harvesting

Research studies report that in areas with low rainfall averages, cultures adapt by devising mechanisms to maximize storage capacities to trap precipitation. These reserves are managed to supplement dry season water supplies.

In the study area, rain water collection involves direct collection into buckets or as runoff from corrugated/plastic roofs. No tradition management base exists in terms of creating artificial runoff or storage mechanisms for rainwater.

History serves to explain why there is little tradition of water harvesting in the study area. Present inhabitants there remember their villages as a land of prosperity when they were children. One generation ago, villages were situated in forests and surface waters were abundant. Today, the forest cover has disappeared, streams are seasonal and finding water is a struggle in the dry season. The villagers do not have a knowledge base concerning rainwater harvesting mechanisms. However, this is an area of great potential for dry season water supply.

Water quality

Water resources hold little value if they are not deemed fit for human consumption. Villagers have their own standards for judging water quality based on colour, presence of sediment, odour and taste preferences. Water placed in storage for drinking is kept a maximum of three days and then diverted for other uses such as cleaning or gardening. Although a borehole indicates that the water source is safer than a traditional source, it will not be used for drinking supplies if the taste is not similar to rainwater or water collected at the river.

Filtering water through sand or by passing it through cloth are the two methods for purifying water at a household level. Water is rarely boiled for drinking because the fire gives it a smoky flavour and the water is not "satisfying". Therefore, the potential for water-borne diseases is present.

External agencies concentrate their resources on supplying water to villages, but pay little attention to the quality of the resource. This is particularly a problem in a region where ground water can be saline. In addition, the onus is placed on hygiene education programmes to inform people on how to improve water quality. If there are different concepts as to how water makes an individual sick, hygiene education programmes will do little to decrease the incidence of water-related diseases.

Delivery system

Women are responsible for transporting water from source to household. Some women will cover water with leaves to prevent spillage during transport but this is being discouraged by the Ministry of Health because of the possibility of transferring parasites into the water.

In times of water scarcity, women recognized as belonging to a "rich" social class will pay other women to fetch their household water requirements. Young men may sometimes be involved in fetching water, mainly from boreholes, if they are paid to collect water or if it is being collected in large quantities to make traditional beer.

If water provision is to remain "safe" mechanisms must be established to educate all participants involved in the delivery of water to the household.

CONCLUSION

This study illustrates how fundamental local knowledge management systems are to everyday lives and routines. The sustainability of any development intervention in water resource management depends upon integration of the related LKMS. The most significant barriers to the procurement of domestic water supplies within the LKMS were gender inequality, lack of historical experience with water shortages and scientific misconceptions. These barriers will have to be addressed before sustainability of community-based water resource management plans or policies can be achieved.

Local knowledge management systems for the procurement of domestic water supply is an area of resource management that will be of grave importance to water stressed and water scarce nations of southern Africa. In the past, water for agriculture has been the main priority of both rural citizens and academics in water management studies. However, as societies are forced to become more and more dependent on cash-based economies and as populations increase, focus will need to be re-directed into satisfying the basic requirements of rural communities. Water management policies and development intervention initiatives must focus upon local mechanisms that support resource management. Before blueprint planning policies can be adhered, there must be flexibility to learn, document and apply local knowledge management systems.

REFERENCES

Chambers, R. *et. al.* (ed.). 1981: *Seasonal Dimensions to Rural Poverty*. London: Frances Pinter (Publishers) Ltd.

Davison, Jean. 1993: Tenacious Women: Clinging to banja household production in the face of changing gender relations in Malawi. *Journal of Southern African Studies,* 19 (3), 405- 421.

Jorgensen, Danny. 1989: Participant Observation: *A Methodology for Human Studies Applied Social Research Methods Series Volume 15.* London: Sage Publications.

Niamir, Maryam. 1990: *Community Forestry: Herder's Decision-making in Natural Resource Management in Arid and Semi-arid Africa.* Rome: Food and Agricultural Organization of the United Nations.

United Nations Economic and Social Council. 1995: Role of Water Scarcity and Water Stress in Addressing the Economic Challenges Facing African Countries at the Dawn of the 21st Century. In *Proceedings of the UNECA and WMO Joint Conference on Water Resources Policy and Assessment*, pp. 20-25. Addis Ababa.

130

Chapter 8

MANAGING PUBLIC WATER STANDPIPES: COMMUNITY-BASED MANAGEMENT OR PRIVATIZATION? LUANDA, ANGOLAN CASE STUDIES.

by Abdi Siad Omar and Farokh Afshar

INTRODUCTION

Water is vital to all aspects of human life. Without a safe and reliable supply, communities suffer and face great difficulty advancing. Because of this, the provision of safe and convenient potable water has been an important sector of development programmes since the 1950s. Unprecedented attention was focused on this sector during the United Nations Drinking Water Supply and Sanitation (UN Water) Decade from 1980-1990. Despite heavy investment from the international community and local governments, up to 70 percent of the water supply infrastructure in developing countries was not functioning soon after construction (Rondinelli, 1991).

In many countries, water supply systems are misused, not repaired, and fail to provide reliable water supply services (Manigin, 1991; Livingstone and McPherson, 1993; Saunders and Warford, 1976). This failure can be traced to a variety of causes, but the primary factor has been identified as a lack of sustainability of the water supply system (Briscoe and de Ferrant, 1988; McCommon *et al*, 1990; Rondinelli, 1991).

It has been recognised that the failure of water supply systems can be attributed to the conventional belief that water supply is a public good which should be supplied free of charge (Briscoe and de Ferrant, 1988; Churchill, 1987). This assumption has led to the establishment of large, centralized government agencies responsible for water provision. These have tended to focus on expanding coverage, but have neglected the operations and maintenance (O&M) of existing infrastructure. The result has been an increasing number of unsustainable water supply stations.

Many governments and international organizations have come to realize that conventional approaches to managing and operating public water services are not suitable. Recently, innovative approaches have been encouraged for public standpipe systems. The most widely suggested models are based on:

- local government management
- private sector participation (PSP)
- community-based management (CBM)

All of these options give importance to supply-driven systems in which cost recovery plays some role. The local government option has not yet established a relevant experience to date.

In this study, private sector participation and community-based management models are examined in the peri-urban setting. These models share a common focus on the importance of the sustainability of the water supply system. They differ in that they employ different methods to achieve sustainability.

The results of this study suggest that specific preconditions must exist within the area before either method can achieve long-term sustainability. This paper discusses those preconditions and examines how both community-based management and privatization-based models have particular advantages and disadvantages. Lastly, the paper discusses how to combine the advantages of both models in order to establish a long-term, sustainable water delivery service.

The following section sets out the basic principals of community-based management and privatization models. The emphasis is on the basic concepts, objectives and the preconditions required for their success. This is followed by an analysis and discussion of the case studies in peri-urban areas in Angola.

ALTERNATIVE MANAGEMENT MODELS FOR WATER DELIVERY SERVICES

It should be noted that, until now, both the private sector participation (PSP) and community-based management (CBM) models have been proposed or applied in different contexts. The PSP model is promoted as an alternative option to public water utilities. Recent experience in Latin America (Argentina, Mexico and Venezuela), in Africa (Ivory Coast and Guinea), in Asia (Malaysia), and in Europe (England and Wales) indicate this is a growing trend (World Bank, 1992 and 1994). The CBM has been employed for many years in rural areas in both developing and industrialized countries (Rondinelli, 1991; McGarry, 1991).

Private sector participation model

Concept and definition: The concept of privatization has emerged as an important institutional or organizational option to operate and manage water delivery services, both in the developed world and the developing countries (World Bank, 1994). The concept is based on the assumption that private sector's management is more efficient, effective, and sustainable than public sector management (Roth, 1987). Despite its popular usage (and perhaps because of it) the term privatization is plagued by problems of definition and misinterpretation. Savas (1987, 277) describes the general problems arising from the concept of privatization:

> The word privatization unfortunately summons forth images from a deep reservoir and causes misunderstanding, premature polarisation and shrill arguments that are beside the point more often than not. Some read into the word a plot to restore a complete free market, with overtone of dog eat dog, exploitation of the weakest and the survival of the fittest. Others interpret the word as an attack on the government and the things government has been doing.

In the water supply sector, the term "privatization" is often equated with the transfer of water ownership and the permanent sales of water supply services to the private sector. This misinterpretation is the result of lack of definition of the term. The term privatization is not clearly defined and has different meanings to different people and in different countries. In many developing countries, privatization is considered as a way for the private sector to participate in the construction, operation, and maintenance of service infrastructure.

In the context of this study, privatization is intended as the involvement of private sector in the operation and maintenance (O&M) of the water delivery services. The terms privatization, public-private partnership, or private sector participation (PSP) are used interchangeably throughout.

Rationale for private sector participation: The rationale for private sector involvement in the provision of water supply services stems from the record of poor performance and mismanagement characteristic of many public water supply services. The main objectives of private sector involvement are to ensure improved management, access to private capital, and greater efficiency, of the water supply and delivery services. Kessides (1993) identifies five main reasons for privatization of the water supply services in developing countries:

- **Managerial skills:** rapid and flexible decision-making due to clear incentive structure (individual reward based on performance);
- **Productive efficiency:** lower production and delivery costs, stemming from the motivation to make profit;
- **Dynamic efficiency:** the motivation to invest in and maintain capital equipment and technological improvement;
- **Accountability to customers:** the motivation and flexibility to adapt production to changing markets and to achieve better service quality;
- **Financial autonomy:** privatization reduces government's financial burden for operating expenditure and debt serving.

Options for private sector participation: The World Development Report of 1994 identifies at least five different privatization options commonly used in the water supply sector, each varying in the degree of involvement such as the duration of the contract, capital investment and commercial risks. These options are: service contracts, management contract, lease system, concessionaire contracts, and built-owned-operated-transfer schemes (BOOT). This section will consider the lease and concessionaire schemes which are the main concern of this study.

- **Lease Contract Option:** Also known as the franchise system, the lease contract option involves arrangements whereby a private firm operates and maintains a state-owned facility at its own financial risk. The public authority remains the sole owner of the assets and is responsible for initial capital investment, debit services, renewals, and replacement of major capital works. The public authority also determines supply tariffs and cost recovery policies. The leaseholder is responsible for working capital and the replacement of short-lived assets such as spare parts. Regarding water supply, the lease contractor collects the water tariff revenue from the customers directly and returns an agreed portion to the public water authority. The profit for the leaseholder is the difference between the gross revenue and the operating costs, and the license fee. Any savings from efficiency improvements are retained by the leaseholder. The lease contract specifies the rates to be charged, usually regulated by a pricing index formula. The contract also specifies the respective roles of the water authority and the leaseholder. The contract generally guarantees reasonable revenue for the leaseholder, but also requires that the leaseholder deposit a performance bond which can be recalled if their performance is below acceptable levels.

▶ **Concession Contract Option:** The concessionaire is entrusted a fixed asset during the concession period and is required to return the asset in a fixed amount of time. Under a concession option, the private contractor or the concessionaire has responsibilities for water supply services, including the operations and maintenance (O&M). The concessionaire is paid for the revenue collected from the consumers, based on contractually set charges. The concessionaire pays the public water authority an agreed portion of the revenue collected and retains the balance for profit. Like the lease contract, the concession terms, conditions, and penalties are clearly spelled out in a written document. The advantage of the concession contract over a lease contract is the combining responsibilities for O&M *and investment* in the same entity. The concessionaire is responsible for investment plans to expand the services and to fund major renewals and replacements to maintain the system. In contrast, under the lease contract, public authority is responsible for capital investment and major repairs. The fixed asset of the investment remain the property of the state or the public authority (Triche, 1990).

Role of the government: In general, the private sector is motivated by profit. On the other hand, the investment objective of water supply services is to provide clean, adequate and affordable water to the community. These two objectives may result in conflict. The government's role then is to balance these objectives. The government should establish an appropriate regulatory framework to monitor and control the operations of the private operator. The primary objectives of the regulatory framework are to ensure compliance with standards of acceptable level of services, to protect the consumers from price inflation, and to create a good business environment for the private operator (Triche, 1990). Basically, the government's function in PSP is to act as "watchdog", safeguarding the interest of the consumers of the water services.

Community-based management model

Definition and concept: Community management is being promoted by international development agencies and governments in the developing world as an effective mechanism for insuring long-term sustainability of water delivery services. Community management is gaining significance with evidence that water delivery services are more sustainable when designed, established, and operated by the community (McCommon *et. al.*, 1990).

Community management approaches represent a shift in community participation from initiation to responsibility. While the community participation concept implies that beneficiaries are involved in development activities, community management refers to the capabilities and willingness of the community to take charge and determine the nature of their development (McCommon *et. al.*, 1990). A community management approach strives to empower communities with the necessary skills and organization to take charge in the operation and maintenance of their water supply facilities. The community exercises responsibilities for decision making and control over the implementation of decisions. McCommon *et. al.* (1990) has identified the following three basic components of community management approach:

‣ **Responsibility:** The community takes on the ownership of and the attendant obligations to the water facility.

‣ **Authority:** The community has the legitimate right to make decisions regarding the water facility on behalf of the users.

‣ **Control:** The community is able to carry out and determine the outcome of their decisions.

These three elements are the distinctive features of the community management approach. The community itself must be the primary decision maker, operator, investor, organizer and overseer (Briscoe and de Ferrant, 1988). Community management is not an ad hoc solution, it is a gradual process of learning, where the local community gradually assumes responsibility.

Rationale for community-based management: Community-based management has been proposed as a key strategy to operate and manage the water supply services for rural and peri-urban areas where incentives do not exist for public and private enterprise (McGarry, 1991). The rationale for CBM is that the maintenance of the water supply services is more effective and the overall performance is better if end-users are involved (McCommon *et. al.*, 1990). As owners and consumers of the improved services, the community will be more motivated to keep the water facility performing efficiently. Control by the community encourages the development of water services which meet the needs of the community. Direct management by the community also increases chances of cost recovery (McCommon *et. al.*, 1990). A further reason for community management is that it may lead to increased confidence of the local community, thus encouraging broader development.

Options for community-based management: CBM is a concept and not a fixed formula. It is very flexible and can take different shapes relevant to the conditions of the local community. It has been recognised that the following preconditions are essential for successful community management of water resources (McCommon *et. al.*, 1990):

▶ There must be community demand for improved water services.

▶ The necessary information required to make decisions must be available to the community.

▶ Technologies and level of service must be commensurate with the community's needs and the capacity to finance, manage and maintain them.

▶ The community must understand its options and be willing to take responsibility for the water system.

▶ The community must be willing to invest in capital and recurrent costs.

▶ The community must be empowered to make decisions to control the system.

▶ The community should have the institutional capacity to manage the development and the operation of the system.

▶ The community should have the necessary human resources to run these institutions.

▶ There should be a policy framework to permit and support community management.

▶ Effective external support services must be available from government, donors and the private sector (training, technical advice, credit, construction and contracts).

The success of CBM depends on the extent to which the above preconditions exist or can be created. It is most unlikely that these preconditions exist in developing countries. The creation of each condition represents an enormous and complex task. However, the preconditions are essential in achieving long-term sustainability of a water system.

Role of the government: CBM requires a significant investment in issues such as training, promotion, mobilization, capacity building, institutional and organizational strength, and the involvement of women. Community management requires strong support from both government and the private sector (Briscoe and de Ferrant, 1988). Government support is essential as the community needs to operate in a legal and administrative framework which encourages community actions. The role of the government should be to facilitate, promote and educate.

It should be based on equal partnership with the community. It is important that government should not try to do what the community can do better (McCommon et. al., 1990). The private sector also has a major role in the community management approach. The private sector can support and provide key services such as the provision of spare parts, fuel, and specific technical skills. The private sector is an effective bridge between the government's limited capabilities and the community's shortage of skills, tools and materials (Briscoe and de Ferrant, 1988).

Prerequisites

Whether CBM or PSP methodologies are used, certain prerequisites must exist in an area for the implementation of a successful water supply system. Five factors are considered essential prerequisites for the sustainability of a public standpipe system:

Adequate institution/organization: This element refers to the capacity of the organization responsible for the O&M of the public water standpipe. Three elements are essential prerequisites for its sustainability.

▶ *Appropriate legal authority:* the managing organization, private or community-based, should have sound legal authority and the mandate to operate and maintain the public standpipe.

▶ *Appropriate incentives, skills and knowledge:* The organization should be motivated to do a good job and should have or develop technical skills for minor repairs and routine maintenance, organizational skills for mobilizing community inputs, and the ability to manage financial resources.

▶ *Appropriate organizational structure:* The managing organization should have clearly defined policies and defined responsibilities for O&M of the public water standpipe. There should also be an appropriate process for monitoring and control of the O&M of the water standpipe.

Financial viability: The operations of the water standpipe should generate *sufficient revenue* to cover at least the O&M cost. This cost should be *affordable* to all community members, particularly the poor. It may happen that a public water standpipe is financially viable due to higher costs which are paid by the few people who can afford it, while the poor may not have access to the benefits of water services. This implies that the operations and management of the public standpipe should be on a *cost-effective basis.*

Appropriate technology: No matter how efficient and effective the managing agency, if the technology used is not appropriate to the needs of the community, it is difficult to achieve long-term sustainability. The technology should be *reliable and easy to maintain*. The technology should provide a *level of service* for which the community is willing to pay. In addition, the technology should be *acceptable* to the socio-cultural attributes of the local community.

Community support: To achieve the development objectives of improved water, the community should be *involved* in the management and the operation of the public water standpipe. The community should *utilize* the benefits of improved services. The operation of the standpipe should be *fairly accessible* to all.

Government commitment: Government should create an *"enabling environment"* that explicitly supports the sustainable O&M of the public standpipe. The government should establish a clear and consistent *policy and legal framework* to encourage the sustainability of the standpipe operations.

The above factors are important preconditions for sustainable O&M of the public water standpipe. The existence and performance of these factors impede or promote the sustainability of the operations and the maintenance of the public water standpipe.

LESSONS LEARNED FROM PERI-URBAN AREAS IN ANGOLA

Peri-urban areas in Angola

Cities in Angola are divided into two zones: the modern urbanized city centre and the unplanned peripheral zone. The modern urbanized area is generally based on an old colonial city centre and is characterized by the presence of the most important commercial activities, government head offices, and middle- and high-income residential areas. The urbanized area enjoys amenities such as piped water, a sewage system, electricity, urban transportation, education and modern health facilities.

In contrast, the unplanned peripheral zones, known also as peri-urban areas, are characterized by "spontaneous habitat" or shanty towns constructed without respect for building regulations. Peri-urban areas are home to about 80 percent of Angola's urban population (DW, 1995). The population of peri-urban areas is continually increasing as more and more people immigrate to urban centres. These areas lack basic services such as water supply, sewage system, removal of solid waste, electricity, modern transportation networks and so on. Furthermore, the peri-urban communities pay more than those in urbanized areas for basic services. For example, the urbanized areas have access to piped water from the provincial water agency at the official rate of US$ 0.002 per cubic metre. Residents in the peri-urban areas pay up to US$ 17.00 per cubic metre for untreated water from private vendors (DW, 1995). Poor communities in the peri-urban areas pay up to 8000 times more than the official price of water.

The peri-urban areas in Angola are not homogenous communities, but can be classified into at least two zones: old marginalized neighbourhoods and peripheral zones. The old neighbourhoods are located within the boundaries of the formalized urban areas. They consist mostly of long-term residents who are involved in the urban economy. In contrast, peripheral peri-urban areas are populated by recent immigrants whose economic initiatives are a mixture of urban and rural activities. The peripheral zones are often more homogenous, in term of education and income, than the old marginalized neighbourhoods.

Description of the case studies

Although five separate standpipe systems were examined in peri-urban areas in Angola, this paper will focus only on two. One demonstrates a community-based management system (CBM), and the other demonstrates use of private sector participation (PSP).

The first case study is located in the peri-urban areas in Luanda, the capital and largest city of Angola. This project was planned and implemented by the *Development Workshop* (DW), an international NGO. DW is a Canadian non-profit organization which has worked in Angola since 1981. DW specializes in the upgrading of human settlements and environmental conditions of the peri-urban areas in Angola.

The water supply project started in 1992 and was expected to terminate by the end of 1998. DW has completed the construction and rehabilitation of 153 public water standpipes in the peri-urban areas in Luanda. DW's program also includes extensive capacity building and technical assistance for the local community, public water authority and water monitors. The public water standpipes are managed and operated by an elected water committee (WC). The elected WC consists of three people: the head, the treasurer and the water monitor. This last person is responsible for day-to-day operations, maintenance and the collection of water fees. DW has established community mobilizers; these are young adults who provide training and support for the elected water committee for a period of six months to one year. The community mobilizers are also responsible for ensuring that standpipes are operating and kept in good condition. The water rate is determined by an agreement between the local government, public water authority and DW. The money collected is divided as follows: 25% for maintenance, 25% for the standpipe monitor, 20% for the local government and 30% for the public water authority.

The second case study is located in the peri-urban areas in Lobito, Angola's second largest city. This water project is part of a large urban rehabilitation project funded and implemented by the World Bank. The project started in late 1992 and the first phase was expected to end in mid 1998. The project has completed the construction of 218 public water standpipes in peri-urban areas of the city. Each standpipe serves about 150 families (800-1000 people) within a maximum distance of about 200 metres. Each standpipe is leased to a private person to operate and manage. The leaseholder is responsible for the O&M of the standpipe. The public water authority (EAST) is responsible for the overall management of the lease contract and the regulatory services to monitor the private operations. The lease contract is for six months duration and can be renewed; it is awarded through an open competition. It specifies in detail the penalties, the price of water and the remuneration for the leaseholder. The contract establishes that the leaseholder retains about 80% of the revenue collected and pays the rest to the public water authority. The contract also establishes a minimum sales of $100/m^3$ of water per month for each standpipe. Sales less than this amount are covered by the water authority to recompense the operational capital of the leaseholder. The provincial government is responsible for fixing water prices at the standpipes.

Analysis and findings

Each project was examined in relation to the five main factors considered prerequisite for sustainable operations and management of the public water standpipes. These factors are institutional/organizational capacity, financial viability, technological appropriateness, community participation and government commitment.

Institutional and organizational sustainability: A sound legal basis is a critical element to operate and maintain public water standpipes. This is possible if the organization responsible for O&M has a clear legal mandate and legitimacy in the eyes of the community to operate and manage the public standpipe.

In the case study of the Lobito PSP model, it was found that the responsible agency had an official legal mandate to operate the public standpipe. The private operator signed an official lease contract with the public water authority. This lease document was attached publicly at the standpipe and provided legitimacy in the eyes of the community.

In the case study of the DW community-based management model, it was found that although the water committees had no legal mandate to operate and manage the public standpipe, their operations were officially recognized by the public water authority, the local government and the community at large. The local government issues an official letter of recognition to the water monitor. In addition, the water monitor is required to hold a community meeting at the standpipe every month to explain the financial and maintenance conditions of the standpipe. These factors give the community a sense of ownership, responsibility and accountability for their water standpipes.

Human resource development is also an important factor that affects the sustainability of the public standpipe (Narayan, 1993). This study examined the skills, knowledge and motivation of all the stakeholders involved. The DW project (CBM) had a component specifically for human resource development. DW recognized that training was fundamental for the success of their water projects. Water committees were provided with on-site training by the community mobilizers. The training enabled the water committees to carry out minor repairs and keep financial and maintenance records. This study found the WCs are able to fully manage and operate their public water standpipe without external support. In the case of Lobito (PSP), most of the private operators hired a local person to clean, and to collect the water charges at the standpipe. The study found that these standpipes were well maintained, thus indicating that there was some success in training the local employees.

The study also looked at the organizational structure and the capacity of other stakeholders such as the community mobilizers of DW and the regulatory team of the public water authority of Lobito. The community mobilizers (CM) were the backbone of DW's water supply projects. CM are young adults living in the peri-urban areas in the city. Their main role is to provide intermediary support to the water committees. They work to build capacity, providing on-site training in management, finances, book-keeping and group decision-making skills for the water committees. It was found that the community mobilizers were effective in their operation. Community mobilizers add significantly to the sustainability of a development project. Their ability to promote and motivate change from within the community is very beneficial.

As discussed earlier, local governments play an essential role in the O&M of public water standpipes. Local governments are recognized as an existing public institution. For this reason, DW involved the local government in the planning and implementation of water projects in Luanda. Despite this effort, it appears that the roles and responsibilities of the local government had not been clearly defined. The study found that local governments were trying to do what the water committees can do for themselves. This study found also that the local governments lack the ability to organize and undertake their expected tasks.

This study also investigated the skills and the organizational capacity of the regulatory agency of the public standpipes in Lobito. It appears that regulatory efforts were ineffective despite the formation of an 18-member team of regulators. Field investigations found that the regulatory team were not aware of the common practice of overcharging. Also, the water meters are not read as specified in the contract. The study found, too, that the agency has no clear procedure to handle community complaints about the private operator. Two of the main difficulties of the regulatory agency are lack of logistical support and lack of motivation. The staff are provincial public employees and receive very low salaries. These factors create an environment where the private operator maximizes his/her profit at the expense of the community.

It was found that both case studies made use of Joint Management Arrangements (JMA). The basis behind joint management is the division and assignment of all tasks and activities related to O&M of standpipe systems in an effective manner (Ostrom *et. al.*, 1993). While traditionally applied to publicly run systems, the phrase applies equally well to privately run systems. The main benefit of JMA is the decentralization of responsibility for O&M away from the public water authority, thus allowing for quicker and more efficient maintenance.

Financial Viability: The second objective of this research was to investigate the financial viability of the public water standpipes. Financial viability is critical for the sustainability of the water delivery services. Three main variables are investigated in this study:

▶ To what extent does O&M of the water standpipes generate sufficient

revenues for the involved organizations?
▶ To what extent are water charges collected efficiently?
▶ To what extent is O&M affordable to the beneficiaries and the water production authority?

Both case studies have established a policy of full cost recovery. Each requires that the beneficiaries pay for the full recurrent costs of the public water standpipes. In the case of Lobito, the private operator buys a bulk quantity of water from the public water authority at the price of 50,000 KWZ (US$ 0.17) per meter cubic of water and resells to the community at the agreed price of 5,000 KWZ (US$ 0.016) per 20 litres of water. The private operator thereby keeps approximately 80 percent of the money collected, and the rest is paid to the public water authority. Some private operators noted that revenue was declining because consumers were purchasing water from people with household connections. This competition was given as the main reason why private operators overcharge for water. A discussion with the public water authority indicated that this competition between the public standpipes and private household connection is undermining the ability to recover the full cost of O&M of standpipes. From the point of view of the public water authority, it appears that the regulatory agency is not making any profit from their share of fees. It was indicated that water rates do not reflect the cost of O&M of the public water standpipe. The public water authority has twice asked the provincial government to increase the water rates; both requests have been turned down.

In contrast, in the case study of Maianga (DW), standpipes generate sufficient revenue for all stakeholders. An interview with the provincial water authority indicated that they are satisfied with the current cost recovery mechanism. One of the innovative aspects of this cost recovery mechanism is that the O&M of water standpipes generates incentives for the local government. The local government receives approximately 20 percent of the total revenue, thus stimulating local government interest to work with the local communities. The study found that water supplied at the DW public standpipes was affordable to the community. This was not found to be the case in Lobito, where overcharging made safe water unaffordable for some.

Technological Appropriateness: Reliability of the water system suggests that the public water standpipe functions throughout the year, with convenient operating hours and only infrequent breakdowns which are easily and quickly repaired. This study found that in both case studies, the public water standpipe operations were quite reasonable, certainly above average for most water supply projects. It was found that although water tap breakdowns were a problem in both locations, repairs were relatively easy and inexpensive.

The study investigated the extent to which the level of services of the technology chosen is appropriate to the needs of the community. In both cases, the chosen technology is acceptable to the needs of the communities in the peri-urban areas. DW's needs assessment project (DW, 1995) gave the beneficiaries an opportunity to analyze and choose from various feasible technology options. The report found that most of the communities opted for the construction of a public water standpipe.

Community Participation: Community involvement in the O&M of the public water standpipe is a crucial factor in achieving long-term sustainability. Community involvement is not intended to be the contribution of free labour in the construction of the water standpipes – it means the full involvement of the community in all stages of the project cycle.

DW adopted a process of community empowerment through extensive campaigns of community awareness, promotion, persuasion and education. While efforts by the community mobilizers were initially well received and the formation of Water Committees resulted, this enthusiasm was short lived. Once mobilizers were no longer involved in the situation, the WC became ineffective and disbanded, leaving the O&M of the standpipe solely to the water monitor. In the other case studies examined but not discussed here, it was found that community participation was a function of the closeness of the community rather than the efforts of the agency (Omar, 1997). The study found also that the standpipes were subject to frequent vandalism and abuse. Thus, the objective of a sense of responsibility and control of the water standpipe has not been achieved. The study also investigated to what extent women are involved in the O&M of the water standpipes. The DW had an explicit objective to involve women in the O&M of the water standpipe. As result of this policy, over 65 percent of DW's water standpipes are operated and managed by women.

In the case of the Lobito water project, the beneficiaries were not involved in the construction, operation or management of the public water standpipe. As mentioned, the standpipes are operated and managed by private leaseholders. Due to high investment costs, most of the leaseholders are people from the formal urbanized city. An interview with the community found that most of the standpipe beneficiaries do not know who the leaseholder is.

Government Commitment: The fifth objective of this study was to investigate the extent to which the government is committed to the sustainability of the public water standpipes. This study discussed the role of government in the provision of sustainable water services.

Until recently, the water supply sector in Angola was characterized by overlapping responsibilities. Since 1991, overall sectoral responsibility has been passed to the Department of National Directorate of Water (DNA). In the case of Luanda, this study found that the Ministry of Finance and Economics has the overall authority to determine water charges. It is not clear what criteria the Ministry uses to fix the water rates. On the other hand, there is lack of collaboration between the different levels of government. It appears that the central and provincial governments of Luanda are more interested in new investment projects, rather than facilitating and supporting ongoing local water projects. A discussion with DNA project managers revealed that they are looking to replicate the experience of the Lobito project in other provinces of the country. These managers appear less interested in the experience of the public water standpipe projects. A discussion with the provincial government of Luanda indicated that they recognize the importance of the NGOs involved in the improvement of water supply services in the peri-urban areas, but they are not committed to develop any coherent policy to institutionalize these activities.

In contrast, the provincial government of Benguela is committed to improving water supply delivery in the peri-urban areas. The provincial government has challenged the central government to achieve the overall mandate of the water supply sector of the province. Through the Lobito project, the provincial government created autonomous municipal water authorities which are responsible for the production and distribution of water supply. The provincial government retains the overall sectoral policies. Although this process is still in its initial phase, it appears that government activity is enhancing sustainability.

CONCLUSIONS

Requirements for successful water supply management

As discussed in the first section of this paper, the need for innovative management techniques of standpipe operations is apparent. This paper examined two such techniques in the peri-urban environment in Angola. The first was based upon a community-based management approach (CBM) which enlisted the efforts of local stakeholders in the operation and maintenance (O&M) of standpipes. The second involved private sector participation (PSP), whereby individuals purchased the right to sell water from a government standpipe. It was discovered that, regardless of the methodology chosen, both CBM and PSP programs have similar goals:

▶ To relieve the burden of day to day operations and management from the public water authority, so that it can concentrate on the tasks of policy-making, planning and sector investment;

▶ To increase efficiency gains. Both CBM and PSP options are in a better position than the public water authority to collect water charges to (at least) cover recurrent costs;

▶ To develop responsive services. Both options are able to establish service levels matching the needs which the community are willing to pay for and support.

To achieve these objectives, both models require that a set of fundamental prerequisites be established in the peri-urban context. With regards to private participation, the following preconditions were identified as necessary:

▶ A clear set of "the rules of the game", committed government policies and guidance for private sector participation;

▶ An effective regulatory service able to ensure monitoring and control of the PSP;

▶ Appropriate incentives for PSP, the regulatory service and the public water authority.

Regarding community-based management options, the essential preconditions were found to be:

▶ A strong sense of community;

▶ A community willing to take responsibility and control over the O&M of the water standpipes;

▶ A capable community to carry out the expected tasks;

▶ Benefits that outweigh the costs of collective action;

▶ Appropriate policy and commitment to facilitate and promote community management.

In addition, both options should have a clear legal and institutional framework that provides appropriate authority, enabling them to function and guaranteeing sufficient autonomy. The establishment and existence of these preconditions determine the extent to which community-based management and private sector participation can achieve their intended objectives.

Although the case studies have established these preconditions to some extent, it appears that many weaknesses still remain.

In the case of private sector management in Lobito, it was found that the current PSP arrangements were weak in all three of the fundamental preconditions for private sector O&M of the public water standpipes. These shortcomings are beginning to threaten the sustainability of the program, prices are increasing and vendors are complaining of low profits. Similar difficulties have been noted in the experience of PSP in Cote d'Ivoire and Guinea (Triche, 1990). Although PSP in these countries has achieved some success, the major weakness remains governments' incapacity to establish realistic water tariff policies. In addition, the provision of safe water is politically sensitive. Many governments may pursue a policy of social equity. However, it appears that governments have difficulty establishing a balance between social equity policy and private sector operations. This suggests that PSP in water supply services is not a simple process and must be handled with care. Gidman et. al. (1995) notes that private sector participation, without careful planning and management, may not save costs or improve services. Similar conclusions were given by Walker (1993). PSP is more likely to succeed where there are well-defined public policy goals and an appreciation of the costs and benefits involved. The findings of this study confirm that the current PSP arrangement has not been carefully planned.

With regard to community-based management options, the findings of this study indicate that the Maianga case study has established the fundamental preconditions of CBM. As discussed earlier, the emphasis has been given to capacity building, motivation, persuasion, communication and co-ordination. These factors are essential for the long-term sustainability of the public water standpipes. However, there remain significant areas for improvement. The local government's lack of capacity and the lack of an institutional framework may hinder sustainability.

The conclusion that emerges from the case studies is that neither CBM nor PSP are a simple process. They require careful planning and the establishment of fundamental preconditions which enable them to function effectively. In determining which system would be most effective in any particular situation, it is of great importance to understand the existence of particular preconditions as they relate to the two methods.

It was found that these concerns were not addressed in the Angola situations, rather particular methods were adopted regardless of the situation in the peri-urban areas. Specifically, it was found that insufficient effort had been given to the following:

▶   Understanding the objectives of improving water services in peri-urban areas;
▶   Analysis of the benefits and costs involved in CBM or PSP;
▶   Analysis of the comparative advantages of PSP or CBM;
▶   Identification of the roles and responsibilities of key stakeholders;
▶   Understanding the capacity and the ability of each stakeholder.

A careful analysis of these factors would have provided a clear understanding of the pros and cons of community-based management and private sector participation in the existing local conditions. If a community were found to have little "sense of community", but did have a well developed economic sense with strong regulatory instruments available, a PSP method may be best suited. If the situation were different, perhaps a CBM system should prevail. CBM or PSP cannot be prescribed in advance, but must evolve in a country context, depending on local capacity, policies and institutions (Watson et. al., 1997). CBM and PSP must be seen as complementary options, rather than opposing approaches. The comparative advantages of both options should be exploited to achieve sustainable O&M of the public water standpipe. The overall objective should not be the establishment of one option or another, but the identification of the best option to meet the users' needs effectively. Both PSP and CBM arrangements can achieve successful results in O&M of public water standpipes in the peri-urban areas in Angola. What is needed is an evaluation of the pros and cons of each option and an appreciation of the costs and benefits involved.

Stakeholder Roles

This research also found that each stakeholder had specific roles to fulfill before a sustainable water supply system could be successful in the peri-urban areas of Angola. The following recommendations reflect the specific experience of the peri-urban areas in Luanda and Lobito; they are by no means complete. However, based on the results of this study, these specific recommendations are thought to be essential for sustainable O&M of public water standpipes:

- **The local community** should be given full responsibility and control of the O&M of the public water standpipe. The community should be given the option to elect a water committee or appoint a private person to operate and maintain the water standpipe. In some neighbourhoods where there is no sense of collective action, the beneficiaries may prefer that one person operate and maintain the public standpipe. The elected water committee and the private operator should sign a written contract with the municipal government (see the following recommendation) to operate and maintain the public standpipe.

- **Municipal governments** should be given the responsibility of regulatory services. The municipal government is closer to the operation and management of the water standpipe than the provincial government. The role of the municipal government should be well-defined and not overlap with the community's responsibilities. It should develop municipal by-laws or a regulatory framework which defines the activities and expectations of the water committees and private operators, as well as the standard and quality of services. In addition, the by-laws should define the penalties for illegal connections.

- **The public water authority** should concentrate on the production of clean, safe and reliable water service. The public water authority should sell water in bulk to the municipalities and should not be responsible for the O&M of the public water standpipes. The water authority should concentrate on the improvement of water treatment plants and the distribution network, as well as collecting water tariffs from those with household connections.

- **Provincial governments** should establish the appropriate policy and legal framework that enables and facilitates joint management between the community, the municipal government and the public water authority. To establish the joint management option as a legal entity, there must be laws authorizing this agreement between stakeholders. The provincial government should develop overall policies and guidance for the O&M of public water standpipes. In addition, the provincial government should define the goals and objectives of improving water supply services in peri-urban areas.

These recommendations indicate the appropriate roles, responsibilities and functions of the stakeholders involved in the O&M of public water standpipes, which are operation and maintenance, regulatory services, water production and policy-making tasks.

Without changes in the management of water standpipes in peri-urban areas, water supply programmes will continue to face high failure rates. This has been recognized by both governments and aid agencies.

This paper presents some of the findings from two innovative approaches to water standpipe operation and maintenance in peri-urban areas of Angola. While each demonstrated some shortcomings and difficulties to overcome, they also demonstrated reasonable success thus far. Most of the difficulties can be traced to failures in achieving the important preconditions described above. Also demonstrated was the need to examine the situation prior to the implementation of such programs, to ensure adoption of the most appropriate and effective method of management of water standpipes.

These projects presented an opportunity to learn about the process and the relevant preconditions required for success. It is hoped that this research will help future projects enjoy greater success.

ACKNOWLEDGMENTS

This paper is a part of research undertaken in peri-urban Angola between May and September 1997. The paper owes much to the Environmental Capacity Enhancement Project (ECEP) of the School of Rural Planning and Development at the University of Guelph which funded this research. The authors are grateful to Development Workshop in Angola and Guelph for their logistic support. We would also like to thank Dr. John FitzGibbon who co-advised this study.

REFERENCES

Brinkerhoff, D. and Goldsmith, M. 1990: *Institutional Sustainability in Agriculture and Rural Development*. New York: Praeger.

Briscoe, J. and de Ferrant, D. 1988: *Water for Rural Communities: Helping People Help Themselves*. Washington: World Bank.

Churchill, A.A. 1987: *Rural Water Supply and Sanitation*. Washington: World Bank.

Development Workshop (DW). 1995: *Samizanga Project: Luanda Peri-Urban Emergency Water and Sanitation. Annual Report 1994-1995*. Luanda, Angola: Development Workshop.

Development Workshop (DW). 1995a: *Water Supply and Sanitation in Luanda: Informal Sector Study and Beneficiary Assessment*. Luanda, Angola: Development Workshop.

Development Workshop (DW). 1996: *Beneficiary Assessment in the Peri-urban Areas of Lobito*. Luanda, Angola: Development Workshop.

Gidman, P. 1995: *Public-Private Participation in Urban Infrastructure Services*, UMP Working Paper Series 4. Nairobi, Kenya: Habitat.

Kessides, C. 1993: *Institutional Options for the Provision of Infrastructure*. World Bank Discussion Paper 212. Washington: World Bank.

Livingstone, A. and McPherson, H.J. 1993: Management Strategies for Rural Water Development: A Case Study from Sudan. *National Resource Forum*, 17 (4), 294-301.

Manigin, J. 1991: Rural Water Supply in Southern Ethiopia: Failures and Alternatives. *Canadian Journal of Development Studies*, 7 (2), 297-312.

McCommon, C., Warner, D. and Yohalem, D. 1990: *Community Management of Rural Water Supply and Sanitation Services*. World Bank Water and Sanitation Discussion Paper. Washington: World Bank.

McGarry, M.G. 1991: Water Supply and Sanitation in the 1990's. *Water International*, Vol 19 (1991), 153-160.

McPherson, H.J. 1994: Issues, Constraints and Principals for Sustainable Operation and Maintenance of Water Supply Systems. In H.J. McPherson (ed.), *Operation and Maintenance of Water Supply and Sanitation Systems: Case Studies*. Geneva: World Health Organization.

Narayan, D. 1993 *Participatory Evaluation: Tools for Managing Change in Water and Sanitation*. World Bank Technical Paper No. 207. Washington: World Bank.

Omar, A. Siad. 1997: *Managing Public Water Standposts: Privatization or Community-Based Management? Lessons from Five Case Studies in Angola*. Unpublished major paper for M.Sc., University of Guelph.

Ostrom *et. al.* 1993: *Institutional Incentives and Sustainable Development: Infrastructure Policies in Perspective*. Boulder, Colorado: Westview.

Rondinelli, D.A. 1991: *Decentralising Water Supply Services in Developing Countries*. London: Oxford University Press.

Roth, G. 1987. *Private Provision of Public Services in Developing Countries*. London: Oxford University Press.

Saunders, R.J. and Warford, J.J. 1976: *Village Water Supply*. Baltimore: Johns

Hopkins University Press.

Savas, E.S. 1987: *Privatization: The Key to Better Government.* Chatham, NJ: Chatham House

Government of Angola. 1993: *Infrastructure Rehabilitation Engineering Project: Water Supply and Sanitation of the City of Luanda, Short Term Master Plan.* Luanda: Provincial Government of Luanda.

Triche, T. 1990: *Private Participation in the Delivery of Guinea's Water Supply.* Policy Research Working Paper No. 477. Washington: World Bank.

Walker, J. 1993: *Preparing for Private Sector Participation in the Provision of Water Supplies and Sanitation Services.* WASH Technical Report No. 84. Washington: WASH.

Watson, G. *et al.* 1997: Water and Sanitation Associations: Review and Best Practices. In S. Ashok *et al* (ed.), *User Organizations for Sustainable Water Services.* World Bank Technical Paper No. 354. Washington: World Bank.

World Bank. 1992: *World Development Report: Development and Environment.* London: Oxford University Press.

World Bank. 1994: *World Development Report: Infrastructure for Development.* London: Oxford University Press.

Chapter 9

FACTORS AFFECTING BACTERIAL CONTAMINATION OF RURAL DRINKING WATER WELLS: COMPARATIVE ASSESSMENT

by Mary Jane Conboy

INTRODUCTION

In rural areas, drinking water is often supplied by wells fed directly by groundwater. This study tested wells in rural Zimbabwe and Ontario, Canada for bacteriological water quality. Total coliforms, fecal coliforms, fecal streptococci and *Clostridia perifringens* were assessed in each well water sample as indicators of contamination. The wells in both countries were comparable in geology and soil type, but differed significantly in well construction and management practices. Sampled during the dry season, 95% of the Zimbabwe wells had bacteria in excess of Drinking Water Objectives (DWO), and 59% of the wells tested positive for *Clostridia perifringens* (an indicator for fecal contamination of animal origin). In Ontario, each well was tested in the early spring when the fields were near saturation after the winter snowfall, and re-sampled in late summer. In the spring, just below 50% of the wells exceeded the Drinking Water Objectives (DWO). This was reduced to 39% in the summer. On both occasions, approximately 20% of the Ontario wells tested positive for *Clostridia perifringens*. The results indicated bacteria of fecal origin moving into well water, and that a significant percentage of the bacteria originated from animal manure.

Results from this overall study were used to select sites in Ontario where tracer studies could be performed to confirm the ability of the selected suite of indicator organisms to predict sources of pollution and aid in isolating the source of fecal contamination. Thirty sites had a tracer study conducted. Three of these sites found the contamination source present within the well structure, and 23/26 sites were successful in isolating at least one source of fecal contamination entering the well.

The suite of indicator organisms selected was found to be accurate in assessing the source of bacterial contamination of drinking water wells in Zimbabwe and in Ontario. The tracer study showed that using animal manure in agriculture has the potential to contaminate groundwater resources used for drinking water very rapidly.

BACKGROUND

Groundwater contamination in Zimbabwe and North America

In rural areas of Zimbabwe, drinking water is often supplied by wells fed directly by groundwater. Bacterial contamination of these potable water supplies in Zimbabwe presents health risks for people and animals coming in contact with this water. Zimbabweans are trying to improve the quality of water in rural areas by improving well structures.

The two main sources of fecal contamination entering rural wells in Zimbabwe are animal manure and latrines. Animal manure represents the main source of nutrients for soil, as it is readily available, less expensive than commercial fertilizers, improves soil structure and enhances crop production, which generates more food for rural farmers. However, current manure management practices cause contaminants to enter drinking water. Food production should be enhanced without degrading drinking water quality. Methods of manure application and garden maintenance should be established to protect well water from bacterial contamination. Other options for protecting the drinking water supply include different well construction methods or water treatment.

Contamination of rural groundwater is also a concern and a focus of investigation in rural North America. The Ontario Farm Groundwater Quality (OFGWQ) survey demonstrated that about one third of wells used to supply drinking water to 1200 farm families in Ontario were contaminated with coliform or fecal coliform bacteria, considered to be indicative of fecal contamination of water (Goss, Barry & Rudolph, 1998). A review of bacteriological surveys of groundwater used for drinking water supplies in the United States revealed that 9 - 51% of the samples examined in the various surveys contained coliforms and 2 - 27% of these same waters contained fecal coliforms (Hagedorn, Hansen & Simonson, 1978). Goss et. al. (1998) reported values between 15 and 45% in more recent well surveys in agricultural regions of the USA.

A study in Ontario looked at the incidence of gastro-intestinal illness as it related to the presence of bacteria in well water. In this study, water was tested at regular intervals and a diary of illness was kept for a year. It was found that families drinking well water that contained *E. coli* were twice as likely to suffer gastro-intestinal illness as families drinking water without this bacteria (Raina *et. al.*, 1996). In the United States, one third of all waterborne disease outbreaks reported from 1971 to 1976 were traced to the consumption of water from untreated groundwater sources (Craun 1978; 1984). This information shows that bacterial contamination of groundwater is not only a relatively common problem, but presents a significant health risk. These surveys show that bacterial contamination of drinking water wells is a serious problem affecting countries throughout the world.

Indicators of groundwater contamination

The main sources of fecal bacteria on farms are: livestock manure, either spread on gardens or seeping from exercise yards, and septic systems or latrines and feces deposited by animals near a well or water course feeding the well. Animals entering the well or water storage tank is another source of fecal bacteria which may affect well water quality. The origin of the contamination must be identified if remedial action is to be carried out.

The use of indicator species is a cost-effective way of identifying contamination and the sources. However, the use of only one or two indicators has not always been successful in locating the source of contamination. The four indicator bacteria selected for use in this study are generally considered to originate in the intestinal tract of warm-blooded animals. The reason for using this number of indicator organisms was to obtain information that would aid in locating likely sources of the contaminant and determining possible timing of the contamination.

Total and fecal coliforms are commonly used by many health organizations as standard organisms for assessing drinking water quality. The presence of these bacteria is considered to indicate contamination by animal wastes or sewage, as these bacteria are present in large numbers in such waste. These bacteria have similar life cycles to pathogenic organisms such as Hepatitis A, and their presence may indicate that other more harmful bacteria are also present. By including these organisms, a direct comparison of results between those found in this study and those from previous studies or studies conducted in different locations was possible.

Total coliforms are always present in animal waste and sewage, but are also found in soil and on vegetation. The presence of total coliforms alone seems to be of very little use in determining timing and source of contamination. Fecal coliforms and fecal streptococci are considered to originate in the digestive tract of humans and warm-blooded animals. The presence of these bacteria in well water indicates that there is a source of fecal matter entering the water supply. Fecal streptococci die off more rapidly in the environment than other indicators (Crane & Moore, 1986), therefore when there are no new additions of bacteria, the proportion of streptococci to coliforms will decrease rapidly. The presence of fecal streptococci indicates that a source has been contaminated by fecal material relatively recently, or that a very high level of contamination was present. The ratio of fecal coliform to fecal streptococci is different in the feces of humans and wild or domestic animals (Geldreich, 1976). A ratio of at least 4: 1 streptococci to coliform has been used to indicate a human source, such as a malfunctioning septic system.

Clostridia perifringens is thought to be unique to animals (Huysman, Van Renterghem & Verstraete, 1993). The presence of these bacteria indicates animal manure entered the water supply at some time in the past. *C. perifringens* forms spores and can remain in the well water for a longer period of time than the other organisms, so it does not provide any information about timing of contamination. In the absence of other bacteria in a well water sample, the well can be considered to be a safe source of drinking water.

To determine the frequency of bacteriological contamination in rural Zimbabwe and to identify the source and relative age of contamination, 150 wells were sampled. The findings were compared with results from a similar survey in Ontario to try to assess risk factors affecting bacterial contamination and to understand different risk factors that may be present due to soil type or geology. This first part of the study used indicator bacteria to prove that bacteria of fecal origin were entering well water. This aids our understanding of bacteria transport.

To effect a permanent improvement in the quality of untreated drinking water in a rural well, the source of bacteria entering the well must be determined and removed. To further clarify bacterial transport to groundwater and to determine if the indicators were providing a clear picture of the sources, a tracer study was undertaken. *Escherichia coli*, which is resistant to nalidixic acid (NAR), has been used as a biotracer in recent studies (Abu-Ashour et. al., 1994). *E. coli* NAR is an environmental isolate. This organism behaves similarly to the fecal indicators assessed in well water with respect to growth and survival (Joy et. al., 1992). The presence of the NAR trait is extremely rare in the environment. This rarity makes it easier to identify the path of E. coli NAR when used in field experiments. It is also not known to have any of the pathogenic characteristics of E. coli and can be considered safe for field investigation. E. coli NAR was used to trace the movement of bacteria through the soil profile into shallow aquifers. Monitoring the movement of this tracer allows a greater understanding of the source, movement and survival of fecal bacteria in the environment. This will confirm the utility and accuracy of the assemblage of indicator bacteria.

The key to groundwater clean-up is an understanding of where pollution is coming from, to ensure the most effective action is taken to improve the quality of the drinking water source. This tracer study will provide very dramatic evidence on the pathways that transport bacteria in the environment and provide information with regards to susceptible stratigraphies or soils.

METHODS

Sample sites

Sites in Zimbabwe were all located in the Goromonzi district, approximately 60 kilometers northeast of Harare. The sample area was underlain by granite, which was exposed in some areas. The soils were predominantly sandy, of varying grain size and composition. In June 1997, three types of wells were sampled in Zimbabwe:

▶ unprotected wells
▶ protected wells, which were dug wells with some type of lining or reinforcement
▶ boreholes

Sites in Ontario were distributed throughout Southern Ontario. No attempt was made to develop a random survey, but a range of wells with known histories of water quality was used. Soil types represented in this study included sand, clay and loam. Wells selected for study included drilled, sandpoint and dug or bored wells and the depth of the wells range from approximately one to one hundred metres. The water quality was examined in late March to early April 1997, and again in late August to early September 1997.

Sample collection and assessment of indicator organisms

Well water samples were collected in sterilized sample bottles, which were kept refrigerated in coolers with ice packs. Bacteria were enumerated within 24 hours of collection. Observations from visual inspection of well condition and the surrounding area were noted, and the landowner was asked about the depth of the well and the presence of manure on nearby gardens. In Ontario, farmers were asked to complete a short questionnaire related to their farming practices, soil type and details of their well construction. Physiographical and geological maps were used to assess the sites sampled in Zimbabwe and Ontario.

Standard membrane filtration techniques were employed for all filtration enumerations (American Public Health Association, American Water Works Association, Water Pollution Control Federation, 1989). One hundred millilitres of water was filtered through a Magna M-PAC Nylon supported grid (0.45gm) (MSI) and the filters were then placed on the appropriate media in a 55 x 15 mm plastic petri plate. All filtrations were performed in duplicate. All results were reported as colony forming units.

Tests were conducted for total coliforms, fecal coliforms, fecal streptococci and *C. perifringens*, according to standard techniques. Each test was replicated twice. At least five samples from each sampling programme were sent to a local public health laboratory for independent bacteriological analysis. In Zimbabwe, the Public Health Laboratory used a Most Probable Number Technique with Maconkey Broth. In all samples, the Public Health Laboratory concluded that the water was unsuitable for drinking, and the counts obtained were very close to the numbers that were obtained by the membrane filtration technique. In Ontario, the Palmerston Laboratory at the Ministry of Health used the same tests as described above for total coliform and fecal coliform bacteria. In all cases, the counts reported by the laboratory were the same as those obtained by the study researchers.

Plates with characteristic growth were submitted to the University of Guelph, Determinative Bacteriology Laboratory. Tests performed by this lab confirmed the identification of indicator organisms.

Tracer study

E. coli NAR was grown and sub-cultured at weekly intervals to prepare biotracer inocula. Biotracer inocula were prepared by growing *E. coli* NAR in nutrient broth for 60 hours. The Biotracer was placed in one-litre amber bottles and transported to sites in coolers with ice packs.

Wells were assessed for history of contamination and vulnerable wells were chosen for the tracer study. Wells were inspected for the presence of cracks or holes in the lining, adequate grading of the well head, and the presence of debris in the well. This was done by lifting the well cover from the well head, where possible, and looking down the well with a strong flashlight. Where the source was not present within the well, a tracer study was conducted. A background water sample was taken prior to inoculating the site. Using information from the well survey, the most likely source of bacteria was identified. If the well water had tested positive for *C. perifringens* on at least one occasion, an animal source of manure was regarded as the most likely source of contamination. Local topography and the flow of nearby streams were also used to identify the most suitable location for tracer inoculation.

Three litres of inoculum were added each time a site was inoculated. The inoculum was spread evenly over the soil in a space approximately 1/2 metre by 1/2 metre, or it was flushed down a toilet. Inoculum spread onto the soil was washed into the soil using approximately ten litres of water. Samples were taken from the drinking water at 1, 2, 6, 12, 24, 48, 72 and 96 hours after inoculation. To provide background concentrations for indigenous *E. coli* cells that were resistant to nalidixic acid and for enumeration of indicator organisms, all sites were sampled before the commencement of an experiment. For every sample, water was run for 60 seconds to clear water standing in the pipes prior to sampling. All samples were transported in a cooler with ice packs to the laboratory, where filtrations were conducted. Values were reported as the number of colony forming units (CFU) per 500 ml.

RESULTS AND DISCUSSION

The results from this study show that fecal origin bacteria are entering well water in significant numbers in both Zimbabwe and Canada. In both countries, the possible sources of these bacteria are livestock manure or human waste disposal systems. The aim was to acquire information from this assemblage of microorganisms, which would aid in locating possible sources of contamination and determine possible timing of bacteria entering well water. The results from the well survey showed that these four indicator organisms were useful in identifying the source and possible timing of contamination. The accuracy of these assessments was confirmed by the tracer study.

In Zimbabwe, 145 wells were tested and in Ontario, approximately 300 were tested. Of the sample wells in Zimbabwe, 95% exceeded the Drinking Water Objectives (DWO). In Ontario, 49% of the wells tested in the spring exceeded the local DWO, and 39% of those tested in summer failed to meet the DWO standard. The DWO used in this study are those set for municipal water supplies. The bacteria tested have similar life-cycles and resistance patterns as pathogenic organisms, therefore where the DWO are not met, there is a risk of pathogens being present in the water. Ontario DWO indicate that there should be five or less total coliforms and zero fecal coliforms present in order for water to be considered suitable for drinking (Ministry of the Environment, 1992).

Source of bacteria

In Zimbabwe, there was very little awareness of the extent of bacterial contamination present in drinking water wells. Scientists working in related fields did not expect the findings to reveal such a high number of contaminated wells or the levels of bacteria in the wells. Many local hospital staff, who were involved with upgrading wells heads, had thought that most contamination was caused by people not washing their hands after using the latrine and prior to handling the pails used to obtain water. Another source was thought to be the rope or pail lying on the top of the well instead of hanging freely.

This study, however, found the contamination is caused by bacteria seeping into groundwater from animal manure or human waste. Groundwater provides a more favourable environment than the soil surface for the bacteria, and they survive longer once they have reached the water table. They remain as a pollution source for an extended period of time or over an extensive distance, depending on the rate of groundwater flow. This reduces the potable water supply and presents health risks for people and animals coming in contact with contaminated water. This is the case in the area sampled in Zimbabwe, where 95% of the wells tested did not meet DWO and should be considered unsafe for drinking water.

The presence of *C. perifringens* in 59% of contaminated wells shows that animal manure is a major source of bacteria contaminating the water in rural Zimbabwe. The presence of more than ten fecal streptococci in 75% of the wells shows that the source was relatively recent. Unprotected wells are very susceptible to animal origin fecal contamination, whereas the borehole construction may reduce the transport of some organisms. The absence of *C. perifringens* could be due to a number of factors, including lack of transport to depth, rapid die-off, damage to spores, predators specific to *C. perifringens* or absence of animal manure. In samples where *C. perifringens* is not present, the fecal bacteria may be of human or of animal origin.

Table 9.1 Results of Zimbabwe well survey

	Total Coliform	Fecal Coliform	Fecal Streptococci	*C. perifringens*
Drinking Water Objective (DWO)	5	0	10	n/a
% overgrown	65	65	15	
% exceed Drinking Water Objective (DWO)	21	28	59	56
% meeting Drinking Water Objective (DWO)	13	5.5	24	

The number of Ontario wells with *C. perifringens* present did not vary between the spring and summer samples. These results show that at least 20% of the wells in Ontario are receiving bacteria from animal manure. This is approximately the same proportion of boreholes in Zimbabwe that were affected by animal manure. The number of wells with more than ten fecal streptococci were lower in Ontario in the spring than in the late summer sampling. This may reflect the age of the source of bacteria. In the spring samples, the manure had been spread the previous fall and then exposed to freezing temperatures. In the summer, manure can be spread more frequently and rain showers may increase infiltration. The conditions in the soil may also be more favourable for bacterial survival.

Table 9.2 Results of Ontario well survey

	Spring Samples n=306				Summer Samples n=305			
	Total Coliform	Fecal Coliform	Fecal Streptococci	C. perifringens	Total Coliform	Fecal Coliform	Fecal Streptococci	C. perifringens
Drinking Water Objective (DWO)	5	0	10	n/a	5	0	10	n/a
% overgrown	9	5	1		16	4	7	
% exceed Drinking Water Objectives (DWO)	26	40	9	20	25	35	25	21
% meeting Drinking Water Objectives (DWO)	64	55	89		59	60	68	

The well surveys showed a significant problem in drinking water quality due to the presence of bacteria. The majority of the wells in Zimbabwe had all four indicators present, were overgrown with total or fecal coliforms, had more than ten fecal streptococci present and tested positive for C perifringens. This represents a significant amount of bacteria entering the well regularly, most of it from animal manure. The wells chosen for the tracer study in Ontario shared these characteristics. The wells in Ontario have been sampled up to 13 times in six years. Where the majority of these tests found bacteria entering the well, the indication is that there is likely a permanent source of fecal bacteria entering the well on a regular basis. This generally would be a manure pit, manure spread on nearby gardens or a septic system near the well.

This study showed that using a biotracer is a very effective means of determining the source of bacteria. It also confirmed that the use of an assemblage of indicator organisms to assess the most likely source, and therefore the best location to apply biotracer, was very effective. These findings are critical to assessing the most effective means of cleaning up well water in Zimbabwe, where 59% of the wells tested positive for C. perifringens, a bacterium confirmed to originate in animal manure.

During the well survey, Zimbabwe wells were checked for animals or debris present within the well itself. In only one case was there any indication that an animal in the well was the source. Where the source is not in the well or water tank, the most likely source of contamination would be nearby·animal manure applied on a garden or field or dropped by livestock.

Gardens represent a very large source of animal origin fecal bacteria, and they should not be built around wells as this severely degrades water quality. If this is unavoidable, a separate well should be used for drinking water or water should be treated.

The source of bacteria was located on almost all of the farms assessed during the tracer study (27/30). In these cases, the biotracer was used as confirmation of the most likely source. The reliability of the predicted source shows that using the information from the assemblage of indicator organisms and a visual inspection of the area in a 150-metre radius from the well head may locate the source of bacteria. All sources of manure should be kept as far from the drinking water as possible. Water should be treated if anyone drinking the water becomes ill due to its consumption.

CONCLUSIONS AND RECOMMENDATIONS

Bacteria of fecal origin move into well water on many farms following normal practices in and around the well. This was observed at the wells sampled in both Zimbabwe and Canada. The depth and construction of the well are very important in determining the extent of bacterial migration into the well water, but it is not the only factor.

Although having livestock on the farm seems to affect the quality of water, many Canadian farms with livestock were found to have acceptable drinking water. By studying these sites where there is little bacterial contamination, despite the presence of some risk factors, it is possible to identify ways to reduce the amount of bacteria entering groundwater.

Zimbabwe was sampled during a dry season, and most of the sites sampled were situated in sandy soils. However, the shallow depth of the wells, the absence of separation between contaminants and well water, and the incomplete lining of most of the wells leads to drinking water with very high levels of bacterial contamination. During this study, colleagues in Zimbabwe commented that chronic gastro-intestinal problems are common in rural areas. Gastro-intestinal problems and other more serious health risks are likely to occur if this water is consumed and many people can be infected. The sites sampled included rural wells supplying single families, small communities, schools and hospitals – where patients with weakened immune systems are especially susceptible to the bacteria in the drinking water.

Biotracer studies were very reliable in assessing the source of bacteria entering well water at sites where bacterial contamination was a chronic problem. The tracer study confirmed that the use of an assemblage of indicator organisms was very useful in identifying the source of bacteria. The presence of *C. perifringens* was also found to be a very accurate indicator of animal origin fecal bacteria. This may be due to manure spread on gardens, grazing animals, manure storage pits or an animal entering the water supply. Of the sites in Zimbabwe, 59% tested positive for *C. perifringens*. The information obtained would indicate that returning to some of these sites to locate and clean up an animal manure source in the vicinity may improve water quality. Where this bacterium was absent, the location of the latrine should be assessed to ensure that the well is not down slope.

Nitrate analysis in Ontario showed that shallow dug or bored wells are most vulnerable to elevated levels of nitrate as well as bacterial contamination. This is the type of well most commonly used throughout rural Zimbabwe. This result confirms the recommendation that efforts should be concentrated on installing boreholes, as they are less likely to be affected by both bacteria and nitrate contamination.

Recommendations for well maintenance and water treatment

Where possible, the source of entry of the organisms into a well should be determined and remedial measures taken to correct the problem. The four indicator organisms used in this study are relatively easy and inexpensive to assess when a lab equipped for microbiological analysis is available. These indicators provide a great deal of information on the source and timing of bacteria entering well water. This will facilitate locating and removing the source of bacteria entering wells.

General recommendations

▶ Efforts should be made to locate and remove the source of bacteria entering well water.

- Sites sampled in Zimbabwe should be assessed to locate the most likely contamination source. Where C. perifringens is present, animal manure is entering the well water. If C. perifringens is absent, latrines and other non-animal sources should be assessed.

- Drinking water should be tested as often as possible and efforts should be made to facilitate this process. Extension workers should impart information on safe drinking water to the rural residents. Eventually, extension workers could collect samples and possibly be trained to perform the bacterial tests.

- Efforts should be made to have local health labs incorporate testing for C. perifringens to help identify the source of bacteria entering well water.

- Money for well improvements should be directed towards installing more boreholes. This will allow residents to obtain safer drinking water, while continuing to use existing dug wells for irrigation.

- Protected well heads must be maintained to ensure that the lining and reinforcement on the well head remains intact. Any cracks or holes should be sealed.

- Wells located in gardens should not be used for drinking water as bacteria is seeping into the well every time the garden is irrigated.

REFERENCES

Abu-Ashour, J., Etches, C., Joy, D.M., Lee, H., Reaume, C.M., Shadford, C.B., Whitely, H. R. and Zelin, S. 1994: *Movement of Agricultural and Domestic Wastewater Bacteria Through Soil.* Final Report for RAC Project No. 547G. Ontario Ministry of Environment and Energy.

American Public Health Association, American Water Works Association, Water Pollution Control Federation. 1989: Microbiological Examination of Water. In *Standard Methods for the Examination of Water and Wastewater*, pp. 9-1 - 9-227. Seventeenth Edition. Baltimore.

Crane, S.R. and Moore, J. 1986: Modeling Enteric Bacterial Die-off: A Review. *Water, Air, and Soil Pollution,* 27, 411-39.

Craun, G.F. 1978: Disease Outbreaks Caused by Drinking Water. *Journal of Water Pollution Control Federation,* June, 1362-74.

Craun, G.F. 1984: Health Aspects of Groundwater Pollution. In G. Bitton and C.P. Gerba (eds.), *Groundwater Pollution Microbiology*, pp. 135-79. Toronto: John Wiley and Sons.

Geldreich, E.E. 1976: Fecal Coliform and Fecal Streptococcus Density Relationships in Waste Discharges and Receiving Waters. *Critical Reviews in Environmental Control,* 5, 3, 349- 69.

Goss, M.J., Barry, D.A.J. and Rudolph, D.L. 1998: Groundwater Contamination in Ontario Farm Wells and its Association With Agriculture, Results from Drinking Water Wells. In *Contaminant Hydrology* (in press).

Hagedorn, C.D., Hansen, T. and Simonson, G.H. 1978: Survival and Movement of Fecal Indicator Bacteria in Soil Under Conditions of Saturated Flow. *Journal of Environmental Quality* 7, 1, 55-9.

Huysman, F.B., Van Renterghem and Verstraete, W. 1993: Antibiotic Resistant Sulphite-Reducing Clostridia in Soil and Groundwater as Indicator of Manuring Practices. *Water, Air, and Soil Pollution,* 69, 243-55.

Joy, D.M., Abu-Ashour, J., Botari, J.L., Etches, C., Lee, H., Whiteley, H. and Zelins, R. 1992: *Microbial Transport in Soils With and Without Macropores.* Proceedings of the Technology Transfer Conference, Ontario Ministry of the Environment and Energy, Toronto, Canada.

Ministry of Environment. 1992: *Ontario's Drinking Water Objectives.* Environmental Information, Summer, Ontario Ministry of Environment, Toronto, Canada.

Raina, P., Pollari, F., Teare, G., Goss, M., Barry, D., and Wilson, J. 1996: *Well-Water Coliform Bacteria and Gastro-Intestinal Illness in Rural Families,* as reported in M.J. Conboy and M.J. Goss, 1997: Is *Escherichia coli* an Effective Predictor of Health Risks and Source of Water Contamination for Rural Populations? *TEN, 4* (5), 156-157.

Chapter 10

DETERMINATION OF RECOLONIZATION POTENTIAL OF THE *OREOCHROMIS SHIRANUS CHILWAE* FISHERY IN LAKE CHILWA AFTER RECOVERY FROM THE SEVERE RECESSION OF 1995

by Aggrey Ambali and Alfred Maluwa

INTRODUCTION

Lake Chilwa is the twelfth largest lake in Africa and the second largest in Malawi. It is centered on 15°30'S latitude and 35°30'E longitude, 100 km to the southeast of Lake Malawi, 50 km to the southeast of Lake Malombe and 35 km to the south of Lake Chiuta (Fig. 10.1). It is the most southerly major African lake (Lancaster, 1979). The total area of the lake is 1,836 km², of which 678 km² is open water, 578 km² is surrounded by swamps and marshes, and 580 km² is grassland that is inundated seasonally (Lancaster, 1979).

The Chilwa-Chiuta basin is estimated to have been formed during the Cretaceous Period, 65-70 million years ago (Lancaster, 1979). The lake is *endorheic,* that is it has no outlet. It is separated from Lake Malawi, Lake Malombe and the Shire River by a narrow watershed. Geological studies suggest that Lake Malawi has never had an outlet via the Chilwa area to the Ruo River. Lakes Chilwa and Chiuta were once a single open lake, now separated by a sand bar which was probably formed during the early Holocene phase (8,000-9,000 years ago) or earlier, by an easterly movement of beach sand across the northern end of Lake Chilwa. The sand bar is about 1 to 1.5 km across, and in places reaches a height of 25 m above the north Chilwa plains (Lancaster, 1979).

Five major rivers drain into Lake Chilwa from the Shire Highlands and Zomba Mountain: Domasi, Likangala, Thondwe, Namadzi and Phalombe. In total, they contribute 70% of the total inflow to the lake. From the Mozambique side, three rivers drain into the lake namely, the Mnembo, Mbungwe and Nchimadzi. Lake Chilwa is shallow, with average depth ranging from four to five meters. Its levels fluctuate seasonally and they are normally restored during the rainy season, which extends from November to April. If the rainfall is below average for a succession of two to three years, the lake may recede, leaving a dry lake bed. The lake went through moderate recessions during the years 1900, 1923, 1931/33, 1943, 1949, 1953/55 and 1960/61 and severe recessions resulting in a dry lake bed in 1914/15, 1966/67 (Morgan, 1971) and 1995 (pers. observation). The basin, however, refills rapidly after heavy rains, as in 1996, when it restored itself to a depth of more than two meters. In 1998, heavy floods were experienced in the northwest part of the lake, in the Namasalima area.

Prior to 1967, during normal lake levels, the Lake Chilwa fishery supported 2,000 fishermen (Morgan, 1971) and prior to the 1995 recession it supported over 36,000 fishermen and middle-men (Kabwazi and Wilson, 1996). Over a period of 10 years, the number of fishermen has increased steadily by 250% so that the receding water in 1995 led to a potential income loss of about US$ 3.4 million among small scale fishing communities (Kabwazi and Wilson, 1996).

Thirteen species of fish were recorded by Kalk (1970), but only three are abundant throughout the year: *Oreochromis shiranus chilwae, Barbuspaludinosus* and *Clarias gariepinus* (Morgan, 1971). *O. sh. chilwae,* a tilapia species, is endemic to the lake and is most susceptible to periodic changes in water conditions, which led to mass mortalities recorded in 1955, 1960 and 1966/67. *C. gariepinus* is the most tolerant species (Morgan, 1971; Furse *et. al.*, 1979). For instance, during the years preceding the 1966/67 recession, the proportion of *O. sh. chilwae* in the catches declined from 50% in 1965 to less than 25% in 1966 and less than 1% in 1967 when gillnet fishing for tilapia was abandoned after June 1967 (Morgan, 1971). It is feared that the 1995 recession might have led to close to complete extirpation of the species in open waters. Limited remnant populations survived in swamps (Njaya *et. al.*, 1996).

The Government of Malawi mandated the University of Malawi to lead in developing a management plan for the lake (Chibambo, 1996), in order to determine measures to mitigate the impacts of the 1995 lake level recession on the biological, chemical and physical limnology of Lake Chilwa and on the livelihood of fishing communities. This study of the fishery of Lake Chilwa is one of several research projects carried out on Lake Chilwa catchment with support from the Environmental Capacity Enhancement Project (ECEP).

Figure 10.1 Lake Chilwa catchment area, southern Malawi

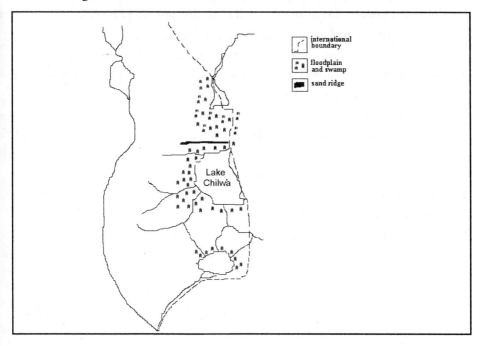

PROBLEMS ADDRESSED BY THE RESEARCH PROJECT

During the 1966/67 recession, the Fisheries Department of Malawi took some precautionary measures before the lake had dried out completely by breeding *O. sh. chilwae* in ponds at National Aquaculture Center. These fish were then used to restock the lake artificially. Additional stocks were collected from reservoirs in the southern region of Malawi after carrying out an intensive survey to identify populations which were morphologically similar to this endemic subspecies. About 300,000 progeny were restocked in the lake during the early months of 1969 (Morgan, 1971; Mathotho, 1975). No such precautionary measures were taken during the 1995 recession, yet it is feared that the impact of the 1995 recession on the subspecies might have been more severe than the 1966/67 drought. There was a need to assess the size of the population and its distribution in the various areas of the lake.

This study, carried out at various sites on Lake Chilwa from March 1997 to March 1998, provided initial indication of the status of *O. shiranus chilwae* in the lake. In particular, the following objectives were addressed:

1. To identify the swamps and lagoons where *O. sh. chilwae* populations survived when the open lake dried completely.

2. To determine the local fishing communities' management practices that the remnant populations were subjected to during the dry period.
3. To compare limnological characteristics of the refuge swamps and lagoons identified in objective 1 to those of open water in the lake and in-flowing rivers.
4. To determine the population structure of *O. sh. chilwae* in the refuge swamps and open waters of the lake.
5. To determine the species composition from various sites in the lake.
6. To determine the dietary shift in a piscivorous species, *C. gariepinus*, which preys on *O. sh. chilwae* fingerlings.

The objectives were covered under three main components:
▶ water quality analysis
▶ fisheries biodiversity analysis
▶ the social structure of the communities involved in the management of fisheries biodiversity in the water and land catchment of the lake.

PHYSICAL AND CHEMICAL CHARACTERISTICS OF LAKE CHILWA

Lake Chilwa dried completely in 1995, forming a dry sand bed on which people could walk across the lake from Kachulu to nearby Chisi Island. Cumulative successive droughts had hit Malawi and the rest of southern Africa through the early 1990s. The drought became more severe in 1995, and the lake water dried up completely. The lake level is traditionally unstable, with wide seasonal fluctuations over long periods of time. The instability of the water level creates changes in the lake chemistry, so that the lake behaves like a freshwater lake when the water is high and like an alkaline lake during dry periods. This seasonal chemical variability creates problems for organisms in the lake.

Lake Chilwa is a continuous sink for materials washed out from its catchment. This factor plus the lack of an outlet for flushing makes Lake Chilwa the most productive lake in the country. Since the country attained independence in 1964, there has been increased agricultural activity in the Lake Chilwa catchment area. The agricultural production include rice, tobacco, cotton and maize. In attempts to increase agricultural production, farmers have increased the use of agrochemicals like fertilizers and pesticides in the catchment, most of which have been washed into the lake due to increased soil erosion. Fertilizers have caused eutrophication in the lake, so that during the 1995 recession there was heavy phytoplankton bloom in the lake and a continuous green scum on the water surface (pers. observation). Water quality analysis was carried out to determine the concentration of various chemicals in Lake Chilwa and to monitor variation in the physical parameters of the water.

Methodology

Sampling for water quality analysis was carried out in three main sites on the lake: Kachulu, Chisi Island and Mchenga (Fig. 10.2). Samplings were taken during the months of April, July, October, January and March. The parameters determined were temperature, turbidity, dissolved oxygen, pH, conductivity, nitrite, nitrate, ammonia, carbonate, bicarbonate, sulphate, phosphorus, chloride, calcium, magnesium, potassium, sodium and alkalinity. All physical parameters and some of the chemical parameters were determined in the field, while the remainder of the chemical parameters were determined in the laboratory. The instruments used for field determinations are listed in Table 10.1.

Table 10.1 Instruments used for field determinations

Parameter	Instrument used
Temperature	Dissolved oxygen meter, model WTW Oxygen Electrode EOT 196
pH	pH meter, Perkin-Elmer Model 500
Dissolved oxygen	Dissolved oxygen meter, model WTW Oxygen Electrode EOT 196
Conductivity	Conductivity meter, HACH Model 44600-00
Ammonia	DREL/5 HACH
Turbidity	Secchi disk
Alkalinity	DREL/5 HACH
Nitrate	DREL/5 HACH
Nitrite	DREL/5 HACH

For laboratory analysis, water samples were collected in plastic bottles, brought to the laboratory and stored at $4^{\circ}C$. No preservatives were used during storage of the water samples. For carbonates and bicarbonates determination, a 100 ml sample was titrated with standard 0.0887 M HCl until phenolphathalein end point was reached. The sample was then titrated after adding 1 to 2 drops of methyl orange until the end point was reached (APHA, 1989).

Standard procedures outlined in APHA (1989) were used to determine sulphate, phosphorus and chloride. Calcium, magnesium, potassium and sodium were determined by acetyle flame atomic absorption spectroscopy. Six standard solutions were prepared for each determination.

Figure 10.2 Lake Chilwa research sites

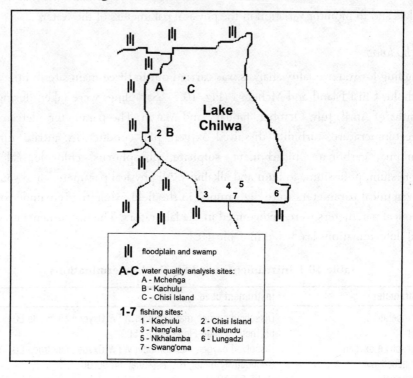

Results and discussion

Mean ± SD values of the various water parameters measured are presented in Table 10.2. Conductivity provides a measure for monitoring changes in dissolved salts. The lake has a higher salt concentration than normal freshwater lakes, for instance the conductivity of Lake Malawi water was 510μ mhos cm^{-1} (pers. observations). Conductivity values were higher on Chisi Island than the other two sampling sites. This could be due to a dilution effect at the other two sites, where the Likangala and Domasi Rivers flow in from the catchment. There is no inflowing river running from the mountain on Chisi Island. Conductivity of the water in the various sampling sites was lower during the cold, rainy periods than during the hot season (Figure 10.3A). This might be due to increased evaporation during the hot season. The rainy season in Malawi begins in November/December and ends in March/April. The period from May to November is dry; temperatures are low during the months of May through to August and increase from September to November.

Overall, the conductivity values observed in this study demonstrated lower

174

conductivity levels in the lake compared to the drying period of 1966 when conductivity readings of more than 4000μ mhos cm^{-1} were reported (Morgan and Kalk, 1970). This was likely due to dilution. The water depth during the period of this study was more than 2 m (Figure 10.3B), while the maximum mean depth between June 1966 and October 1967 was 0.67m. This would explain the higher salt concentration in 1966-67 compared to that found at the time of this study.

In March 1998, it was observed that there was no significant variation in conductivity and pH within a 1 km distance off the shore of the lake at Kachulu (Figure 10.3C). Conductivity ranged from 1100 to 2200μ mhos cm^{-1} and pH from 7.5 to 8. pH values were all higher than neutral (Table 10.2); they were more on the alkaline side than acidic. This is primarily due to high bicarbonate content in the waters of Lake Chilwa (Figure 10.4A). The common rocks in the Lake Chilwa catchment are predominantly syenites and volcanic breccia (Morgan and Kalk, 1970), whereas carbonate and limestone dominate on the islands.

Temperatures were stable at all sampling sites; mean values ranged from 24.4 to 27.3°C. Secchi disk visibility was generally higher on Chisi Island than Kachulu and Mchenga, implying that turbidity was higher in the littoral zones close to the mainland than around the islands. This could be due to strong waves striking the mainland shores, causing considerable amounts of turbulence. The sampling site on Chisi Island was on the leeward side of northeasterly winds.

Dissolved oxygen and ammonia concentrations were within the tolerance range for normal fish growth (Boyd, 1988). The low ammonia content correlates with a non-detectable low nitrite content in the water. This is expected because in aerobic conditions like those found in Lake Chilwa, which is polymictic, ammonia would have been converted to nitrite. Nitrate levels of more than 3 mgl^{-1} could have been the result of agricultural chemical use in the catchment. The observed levels of nitrate were lower than the maximum allowable limit of 10 mgl^{-1} for drinking water (HACH Company, 1987).

Of the ions determined in this study, the most predominant in the lake were chloride, bicarbonate and sulphate, while the most dominant cation was sodium (Table 10.2 and Figure 10.4). Chloride levels observed were higher than the maximum allowable concentration of 250 mgl^{-1} in drinking water (HACH Company, 1987). The level of sulphate was within the allowable maximum of 250 mgl^{-1} (HACH Company, 1987). The phosphorus content of Lake Chilwa water was high and this could contribute considerably to the high productivity of the lake.

The ionic profile observed in this study shows a similar pattern to those observed in the 1970s, when the major ions in the lake were Na^+, Cl^- and HCO_3^- yielding alkaline water with pH range of 8 to 9. The major source of chloride could be from three underground hot salt springs located in the lake catchment. These high concentrations were also observed to reach Chisi Island.

The main source of salts are the feldspars and napheline syenites, the volcanic intrusions from mountains in the catchment, and the alluvia over which rivers flow on the floodplain. Lake Chilwa has alkaline igneous intrusions, volcanic vents and dykes of a distinctive composition. The intrusions are granites, syenites and napheline syenites. Napheline syenites are rich in sodium and potassium. The volcanic vents have distinct composition; to the south of the lake there is a complex of alkaline silicate rocks, carbonates, rocks rich in sodium and calcium carbonates and agglomerates. Chisi Island is the largest carbonite center (Lancaster, 1979).

Table 10.2 Mean ±S.D of water quality parameters determined at three sampling sites of Lake Chilwa

PARAMETERS MEASURED	SAMPLING SITES		
	MCHENGA	**CHISI**	**KACHULU**
Conductivity μmhos cm^{-1}	1265 ± 149	2040 ± 1004.09	1534.5 ± 280.9
Temperature °C	26.6 ± 1.7	24.4 ± 2.3	27.3 ± 0.6
Secchi disk visibility cm	7.5 ± 0.71	9.5 ± 0.7	7.5 ± 1.4
pH	8.0 - 8.6	8.3 - 8.5	8.6
Dissolved oxygen mgl^{-1}	5.9 ± 0.3	6.4 ± 0.6	6.8 ± 0.1
Alkalinity mgl^{-1}	432 ± 74.95	457 ± 71.84	482 ± 2.83
Ammonia mgl^{-1}	0.3	0.15	0.1
ANIONS			
Chloride mgl^{-1}	455.5 ± 48.8	457 ± 43.1	461.0 ± 33.9
Bicarbonate mgCaCO$_3$l^{-1}	533.5 ± 71.4	521.5 ± 16.3	545.0 ±·41.0
Sulphate mgl^{-1}	234.5 ± 7.8	234 ± 8.5	236.0 ± 22.6
Carbonate mgCaCO$_3$l^{-1}	44.3 ± 25.0	38 ± 8.5	33.8 ± 5.4
Phosphorus (PO4-P) mgl^{-1}	3.6 ± 2.0	2.5 ± 0.8	3.9 ± 2.8
Nitrite (NO$_2$) mgl^{-1}	0	0	0
Nitrate (NO$_3$-N) mgl^{-1}	3.4 ± 2.2	3.3 ± 2.3	3.0 ± 1.8
CATIONS			
Sodium mgl^{-1}	262 ± 107.5	322.5 ± 99.7	321.0 ± 8.4
Magnesium mgl^{-1}	27 ± 19.8	8.5 ± 3.5	6.8 ± 4.5
Calcium mgl^{-1}	26 ± 11.3	16.5 ± 2.1	11.0 ± 7.1
Potassium mgl^{-1}	13 ± 4.2	14.0 ± 2.8	10.5 ± 4.9

Figures 10.3A-D Variation in water quality variables at Kachulu

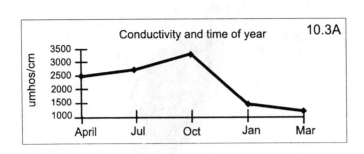

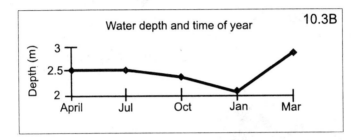

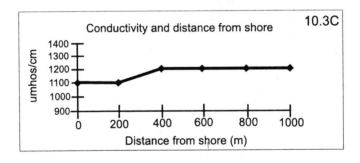

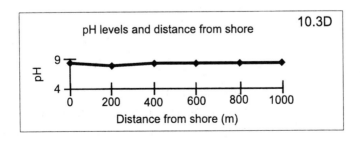

Figure 10.4

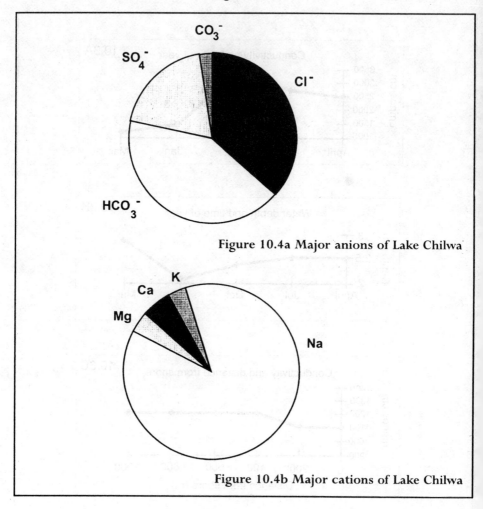

Figure 10.4a Major anions of Lake Chilwa

Figure 10.4b Major cations of Lake Chilwa

Evaluation of the suitability of Lake Chilwa as habitat for biotic resources

The physical and chemical parameters determined in this study are within tolerable ranges for successful recolonization of the lake by fish and other biotic communities. Beadle (1974) indicates that "Within the freshwater range, mineral composition has little to do with the distribution of plant and animal species ... [because] the biota of freshwater all have ionic regulation mechanisms which normally maintain body fluids hypertonic to the environment." The salinity range suitable for most freshwater animals is about 350 - 5000 μmhos cm^{-1}. Conductivity values observed in this study are all within this range, the lake is therefore a suitable habitat for fish. The main limiting factor could be the high turbidity due to continuous mixing of the waters and the high rate of eutrophication. The chemical flushing from agricultural activities in the catchment promotes high phytoplankton blooms in the lake water.

FISHES OF LAKE CHILWA

Lake Chilwa contributes between 16.7% to 43.1% of total fish production in Malawi. During the past twenty years, catches have ranged from 1,260 to 25,800 metric tonnes per annum (Fisheries Department, unpublished catch statistics). Oral interviews carried out among local fishing communities at Lake Chilwa indicate that there were differences between the 1966/67 drought and 1995 drought in terms of fish biomass stranded on the exposed lake bed. During the 1966/67 recession, more fish were caught as they were stranded in the mud, while during the 1995 drought, catches in the lake kept declining and there were no fish stranded in the mud. This information suggests that although the drought may have exacerbated the collapse of the fishery, the lake was likely already overfished by 1995. The focus of this study was to monitor the possibility of recovery of *O. shiranus* and other species in Lake Chilwa.

O. shiranus has been subdivided into two subspecies based on morphological characteristics (Trewavas, 1983). This subdivision is supported by DNA analysis (Ambali, 1996). The two subspecies are *O. sh. chilwae* and *O. sh. shiranus*. *O. sh. shiranus* is found in Lake Malawi, its tributary rivers, streams, lagoon as well as the upper Shire River and Lake Malombe. *O. sh. chilwae* is endemic to Lake Chilwa and probably Lake Chiuta. Detailed biology of the subspecies is provided in Kirk (1967). Progenies restocked in 1969 were collected from reservoirs in the southern region where pure stocks of the subpopulation were stocked between 1955 and 1960 (ICLARM and GTZ; 1991). It has, however, been reported that during the 1970s, several other tilapia species were restocked in some of the reservoirs in the region; these species included *O. sh. shiranus, O. mossambicus, O. placidus* and *O. Nyasalapia* (Mathotho, 1975). There is no record of the actual reservoirs where these other species were stocked. Interspecific hybridization has occurred so that populations in some of the reservoirs in the country are no longer genetically pure (Ambali, 1996). The hybrids show intermediate morphological characteristics rendering identification of pure stocks of *O. sh. chilwae* difficult when using morphometric techniques.

As noted earlier, Lake Chilwa was restocked in 1969 with *O. shiranus chilwae*. From a conservation genetics perspective, this recolonization effort created problems for the genetic diversity of the subspecies in the lake. Ambali (1996) observed a considerable decline in microsatellite DNA allelic diversity in the Lake Chilwa population of *O. shiranus* sp, compared to populations from other natural water bodies in the country. For instance, a mean effective number of alleles of 3.87 ± 1.67 was observed in the Lake Chilwa population, while populations means of 7.22 ± 2.55 and 6.56 ± 2.40 were observed in Lakes Chiuta and Malombe respectively. This decline in genetic biodiversity is due to an historical bottleneck that the Lake Chilwa population was subjected to. These observations allude to the fact that the absolute number of progenies restocked is not the only important factor in a restocking programme. Also important are the within and between population genetic diversity of founder populations. These two levels of genetic variation not only enhance the fitness of the species within a particular habitat, but they also promote colonization and expanded distributional ranges due to an increase in tolerance across a wider range of environments resulting from greater genetic diversity (Meffe, 1986).

Success of the 1969 restocking was not without mixed reactions. Morgan (1971) bred and reared 300,000 fingerlings in the Fisheries Department culture ponds and stocked them in Lake Chilwa. Although some were marked by fin clipping, no trace of them was ever found. Despite the effort, the population of *O. shiranus* did not approach its former density until two years later. Low survival may have been due to inappropriate and non-genetic strategies for establishing a founding population. Wild progenitors might have been crossed with domesticated broodstock in culture ponds. This would have led to outbreeding depression, whereby the existing and potentially adaptive combinations that occurred in the wild population were broken in subsequent generations. As a result, the fingerlings that were stocked would not survive favourably in the natural water body where environmental factors were not controlled. These results suggest the need to determine the potential of the remnant population in the lake to re-establish itself without substantial decline in genetic diversity due to bottlenecking. The study covered several sites of the lake in order to determine whether *O. shiranus chilwae* stock was recovering.

Methodology

Fish sampling was carried out to collect the following variables:
number and individual weight of fish caught
percentage composition of each taxon
total length of a sample from each taxon
sex ratios

Seven sites spread across various parts of the lake were sampled: Kachulu (Kach), Chisi Island (Chisi), Nkhalamba (Nkhal), Nang'ala (Nang), Nalundu (Nal), Lungadzi (Lunga) and Swang'oma (Swang) (see Figure 10.2). Samples from Kachulu and Chisi Island sites were used to derive length-weight relationships. Sampling at these sites was conducted four times, in May, August and October 1997 and January 1998. For species composition, all seven sites were sampled twice. Each sampling round was conducted within a week, in order to minimize the effect of the sampling period on species composition. These two samplings were carried out in October 1997 and January 1998. Due to irregularities in the fishing effort during the October sampling, only January data has been used in the analysis. Fishing effort in all the sites was the same. Only one haul was made on each sampling day.

All fish caught were placed in containers and transported to the laboratory where they were frozen. In the laboratory, each catch was sorted into species before counting. Total length, and body weight were recorded. In the case of *O. shiranus chilwae*, large individuals were sexed in order to determine sex ratios. Those fish caught at sites which required overnight stay were processed on the same day and only length measurements were taken.

Data Analysis

Diversity: Species diversity was assessed using the Simpson index (D) and the Shannon index (H):

$$D = S(p_i)^2 \text{ and } H = p_i \ln p_i$$

where pi is the proportion of individuals in a community, which are members of the ith species. In addition, the evenness indices E for Simpson index and J for Shannon index were determined:

$$E = (S(p_i)^2)^{-1} S^{-1} \text{ and } J = (-S\, p_i \ln p_i) (\ln S)^{-1}$$

where S is the total number of species observed in the community.

Coenological analysis: Frequency tables and graphs were used to describe the species composition of fishes caught in the various sampling sites. Similarity between sites was calculated using the Marczewski and Steinhaus (1958) equation

$$s = (100w)(a + b - w)^{-1}$$

where s is similarity of two collections, w is the total of the lower numbers o specimens of each pair of species common for two given analyzed sites, a is the tota number of specimens of a species at the site A, and b is the total number o specimens of a species in site B. In the determination of similarity values, specie: represented by one specimen at one site only were omitted from the calculation The similarity values were used to construct a branched, two dimensional dendrit of sites which was then transformed into a linear dendrite. The two-dimensiona dendrite was constructed using only the highest values in Table 10.7 (bol numbers) to connect sites. To change into a linear dendrite, the weakes connections were separated in order to insert, between the sites connected b' weaker linkages, others with higher similarities to them. Quotients were calculatec between decreasing similarities of neighbouring sites except for the border ones These are supposed to differ slightly and if in between their series a quotient occur. that differs from the neighbouring ones then its dividend constitutes the lowe bound of a similarity for defining clusters. All clusters below that value of similarit' were considered separately.

Length-weight Relationship: This analysis was carried out for *O. s. chilwae* *C.gariepinus, Barbus* sp and *H. calliptera.* Length and weight data were lo transformed and least squares linear regression was performed on th transformation data with W as the dependent variable, following the well know length-weight relationship log W = log a + b log L (Beckman 1948). Linea regressions on logtransformed data were highly significant (p<0.001) for a species.

Results

In all the sites sampled, nine species of fish were observed and these are presentec in Table 10.3. The tenth species *T. rendalli* was not caught in any of our samplings but was observed in fishermen's catches starting from February 1998. Four majo species were observed in most of the sites and these are *O. s. chilwae, C. gariepinus B. paludinosus* and *calliptera.*

Table 10.3 Fish species observed in Lake Chilwa during sampling and fishermen's catch

Family	Latin Name	Chinyanja Name	Lake	Rivers & Marsh
Cichlidae	*Tilapia rendalli*	Chilinguni	+	-
	O. shiranus chilwae	Makumba	+	-
	Haplochromis calliptera	Makwale	+	+
Clariidae	*Clarius gariepinus*	Mlamba	+	+
Schilbeidae	*Pareutropius longifilis*	Ntchenjeta	+	-
Mormyridae	*Gnathonemus catostoma*	Mphuta	+	+
Characidae	*Brycinus imberi*	Mkhalala	+	+
Cyprinidae	*Labeo cylindricus*	Chonjo	+	+
	Barbus_paludinosus	Matemba	+	+
	B. trimaculatus	Matemba	+	+

+present in the lake and/or rivers
- absent in the lake and/or rivers

The most dominant species observed in all sites was *B. paludinosus*. Other species of cyprinids were observed, such as *B. trimaculatus* and *L. cylindricus*, but these were in smaller quantities than *B. paludinosus* (Tables 10.3 and 10.4). The trend observed in most of the sites was that *O. s. chilwae* continued to be one of the dominant species compared to *C. gariepinus* and *H. calliptera*. *P. longifilis* was found to be abundant at Nang'ala and only three individuals were observed at Kachulu. Other rare species in the catch included *G. catostoma*, and *B. imberi*.

Table 10.4 Species composition of Kachulu and Chisi Island sampling sites

Species	May		July		September		January	
	Kach	Chisi	Kach	Chisi	Kach	Chisi	Kach	Chisi
T. rendalli								
O. shiranus chilwae	16	12	12	34	16	21	38	625
H. calliptera		19	19	9	2		38	85
C. gariepinus	57		41	30	27	208	59	28
P. longifilis							3	
G. catostoma		2	2					
B. imberi							1	
L. cylindricus				1		1	1	
B. paludinosus	469	1117	1111	182	1000	1082	14865	2287

Catches at each site are presented in Tables 10.4 and 10.5. Two indices of diversity were used because Simpson's index is weighted in favour of dominant species, while the Shannon index favours rare species. The indices show that Lake Chilwa has low species diversity throughout all the sites where sampling was carried out. The least diverse site was Kachulu whereas Nkhalamba, Chisi Island and Swang'oma showed relatively high species diversity (Table 10.6). The dendrite of the investigated sites fell into two clusters of sites; site one being Kachulu, Lungadz and Nang'ala and site two being Nalundu and Nkhalamba. Swang'oma and Chis were separate sites, that did not belong in any cluster. The abundance of B puludinosus contributed significantly to the clustering of the sites. The first cluster comprised sites with more than 92% B. paludinosus by composition while the other cluster had less than 92% but instead had a high composition of O. s. chilwae, H calliptera and C. gariepinus. The linear dendrite is presented in Figure 10.5. It is clear that neighbouring sites had differences in species composition, mostly in the abundance of B. paludinosus (Table 10.7).

Table 10.5 Number of fishes collected in the sites sampled

	Kach	Chisi	Nkhal	Nang	Nal	Lunga	Swang
O.s. chilwae	38	625	1071	260	104	823	8
H. calliptera	38	85	403	214	283	155	
C. gariepninus	59	28	98	44	106		
P. longifilis				42			
B. paludinosis	14865	2287	5536	10264	5000	12800	520
B. imberi	1		1				94
Total	15001	3025	7109	10824	5493	13876	622

Table 10.6 Simpson (D) and Shannon (H) diversity indices and evenness indices E and J

	Kach	Chisi	Nkhal	Nang	Nal	Lunga	Swang	Mean ±SE
D	1.02	1.63	1.58	1.11	1.20	1.17	1.39	1.30±0.09
E	0.20	0.33	0.32	0.22	0.24	0.23	0.28	0.26±0.02
H	0.06	0.68	0.70	0.26	0.39	0.39	0.49	0.42±0.09
J	0.03	0.42	0.44	0.16	0.24	0.24	0.45	0.28±0.06

Table 10.7 Similarity of sites in terms of species abundance

	Kach	Chisi	Nkhal	Nang	Nal	Lunga	Swang
Kach	100.00	15.29	34.51	67.25	33.43	**81.14**	4.15
Chisi		100.00	42.55	25.43	**50.36**	21.80	18.01
Nkhal			100.00	**50.96**	77.07	46.00	4.84
Nang				100.00	48.94	**76.72**	48.36
Nal					100.00	4.63	9.45
Lunga						100.00	3.78
Swang							100.00

Figure 10.5 Linear dendrite for the sales sampled based on similarities in Table 10.7

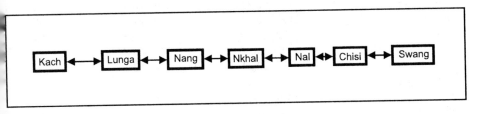

Weight-length analysis is presented in Tables 10.8 and 10.9. Mean total length of *B. paludinosus* was not significantly different among sites: mean weight was 2.37 ± 0.03 g. *O. s. chilwae* ranged in length from 1.7 cm to 21.0 cm with a mean weight of 24.87 ± 3.49 g. *C. gariepinus* had a small size distribution with mean weight of 14.83 g and length ranging from 5 to 41.5 cm. Regression coefficients for the cichlids were higher than those of cyprinidae and clariidae, and there was no significant difference in the value of log a.

Table 10.8 Lengths of three major species caught in the samples

	Mean ±SE TL	Range	n
Barbus sp			
Kachulu	5.70 ±0.08	4.0 - 10.3	209
Chisi Island	5.86 ±0.09	2.6 - 10.1	220
Nang'ala	5.85 ±0.08	3.2 - 9.8	197
Nkhalamba	6.51 ±0.09	3.7 - 10.5	202
Nalundu	6.51 ±0.09	3.2 - 9.7	150
Swang'oma	5.54 ±0.09	2.1 - 8.9	185
Lungadzi	5.55 ±0.06	2.8 - 9.0	150
O.s. chilwae			
Kachulu	11.79 ±0.68	4.7 - 19.0	38
Chisi Island	7.26 ±0.36	3.1 - 17.2	149
Nang'ala	6.46 ±0.29	3.0 - 20.5	176
Nkhalamba	8.25 ±0.39	1.7 - 21.0	180
Nalundu	14.50 ±0.17	11.0 - 18.5	64
Swang'oma	14.01 ±0.59	10.5 - 16.1	8
Lungadzi	5.86 ±0.24	2.9 - 18.4	210
C. Gariepinus			
Kachulu	15.19 ±0.45	7.1 - 26.7	59
Chisi Island	15.60 ±0.94	10.0 - 30.3	28
Nang'ala	14.56 ±0.51	5.0 - 25.0	44
Nkhalamba	15.18 ±0.33	9.8 - 30.3	98
Nalundu	14.25 ±0.34	9.5 - 41.5	109
Swang'oma	-	-	-
Lungadzi	16.34 ±0.34	10.2 - 29.3	96

Table 10.9 Regression coefficients for length/weight relationship (with standard errors in parenthesis) for four fish species

Species	r² (all significant at P<0.001)	b, slope of regression (S.E)	Log a, intercept of regression (S.E)
O.s. chilwae	0.86	2.925 (0.114)	-1.734 (0.109)
B. paludinosus	0.85	2.615 (0.055)	-1.778 (0.061)
C. gariepinus	0.62	2.553 (0.041)	-1.745 (0.033)
H. calliptera	0.85	3.010 (0.243)	-1.876 (0.220)

Sex Ratio of O. s. chilwae and piscivory of C. gariepinus

Most of the *O. s. chilwae* caught were small and could not be easily sexed. For the few individuals that could be sexed, male vs female sex ratio values ranged from

0.71 at Kachulu to 11.8 at Nalundu (data not shown). The fact that more males were observed in this particular study may be due to the effect of sexual dimorphism; males grow faster and to larger size than females, hence more males reached a large size and could be more easily sexed than most females.

Most of the *C. gariepinus* caught in this study were small and their piscivory could not be well established.

Discussion

Traditionally, the fishery of Lake Chilwa has been dominated by three main species, *B. paludinosus*, *C. gariepinis* and *O. s. chilwae*. Past catch statistics show that they each contribute 47.5%, 30.5% and 12.5%, respectively (Unpublished data; Fisheries Department). Although the lake dried out completely in 1995, it is observed that the three species have resumed their status as the main species of economic importance in the lake. The recovery of *B. paludinosus* has been the fastest; the populations of *C. gariepinus* and *O. s. chilwae* are also increasing. It is interesting to note that when the lake overflooded in January/February 1998, at sites which were sampled more than four times, stocks of fish showed continuous increase.

During all the sampling programme conducted at the lake, we did not catch any specimen of *T. rendalli*. Furthermore, during the period March to December 1997, we never saw any specimens of the species in the fishermen catches. However, in February and March 1998, fishermen caught a few specimens of the species in their gillnets. It is not unusual for *T. rendalli* to be rare in the lake. Even in the 1970s, Furse *et. al.* (1979) reported that in two years of trawling (1971-72), only two specimens of *T. rendalli* were caught. The species is usually caught during the years of very high water level, when it is found in open water. The 1997/98 rainy season was particularly high in the Lake Chilwa catchment and the observed specimen coincided with period when the lake was at this high level.

Sites in the southern tip of the lake harbour considerable numbers of *O. s. chilwae*. This was primarily due to a founder population which survived in Mpoto Lagoon in the southwest area of the lake. The lagoon overflooded during the 1996 rainy season and a population of *O. s. chilwae* recolonized the lake, which had recovered from the severe drought. The species has been found to survive in the marshes, but is rarely found in the inflow rivers on the Malawian side. The fact that *O. s. chilwae* was of average length (i.e. <9.0 cm) in most of the sites might imply that the populations were mainly recruits from recent breeding. Large individuals were fewer than fingerling size. A similar case also applies to *C. gariepinus*, where most of the individuals observed were in the small size range.

The diversity indices suggest that Lake Chilwa has low fish species diversity. There are several species of fish found in the catchment of Lake Chilwa, but most of them are restricted to the swamp and streams around the lake. In Lake Chiuta they live in the open water. This distribution is due to high conductivity of the lake which makes it inhospitable to palustrine and riverine fishes, especially in the dry season (Furse *et. al.*, 1979).

The site clusters show some element of independence from geographical distance between sites. The major factors in the sites were closeness to tributaries. It was observed that sites close to the mouth of rivers were similar because there were large populations of *B. paludinosus*. The first cluster comprised sites which were on the mainland and were close to the mouth of inflow rivers. The Kachulu site was close to Likangala River, Nang'ala was close to Namadzi and Lungadzi was close to Mulira River. The second cluster comprised sites which were close together on an island in the southern part of the lake. There were no common characteristics between Chisi Island and Swang'oma and they did not form a cluster based on species abundance and evenness.

SOCIO-ECONOMIC SETUP OF THE LAKE CHILWA COMMUNITY AND ITS RELEVANCE TO CONSERVATION OF FISHERIES BIODIVERSITY

Lake Chilwa supports more than 30% of the population in the country. Within a radius of 60 km of its catchment it encompasses five districts: Zomba, Mulanje, Phalombe, Machinga and Thyolo. The lake provides supplies to the communities in these districts and several other districts outside the catchment. Although the lake is the most productive in the country, it has been traditionally exploited by small-scale fishermen operating with minimal capital investments in the fishing business. Declines in the lake stocks have severe consequences on low-income rural communities which earn their income by fishing and can not easily afford other expensive forms of animal protein like beef, pork etc.

The rains of 1996 and 1997 refilled the dry bed of Lake Chilwa to normal levels and in 1998 floods occurred in the northern part of the lake. Results from our surveys suggest that fish stocks are recovering and, more importantly, that there is recruitment of all major species in the lake. The situation in the lake looks healthy for now, but there is a need to devise management systems which will promote sustainable conservation and management of the stocks. This component of the study was designed to determine the social structure in the catchment that would support sustainable utilization and conservation of the fishery.

The Department of Fisheries of the Government of Malawi is one of several government departments operating in the Lake Chilwa catchment. The Department activities include: licensing, restriction of mesh size, etc. Prior to 1996, the Department carried out no enforcement work. The lake management differed from that of other lakes in the country. At Lakes Malawi and Malombe, there were closed seasons and gear restrictions. Because there were no restrictions on Lake Chilwa, fishermen from the other lakes migrated to there when their lakes were closed, putting high pressure on the Lake Chilwa stocks. These migrant fishermen brought in new and more destructive fishing gear such as *nkacha* which were uncommon in the history of traditional fishing in Lake Chilwa. In this study, we were interested in determining the activities the Department has undertaken in an attempt to conserve the stocks of Lake Chilwa.

The traditional extension methodology in the country has taken a top-down approach, with government institutions providing the information and rural communities on the receiving end. This study wanted to determine whether or not the people of Lake Chilwa knew how to manage their own stocks and understood that fish are a finite resource.

Methodology

Group focus interviews were carried out among local fishing communities at Lake Chilwa. These interviews involved the researchers, Fisheries Department officials, local leaders and fishermen at the lake. The questions focused on:

▸ where the remnant populations that have recolonized the lake survived during the 1995 recession

▸ how these locations were managed by the local communities themselves

▸ how these locations (i.e. wetlands) and the open water lake are being managed, now that the lake has refilled and stocks are building up.

Results and discussion

A major change in the country's natural resources management was introduced in the mid-1990s, when the Government of Malawi revised several of its environmental laws. One such law is the Fisheries Conservation and Management

Act of 1997, which was passed by Parliament on October 20, 1997 and enacted on November 13, 1997. Of special interest is the fact that the act provides for local community participation in the conservation and management of fisheries in Malawi. Fisheries management committees have been formed in the Lake Chilwa catchment. These are of two forms: (1) River Committees (RCs) and (2) Beach Village Committees (BVCs).

RCs manage rivers and they are comprised of the group village headman (GVH) and the village headmen (VH) of a particular area. RCs are distributed on various sections of the lower courses of the inflowing rivers on Lake Chilwa; for instance, there are seven RCs on Likangala River. In 1995, some of the lower courses of these rivers did not dry out completely and, as a result, fish species, predominantly *Barbus* sp., sought refuge in these rivers. The committees were set up with the aim of conserving the remnant populations of these fish.

There are nine such committees on Lake Chilwa and they are chaired by the GVH so that each RC is known by the GVH's name (Table 10.10). The RC system is a revamp of the old traditional system that operated prior to 1995. The chiefs used to control fishing and use of other natural resources in the rivers. Village members were only allowed to fish using fish traps or hook and line and were not allowed to use poisonous herbs during the dry season. However, the system was disrupted after a 1991 rock avalanche, known as the Phalombe disaster, brought about changes in the social structures on some of the rivers such as the Likangala.

Table 10.10 River Committees on Lake Chilwa

Group Village Headman River Committee	
Nyanya	Mbalu
Nambesa	Kimu
Chirunga	Makawa
Mindano	Kwindimbule
Kadewere	

The RC system introduced in 1995 operates under similar terms as those in the past. The chiefs put in place regulations which they enforce jointly with members of their villages. The regulations prohibit:

> the use of closely spaced fish traps which would catch juveniles

▶ the construction of a fence for setting fish traps across the river during the closed season
▶ the use of poisonous herbs to kill fish during the dry season when the water level is low.

The RC have set a closed season for the rivers from April to October of every year. Fishing is open during the rainy season.

Although the main genus of interest for conservation is *Barbus* sp., it is a multi-spawner, spawning throughout the year. Therefore it requires no special habitat or spawning requirement during the rainy season. The basis for closing during the dry season is because water levels in the rivers drop and historically during the dry season most villagers applied poisonous herbs to kill fish in the rivers. This was a major threat to the populations of *Barbus* in the rivers.

RCs have played a role in conserving river stocks which later recolonized the lake. The committees have continued to operate although the lake has recovered. The local leadership has been informed that RCs are legally constituted according to the Fisheries Act. The village headmen feel that they will have to re-introduce their powers over control of fisheries resources in the rivers.

After independence, the RC system was one of the systems abolished in the country. A notable example is Lweya River in the Nkhata Bay district, where there is a site known as Chiwandama. This site was controlled by a chief. Fishing at Chiwandama without the chief's consent was prohibited. People believed that mystical powers were bestowed on the chief to guard the site. It was believed that anyone who fished illegally in the area would be caught by crocodiles (D.B. Phiri, pers. comm.). Each year, fishing was conducted only after the chief had performed some traditional rituals. This was an effective traditional system which conserved the cyprinid population in the river. Since the RC system was abolished, the cyprinid population has declined drastically.

BVCs are lake-based committees which liaise between the fishing communities and the Department of Fisheries. BVCs are controlled by village headmen, although the actual leadership is based on members who are fishermen. BVCs were formed in 1996 after the lake refilled. There are currently 49 BVCs spread throughout the lake (Table 10.11). The BVCs set regulations, which they also enforce jointly with Fisheries Department personnel. Since the introduction of the BVC system, a number of fishery regulations have been established on Lake Chilwa. These include:

- a closed season from December 1 to March 31
- gear restriction
- prohibition of the construction of shelters in open water.

The BVCs have established a closed fishing season on Lake Chilwa. The first closed season was introduced in the 1997/98 rainy season. Fishing gear such as beach seines are prohibited. Fishing at night is also prohibited during the closed season. The December to March closed period coincides with the rainy season, which is the peak breeding period for *O. s. chilwae* and *C. gariepinus*. Operators caught fishing illegally during the closed seasons have their gear confiscated and are tried by the Traditional Authority. By February 1998, seven gears had been confiscated by various BVCs. The gear was deposited at Fisheries Department offices for safe-keeping pending the trials.

The BVCs have also introduced a fishing gear restriction system on Lake Chilwa. Gear such as gill nets, fish traps, long lines, handlines and cast nets can be used throughout the year without any restrictions. Beach seining is prohibited during the closed season, but can be used from April to November. *Nkacha*, a locally known gear introduced by migrant fishermen from Lakes Malawi and Malombe, is prohibited in Lake Chilwa. The gear had not existed in Lake Chilwa but was introduced by migrant fishermen who took advantage of the fact that there was no closed season on the lake.

There are also restrictions on the mesh size of the nets. For instance, beach seine minimum mesh size is 12 mm, maximum headline length is 5 m. For gillnets, minimum mesh size is 70 mm and maximum headline length is 3 m. As far as *O. s. chilwae* population in the lake is concerned, the closed season protects recruits from exploitation and, because of the large gill mesh size, only large individuals are removed from the stock. As gillnets do catch great quantities, the gear is not very destructive. Several fishermen have now acquired gillnets so that they can maintain their fishing operation throughout the year.

Table 10.11 Beach Village Committees on Lake Chilwa

Site of the lake	Name of the BVC	
Lake Chilwa North	Mkumba	Mkwate
	Mpilanjala	Chitembo
	Chipakwe	Makawa
	Nyanya	Lingoni
	Namanja	Zumulu
	Milalo	Masinde
	Mgwalanga	Mtila
	Pawaya	Makate
	Khuzumba	Neula
	Likhonyowa	Mpheta/Chisani/Damasi
	Mchingudza	Chilumo
	Mapila	Mtubula
	Msikawanjala	Chiwanga
Lake Chilwa West	Kachulu	Tiyese
	Naphali	Mtolongo
Lake Chilwa, S. Marsh	Swang'oma	Changa
	Malunguni	Nthambala
	Lungani	Njalo
	Mtemanyama	Thanga
	Malagani	Ngangala
Lake Chilwa East	Chinguma	Muluma
	Ngotangota	Tsekwa
	Chitula	

Prior to 1997, *Nkacha* operators constructed temporary shelters in the open water where they used to operate. These were locally known as *zimbowera*. The BVCs have banned construction of these shelters so that operators do not use the gear at night. BVCs also argued that the use of *zimbowera* polluted the lake because inhabitants dumped all their waste directly into the lake, promoting eutrophication.

In accordance with the provision of the Fisheries Act, the BVCs have the mandate to restrict the number of licenses that are issued for beach seine and gill nets.

The Relationship between RCs and BVCs

RCs were established before the BVCs, but it was observed from the focus group interviews that members of the two committees did not clearly understand how the committees were related. The issue of relationship is important for the sustainability of the two committees. The current position is that the RCs protected the fish stocks that subsequently re-established the lake population after the drought. Since the lake recovered from the drought and the BVCs now manage the stock, they believe that they now own the stock. Given this point of view, the arrangement has not been without conflict. The RCs claim that they protected the stock during the drought period and now members of the BVCs are over-exploiting the stocks. It is felt the BVC has not appreciated the RCs role in conserving the remnant fish populations and there has been a lack of reciprocity. The element of benefit sharing is not properly defined.

Considering the instability of Lake Chilwa, there is a need to establish a mechanism to ensure the RCs receive remuneration from the BVCs. There is provision in the Fisheries Conservation and Management Act, 1997 for establishment of Fisheries Funds. The Act further provides for district fees from levy of licenses, permits, etc. which "... shall be used for the benefit of the people in the fishing district in respect of which the license, permit or other matters for which the fees was paid relates". This study would recommend that the Department of Fisheries devise a way to use the levy collected from fishing licenses to support the activities of both the BVCs and RCs.

Conclusion

The local community participation which has been introduced in Lake Chilwa and all other lakes should be promoted because the stakeholders are directly involved in the management of resources. In order to promote sustainability, conservation and utilization of fisheries biodiversity, there is a need to involve the custodians of the resources. The BVCs and RCs are fora where the voices and actions of the local communities render services to resource management. Since the benefits of their involvement are obvious, they are likely to support the programme. If the management system is to be sustainable, the Department of Fisheries will need to give the committees financial autonomy in order to support their own management and conservation activities.

ACKNOWLEDGMENTS

We are grateful to the Environmental Capacity Enhancement Project for providing funding for this study. We also extend gratitude to various members of the Fisheries

Department and the University of Malawi for the assistance they rendered during data collection at Kachulu as well as in the laboratory.

We also thank Melda Lipenga, Mabvuto Gondwe, Gift Changadeya and Nsano Mandalasi, final year Bachelor of Science students at Chancellor College, for their participation in our sampling programme and for enduring odd hours of travel to Lake Chilwa.

References

Ambali, A.J.D. 1996: The relationship between domestication and genetic biodiversity of mouthbrooding tilapia species in Malawi: *Oreochromis shiranus shiranus* (Boulenger) and *Oreochromis shiranus chilwae* (Trewavas). Ph. D. Thesis. Department of Biology, Dalhousie University.

American Public Health Association, American Water Works Association, and Water Pollution Control Federation. 1989: *Standard Methods for Examination of Water and Wastewater,* Washington, D.C.: APHA.

Beadle, L.C. 1974: *The Inland Waters of Tropical Africa. An Introduction to Tropical Limnology.* New York: Longmans.

Beckman, W.C. 1948: The length-weight relationship, factors for conversion between standard and total lengths, and coefficients of condition of seven Michigan fishes. *Transactions of the American Fisheries Society* 75:237-256

Boyd, C.E. 1988: *Water Quality in Warmwater Fish Ponds.* Alabama: Agricultural Experiment Station, Auburn University.

Chibambo, Z. 1996: The official opening speech delivered by the Minister of Natural Resources, Hon. Ziliro Chibambo. In F.J. Njaya, S.S. Chiotha and H. Kabwazi (eds.), *Management Plan for Lake Chilwa and its Catchment*, p. 5. Proceedings of a workshop jointly organized by the Department of Fisheries and University of Malawi, held at Chancellor College, Zomba, Malawi, 11-12 January 1996.

Furse, M.T., Kirk, R.G., Morgan, R.P. and Tweddle, D. 1979: Fishes: distribution and biology in relation to changes. In M. Kalk, A.J. McLachlan, and C. Howard-Williams (eds.), *Lake Chilwa: Studies in a Tropical Ecosystem,* pp. 175-208. Monographiae Biologicae, 35.

HACH Company. 1987: *Water Analysis Handbook, 1987 Edition.* Loveland: Systems for Analysis.

ICLARM and GTZ. 1991: *The Context of Small-scale Integrated Agriculture-Aquaculture*

Systems in Africa: a Case Study of Malawi. ICLARM Studies and Reviews 18. Manila: ICLARM and Germany: GTZ.

Kabwazi, H.H. and Wilson, J.G. 1996: The fishes and fishery of Lake Chilwa. In *Lake Chilwa RAMSAR Study Summary Report*, pp. 1-14. Department of Biology, University of Malawi.

Kalk, M. 1970: *Decline and Recovery of a Lake.* Zomba: The Government Printer.

Kirk, R.G. 1967: The Fishes of Lake Chilwa. *Soc. Mal. J.,* 20(l), 35-48.

Lancaster, N. 1979: The environmental setting: the changes in the lake level. In M. Kalk, A.J. McLachlan and C. Howard-Williams (eds.), *Lake Chilwa: Studies in a Tropical Ecosystem,* pp. 41-58. Monographiae Biologicae, 35.

Marczewki, E. and Steinhaus, H. 1958: On a certain distance of sets and the corresponding distance function. *Coll. Math,* 6, 319-327.

Mathotho, A.J. 1975: *A simple guide to rearing fish in small dams in Malawi.* Fisheries Bulletin, Malawi Department of Fisheries.

Meffe, G.K. 1986: Conservation genetics and the management of endangered fishes. *Fisheries* 11(I), 14-23.

Morgan, P.R. 1971: The Lake Chilwa tilapia and its fishery. *Afr. J. Trop. Hydrobiol. Fish.* 1(l), 51-58.

Morgan, A. and Kalk, M. 1970: Seasonal changes in the waters of Lake Chilwa in a drying phase, 1966-68. *Hydrobiologia* 36, 1-23.

Njaya, F.J. 1996: The development of a fisheries co-management programme for Lake Chiuta in Malawi. In F.J. Njaya, S.S. Chiotha and H. Kabwazi (eds.), *Management Plan for Lake Chilwa and its Catchment,* pp. 42-45. Proceedings of a workshop jointly organized by the Department of Fisheries and University of Malawi, held at Chancellor College, Zomba, Malawi, 11-12 January 1996.

Trewavas, E. 1983: *Tilapiine Fishes of the Genera* Sarotherodon, Oreochrornis *and* Danakilia. British Museum, Natural History.

Chapter 11

WETLAND BIODIVERSITY AND IMPLICATIONS FOR LAND USE

by James Bogart and Alan Channing

INTRODUCTION

This study undertook an assessment of the amphibian populations in wetland habitats in South Africa, Zimbabwe, Zambia and Namibia from November 1996 to January 1997. The health of a wetland environment is often assessed by the diversity of animal and plant species the wetland supports, but the simple estimation of diversity may not be sufficient. The diversity of the amphibian species community provides sensitive indicators of the health of the wetlands due to the wetland niche which they occupy. Accordingly, the diversity of amphibians was estimated using observation, tape recordings of their calls, and by examining the tadpoles in ponds. Thirty-eight species of frogs were found in 25 wetland populations. Individuals of *Tomopterna* were selected as being the best indicators of suitable wetland habitat. Cytogenetics, isozyme electrophoresis and DNA sequences were used to identify and to examine the genetics of populations of *Tomopterna*. The molecular genetic data show that most of the wetland population examined have been isolated for considerable periods of time. Loss of habitat, as a result of human activity or other intrusion, can have serious implications for endemic populations. In order to maintain the diversity of this community and protect the health of the wetland, certain populations should be protected, while habitat restoration and rehabilitation will contribute to enhancement of others. Monitoring should be undertaken to provide for management of these areas and the sensitive amphibians which occupy them.

Background

Southern Africa presents a diversity of habitats and is home for many amphibian species that are mostly endemic to that region (Passmore and Carruthers, 1979). The species that inhabit a particular wetland are responding to present environmental conditions but historical conditions are also very important. Amphibians, and in particular the frogs that inhabit wetland communities, provide very good indicators of environmental health because they are known to be susceptible to a diversity of water and air borne contaminants (Dunson *et. al.*, 1992; Lambert, 1997) (Table 11.1).

Amphibian populations have been observed to be declining on a worldwide scale (Wake, 1991). They are relatively immobile and unable to escape from areas of habitat degradation. Some species of frogs or even some populations of the same species may be more resistant to changes in the environment than others. The differences are related to a number of factors, such as behavioural differences of the species, genetic resistance, food availability, micro-habitat preference, or time-related factors (life expectancy, time in the tadpole stage, time spent in the breeding ponds). Thus, determining the factors that affect diversity is a complex problem that requires fundamental knowledge of the species' life history, genetics, ecology, vagility and evolution. For example, the diversity of frogs is found to be reduced in a dam (or pond) in the dry areas of Namibia, when compared to a dam on the southern coast. The Namibian locality might be suitable habitat for species that never immigrated to that area or historical populations may have been eliminated, leaving the individuals that could tolerate altered conditions. Short-term answers to such long-term questions can only be estimated by comparing the species composition of several populations and by using population genetics to estimate isolation and vagility of particular species.

Table 11.1 Characteristics of amphibians as bioindicators of pesticides and other environmental contaminants

---

a. Complex life cycles (aquatic and terrestrial life stages) expose them to pollutants in either or both habitats.
b. Rapid aquatic larval growth rates to achieve metamorphosis render them useful for bioassaying for pollutants when defects are soon detectable.
c. High intra- and inter-specific competition for resources, especially in larval stages, rapidly reflects differences from pollutants between species; adult stages of some species are terrestrial.
d. Permeable eggs and gills or skin that are highly vascularized and in close contact with the environment increase susceptibility to pollutants.
e. Important trophic cycling role in such temporary pond ecosystems in which changes caused by pollutants are quickly detectable.
f. Cold-bloodedness or ectothermy render them dependent on temperature when responding physiologically to pollutant levels in the environment; poor ability to metabolize pesticide residues

results in accumulation in body tissues.

g. Simple enzyme systems, as relatively primitive vertebrates, result in poor ability to degrade or detoxify complex chemical compounds like pesticides whose residues, in combination with low metabolic rate, then accumulate in body tissues.

h. Aestivation or hibernation, in soil and mud, potentially expose them to toxic conditions when they may be unable to respond. .

i. They are versatile for experimental use in the laboratory, semi-natural conditions, and in the field.

j. Insectivorous, they are subject to the intake (also through inhalation) of such contaminants as pesticides with their prey.

k. Many species form an important link in food chains with raptorial birds and other vertebrate predators in aquatic and terrestrial ecosystems.

1. Many species are active and both visually and vocally conspicuous, especially at breeding ponds during wet seasons, facilitating population monitoring in the field.

In spite of efforts made to identify and characterize frog species in southern Africa (Rose, 1962; Wager, 1965; Passmore and Carruthers, 1979; Channing and Griffin, 1993; Channing, 1998), new species are frequently encountered and the ranges of southern African species are constantly being revised (Channing, 1993; Channing et. al., 1994; Channing and Bogart, 1996; Visser and Channing, 1997). Prerequisite to any analysis of diversity or comparative evidence of habitat change is an understanding of the species that occur in the populations and the species' ranges in southern Africa.

RESEARCH OBJECTIVES

▶ To select representative species of frogs that depend on wetland habitats in southern Africa for their existence. Such species should be wide spread and be known to be relatively intolerant of habitat degradation.

▶ To relate the biodiversity of the wetlands studied in terms of their land use considerations.

▶ To make a balanced appraisal of the value of the wetlands that could be used by land owners and managers to maintain suitable wetland habitat for frogs and the associated flora and faunal components.

METHODOLOGY

Field trips were taken between November 1996 and January 1997 to wetland habitats in southern Africa. An inventory of the amphibians was taken at each examined locality. Most of the inventories were taken at night when the male amphibians were vocalizing. Tape recordings were made of the mating calls and the species were collected and identified. Because most of the wetland populations were discrete ponds, it was possible to examine and identify most of the adult individuals present as well as tadpoles in the water. Representative voucher specimens were taken for the genetic examination of individuals found in the populations.

A species that was especially important and of great interest to this research was the newly discovered (Channing and Bogart, 1996) tetraploid sand frog, *Tomopterna tandyi,* that was thought to occur in a small area on the southern Cape. Cytogenetics, isozyme electrophoresis and DNA sequences were used to identify and to examine the genetics of populations of *Tomopterna.* By examining the chromosomes of specimens during field studies, it was possible to both extend the range of this species and to follow tetraploid populations throughout southern Africa.

Other methods were used to estimate the relative importance of wetland habitat. The sounds were recorded from populations that were not easily accessed in order to determine what species were present. Amphibians were observed on roads in areas where ponds were not obvious. These data were used to determine possible ranges of particular species that were uncommon or not in breeding congregations. Where possible, the identification of plants at a site and the presence of other animals was information that was used to compare wetlands. In many cases, land uses could be identified, i.e. if the wetland was maintained by a land owner as a source of water for livestock or the water was used for irrigation during dry periods.

RESULTS AND DISCUSSION

Twenty-five wetland habitats were examined in southern Africa (Table 11.2) and 38 species of frogs were found. To compare wetland environments in southern Africa with respect to degradation and perturbation in order to suggest possible enhancement methods, the depth of analyses was restricted to those species or genera that did use discrete wetlands and were widespread. Some of the species are relatively uncommon and have a very restricted range (e.g. *Hemisus marmoratus).* Many of the species found were only present in one wetland (Table 11.3) and were not useful for broad comparisons. The most suitable species for the present investigation were species in the genus *Tomopterna,* the sand frogs. At least one species of *Tomopterna* occurred in South Africa, Zambia, and Namibia

(Table 11.3), and they were common enough to ensure that the research team would encounter them if they resided in a particular wetland. Because *Tomopterna* species often did occur with many other species, it was assumed that a wetland possessing one or more species of *Tomopterna* would be suitable amphibian breeding habitat.

Table 11.2 Wetland habitats examined for the presence of individual frog species

SOUTH AFRICA:
1.   Ponds, dams, and river courses around Stellenbosch.
2.   Jeffrey's Bay, close to the coast on the southern Cape
3.   Nature Reservation (Andris Voslos Kudu Reserve) north of Grahamstown
4.   Ponds and dams between Grahamstown and the coast
5.   River edge in Lainsburg
6   Ponds around Aliwal North
7.   Ponds around Bloomfontein
8.   Ponds between Burgersdorp and Venterstrad
9.   Springbok
10.   Hazeyview
11.   Kruger National Park, pans and several ponds
12.   Pietersberg, several dams
13.   Mefete River south of Pietersberg

ZIMBABWE:
14.   Stream at Inyanga Mountain
15.   Ponds in La Rochele, Penhalonga
16.   Wetland on slope of mountain by World's View
17.   Stapleford
18.   Ponds west of Mutare
19.   Wetlands close to the banks of the Zambezi River

ZAMBIA:
20.   Wetlands close to the banks of the Zambezi River
21.   Zambezi River (banks and pools in rocks)
22.   River bed and pools west of Victoria Falls

NAMIBIA:
23.   River bank and associated wetlands of the Okavango River near Runtu
24.   Wetland east of Grootfontein
25.   Hardam and a wetland irrigation area (the Scheme)

Table 11.3 Species found to be present in the wetland sites that were examined. The wetland sites (in parentheses) are numbered (from Table 11.2)

Species	Wetland Sites
Afrana angolensis	(11, 13, 15, 16)
Afrixalus aureus	(11)
Afrixalus crotalus	(15)
Arthroleptis stenodactylus	(15)
Bufo gariepensis	(4)
Bufo gutteralis	(4)
Bufo pardalis	(4)
Bufo rangeri	(1, 4)
Breviceps fuscus	(3)
Breviceps verrucosus	(4)
Cacosternum boettgeri	(2, 3, 4, 25)
Cacosternum nanum	(2, 4)
Chiromantis xerampelina	(10, 11)
Hemisus marmoratus	(10)
Hyperolius broadleyi	(15)
Hyperolius marmoratus angolensis	(20)
Hyperolius marmoratus aposematicus	(20)
Hyperolius marmorata marmorata	(1, 2, 3, 4)
Hyperolius marmorata rhodesianus	(19)
Hyperolius nasutus	(20)
Hyperolius pusillus	(10)
Kassina senalagensis	(11)
Phynobatrachus natalensis	(20)
Phynobatrachus mababiensis	(11)
Ptychadena anchitae	(11)
Ptychadena oxyrhynchus	(10)
Pyxicephalus adspersus	(8)
Rana fuscigula	(9)
Rana inyangae	(15)
Schoutedenella stenodactylus	(17)
Strongylopus grayi	(1)
Tomopterna cryptotis	(7, 13, 20)
Tomopterna delalandii	(1, 2, 4)
Tomopterna krugerensis	(11)
Tomopterna marmorata	(13)
Tomopterna natalensis	(3, 11, 13)
Tomopterna tandyi	(3, 4, 6, 7, 8, 12, 24, 25)
Xenopus laevis	(1, 11, 12)

Tomopterna were not found in Zimbabwe but that was not unexpected. Sand frogs are considered to be arid adapted frogs that range through the drier regions of southern Africa. *Tomopterna kruge-rensis, T. marmoratus* and *T. natalensis* are more tolerant of mesic environments than are *T. cryptotis* and *T. tandyi*, but still breed in the drier regions of eastern South Africa. A faunal change occurs in the wetter regions of Zimbabwe and results in many more frog species. Pond environments in the more mountainous regions are limiting, but very important to many species. Ponds were examined in the grounds of La Rochelle Hotel in Penalonga. At this locality, a botanical garden is maintained and the river is dammed and diverted to form a series of ponds. The amphibian diversity at this locality was much higher than other wetlands in the vicinity. The botanical garden is a focal point for tourists and local inhabitants in the region of Mutare and should serve as a model for future development of wetland habitat in that region.

The identification of species of *Tomopterna* is confounded by the fact that individuals of all the species have considerable morphological variability. They can be correctly identified using genetic markers and by observing the chromosomes which will identify the tetraploid species, *T. tandyi*. Using these techniques, the ranges of the species have been corrected, in addition to the discovery of genetically distinct populations, demonstrating that undiscovered species exist in the genus. These same techniques show that many of the populations we studied (Tables 11.2 and 11.3) have been isolated a very long time and there has not been recent communication through immigration and emigration. These data are relevant to environmental enhancement because it is very likely that populations living in the drier regions of Namibia or in the Karoo could not be re-established if they are lost.

Information obtained can be used to document the fact that certain wetland populations in southern Africa should be recognized and afforded protective measures. At least two new species have been encountered and the distributional records for several species have been improved. These data will improve the estimation of species diversity in wetland habitats in southern Africa.

Some of the questions that need to be addressed follow.

What are the priorities for protecting wetland habitat?

Rather than concentrating on a few wetland communities, information from 25 sites in four countries was collected. It was important to obtain an overview of wetland habitat, but the study was compromised because many sites could only be visited once and at one time of year. More time at any particular site would have provided a better estimate of the diversity at that site. Also, it is not known how annual fluctuations in rain fall would impact on the populations or how the wetland is used by local residents over the years. The indicator species that were used served as an indirect test of long term environmental conditions. If an indicator species was able to successfully breed in a wetland site, there must be suitable environmental conditions. Even in the cursory examination, researchers could document present and future problems with respect to environmental degradation.

Human encroachment was an obvious problem, as was the associated use of wetland habitat for garbage dumping. It was more difficult to document problems in some rural environments because water sampling, which would have detected herbicides or pesticides as possible contaminants in these wetlands, was not performed. It is of interest that Lambert (1997) found highly elevated concentrations of organophosphates that were bioaccumulated in tissues of *Tomopterna cryptotis* following a spillage event in Somaliland. He suggested the use of amphibians as bioindicators of environmental contamination because of their ability to absorb chemical compounds from water and soil.

Based on the examination of the wetland habitats in southern Africa, the following wetland sites were of particular concern:

▶ **Jeffrey's Bay, Grahamstown, South Africa.** There is a large pond in the middle of the town that was found to be the breeding site for five frog species. This pond is surrounded by houses and is used by local residents as a dumping site for garbage. Other ponds to the north of the town are not as active and have fewer species.

▶ **Springbok, South Africa.** The wetland in Springbok is a small river course that passes through the middle of the town. The river is dammed in steps down the valley that provide pond-like habitat and then emerges from the town onto a flood plain. Previous records indicate a much higher diversity of amphibians than the single species that was found to be living in the river. The ponds are used for ducks. Springbok is in a dry region of South Africa and the expansion of the town has probably reduced the available water and restricted the flow and the size of the water course.

▶ **Grootfontein, Namibia.** A wetland area exists to the east of the town. This is a small river course that floods flatland and leaves temporary ponds when it subsides. This is the most active amphibian breeding site in a very large area. This site also appears to be undergoing development and there is fear is that the main river channel will be deepened for more rapid draining of the surrounding area.

What additional information is needed?

This study was conducted in a relatively short time period and complete inventories of the wetland habitats were not established. Additional monitoring is especially required in wetlands that were found to be of special interest. It would also be important to engage in a more intensive investigation of wetland habitats that should include estimations of reproductive success, immigration and emigration, and meta-population dynamics that would be important for extensive wetlands or ponds in close proximity. A major part of the study was to train students to engage in wetland evaluations and to communicate with farm owners and local populations. Abeda Dawood, a PhD student at the University of the Western Cape, joined the field trips, was trained in molecular techniques and is continuing to analyze the data that were obtained. Information obtained by other students throughout southern Africa who can more easily monitor nearby wetlands would be a necessary and significant next step to address future wetland evaluations.

How is community involvement achieved?

The most difficult aspect of studies related to environmental protection or enhancement is to ensure the implementation of a monitoring or management plan. The best analyses do little if recommendations are not heeded. From interaction with land owners and colleagues in southern Africa, it is perceived that there is a growing interest in environmental issues that will lead to programmes designed to protect and to preserve wetland habitat. This study will result in papers published in scientific journals and presentations to scientific societies, but this information must also be provided to a more general audience. Co-author Alan Channing is the regional co-ordinator for the Southern African Frog Atlas Project. This project is supported by a very active group of naturalists who are documenting and monitoring populations of frogs throughout southern Africa. If adequate data are available, wetland habitats can be monitored using this network and pressure can be applied to protect and preserve environments at a fairly local level. Channing also publishes information relating to the conservation of taxa and of wetlands in popular southern African publications such as Madoqua and in his new Field Guide to the Frogs of Central and Southern Africa. Communicating to the general public and to naturalist groups will ensure that the public is aware of the problems associated with wetland conservation and will encourage proactive management policies.

CONCLUSION

This research has illustrated that the study of amphibians as bioindicators of ecosystem health may be a credible approach to water resource and land-use management in southern Africa. The acquisition of scientific data and the communication of knowledge gained from such data to community land-users pose challenges for the implementation of this approach. However, the authors feel there is a growing interest in environmental issues in southern Africa which is a key element in encouraging community involvement and promoting proactive management policies.

ACKNOWLEDGMENTS

Abeda and Ania were adept in the laboratory and proved to be almost as good in the field. Martin Pikersgill assisted with an early field trip and provided interesting and humorous conversation. Jenny, Alison and Catherine Channing cheerily put up with travelling in cramped conditions and were indispensable in the field. Accommodation during our field trips was kindly offered and gratefully received from Bill Branch, Marius, Les Minter, Judi and Arthur, Mark and Charlie. Marius assisted us in our fieldwork around Grahamstown, Louis duPrez assisted us in Bloemfontein. Harold Braack and Nick helped us perform field studies in Kruger Park.

REFERENCES

Bogart, J.P. 1981: Chromosome studies in *Sminthillus* from Cuba and *Eleutherodactylus* from Cuba and Puerto Rico (Anura: Leptodactylidae). *Life Sci. Contr. R. Ont. Mus.* No. 129, 1-22.

Channing, A. 1993: A new grass frog from Namibia. *S. Afr. J. Zool*, 28, 142-145.

Channing, A. 1998: *Field Guide to the Frogs of Central and Southern Africa*. Cape Town: Cottage Press.

Channing, A. and Griffin, M. 1993: An annotated checklist of the frogs of Namibia.

Madoqua, 18, 101-116.

Channing, A., Hendricks, D. and Dawood, A. 1994: Description of a new moss frog from the southwestern Cape (Anura: Ranidae). *S. Afr. J. Zool*, 29, 240-243.

Channing, A. and Van Dijk, D.E. 1995: Amphibians. In G.I. Cowan (ed.), *South African Wetlands*, pp. 193-206. Dept. of Environmental Affairs and Tourism.

Channing, A. and Bogart, J.P. 1996: Description of a tetraploid *Tomopterna* (Anura: Ranidae) from South Africa. *S. Afr. J. Zool*, 31, 80-85.

Dunson, W.A., Wyman, R.L. and Corbett, E.S. 1992: A symposium on amphibian declines and habitat acidification. *J. Herpetology*, 26, 349-352.

Lambert, M.R.K. 1997: Effects of pesticides on amphibians and reptiles in sub-Saharan Africa. *Reviews of Environmental Contamination and Toxicology*, 150, 31-73.

Passmore, N.I. and Carruthers, V.C. 1979: *South African Frogs*. Johannesburg: Witwatersrand University Press.

Rose, W. 1962: *Reptiles and Amphibians of South Africa*. Maskew Miller.

Visser, J. and Channing, A. 1997: A new species of river frog from the Swartberg, South Africa (Ranidae: *Afrana*). *J. Afr. Zool*, 111, 191-198.

Wake, D.B. 1991: Declining amphibian populations. *Science*, 253, 860.

Wager, V.A. 1965: *The Frogs of South Africa*. Cape Town: Purnell and Sons Ltd.

Chapter 12

QUESTIONS ANSWERED, QUESTIONS RAISED: BUILDING AN AGENDA FOR THE FUTURE

by John FitzGibbon

INTRODUCTION

There has been significant progress in the development of the science and management of watersheds and wetlands in Southern Africa in the past 25 years. As with many things, the more we know, the more we realize we need to know. This moves us to new studies to fill in the gaps, to improve our skills and improve methods and technology which increase our capacity to know and manage. The outcome of the research provided in this volume indicate directions for future research and capacity building. The research has provided answers to some of current challenges and an agenda for future action.

The limitations of research are most often found in implementation of that research in practice. Thus the test of the utility of what has been accomplished here will take place over the coming years as research assists development. Each study contributes a small piece of the understanding required for successful implementation. Research tends to reduce complex issues to small problems which are soluble. Practice on the other hand has to respond to all of the complexities of the ecosystem under both present and future conditions. In so doing practice must integrate. It requires knowledge of the resource and its natural functioning, the community which currently uses the resource and the environment in which it resides as well as an understanding of the dynamics of both the system producing the resource and the demands placed on it.

The contributions in this volume fall into the areas of watershed and wetlands assessment, water supply assessment and aquatic biodiversity assessment. Each study focuses on a particular research problem but taken as a whole they provide a significant foundation for the management of watershed ecosystems, water supply systems and aquatic systems in Eastern and Southern Africa.

CONTRIBUTIONS OF THE RESEARCH ON WATERSHEDS AND WETLANDS

The research papers on watersheds and wetlands all deal with the complexities of the water cycle and its relation to other factors such as water supply, erosion, sedimentation and land degradation. They share the problems of large complex data sets derived from a wide variety of sources and face the challenge of developing an integrated data base which can accommodate both quantitative (Kelbe, *et al.*) and qualitative (Brown & Kalindekafe) data which is easily accessible and can provide the information needed for decision making. These problems are to some degree dealt with by the development of appropriate data structures and organization (Chapman & Kreutzwiser) as well as through the use of digital data base management tools (Kelbe, *et al.*) The area of need for further research is in the integration of the data so that characterization of environments (Chapman & Kreutzwiser) can be used to select appropriate models (Kelbe, *et al.*) which can effectively employ the data for prediction of the behavior of the watershed or wetland. The linkage to decision making can be made through the provision of scientifically generated management scenarios (Kelbe, *et al.*) or through the process of community consultation and local knowledge of the systems behavior (Brown & Kalindekafe).

CONTRIBUTION OF WATER SUPPLY RESEARCH

The research on water supply provides an understanding of the problems of dealing with water quality and quantity and the protection and management of that supply in areas of scarcity. Management of water supply requires the identification of the sources of water (Maseka & Nyambe, Henschel, *et al.*, Simpson) and to understand the variability and vulnerability of those sources of supply (Maseka & Nyambe, Simpson, Omar & Afshar, Conboy). It is also clear that effective management requires an understanding of the pathways by which water moves from source of supply to the point of capture (Maseka & Nyambe, Conboy). This allows initiatives to prevent intervention with the source of supply which might reduce either the quantity or quality supplied. Capture and delivery of water is a critical point of intervention. Due to the unpredictable (Henschel, *et al.*) nature of many sources of water in the region much ingenuity (Henschel, *et al.*) and knowledge (Simpson) are required to achieve an adequate water source. Delivery of water to the user is often a key factor in the success of a supply system. It can also be one of the elements that is most difficult to manage (Omar & Afshar). The development of a vested interest in the part of the consumers most effected is an element which ensures that such a system can be maintained (Simpson, Omar & Afshar).

CONTRIBUTION OF RESEARCH ON BIOLOGICAL DIVERSITY

It has been said that the function of the ecosystem is to provide for the existence of living creatures. An indicator of the ability of an ecosystem to fulfill this function is biodiversity (Conway, 1991). Biodiversity is impacted by both natural stresses and by those created by human activity. Ambali and Maluwa have provided insight into the recovery of a diversity of fish species in Lake Chiuta after drought. The recovery is a measure of the adaptation of the fish species to drought conditions and is also a measure of the resilience of the ecosystem after severe stress. Such studies provide an understanding of the biological indicators of ecological stress. They can provide valuable information on the health of the system and sustainablity of development in an area. Bogart and Channing have provided insight into the regional response of amphibians to loss of habitat due to human activity. These sensitive creatures prove valuable as early warning indicators of degradation.

INTEGRATION

The discussion above has attempted to provide a sketch of the logical linkages between the research conducted in these different studies carried out on different aspects of the watershed ecosystem. It is clear that a contribution to our knowledge has been made, however there remains a concern that the pieces of the puzzle are still fragmented. The question arises how the dimensions of the human ecosystem can be integrated with those of the natural ecosystem so the science can provide for sustainable development of both the community and the environment on which it depends. The reader might wonder what differences would have occurred if the research had been conducted in a single watershed, if the data collected by one study had been shared with the others, if the methods of inquiry had been brought together and integrated, if the community that will ultimately be impacted by this science had been involved in the development of the knowledge and if the results had been shared.

An approach developed in the International Hydrologic Decade (the 1970s) was that of the **experimental watershed**. Many advances in our understanding of watersheds and wetlands were developed in that period and the initiation of multidisciplinary integrated research began at that time. The approach is now out of favour but it may be that with our emphasis on holistic approaches to understanding the environment and the use of the ecosystems approach in management of the natural environment it is time to revisit the experimental watershed and to begin to undertake a more participatory approach to watershed and wetland research and development.

REFERENCE

Conway, G. R. 1991: *Sustainability in Agricultural Development: Tradeoffs with Productivity, Stability and Equitability*. A paper presented at the 11th Annual AFSR/E Symposium, Michigan, Oct. 5-10.

INDEX

Manure management, 156
Marshes, 42
Mathematical models, 15
Measures of sustainability, 34
Mechanical catchment management, 28
Mfuli catchment, 21
Mhlatuze catchment, 17
Mhlatuze hydrological project regions, 18
Mhlatuze River, 17
Mhlatuze River catchment area, 11
Migrant labour, 123
Mineral cycling, 6
Miombo woodland, 78
Mobilization, 65
Model application, 17
Monocropping, 121
Most Probable Number Technique, 160
Mpongwe Mission, 84
Municipal government see local government
Mutare, 203

NAMFOG Project, 93
Namib desert, 91, 92, 94
Namib fog, 97
Namib Naukluft Park, 103
Namibia, 91, 92, 198
Namibia - wetlands, 197
Namibia Department of Water Affairs, 102
Namibia Desert Research Foundation, 91
Namibia water supply and sanitation sector policy, 107
NAR trait, 159
Natural ecosystems functions, 6 (TOP)
Natural resources management, 189
New technologies, 8

Storage capacity, 65
Storms, 46
Stratus cloud, 95, 96
Stream flow, 15
Stream flow augmentation, 52
Stream flows, 80 (BOP)
Stream gauging, 80
Substrate, 68
Succession, 6
Surface water, 125
Surface winds, 95
Sustainable action in land use, 27
Sustainable development, 1 (BOP)
Sustainable human ecosystem science, 5
Sustainable land use, 27
Sustainable water supply, 132
Sustainable watershed management, 4
Swamps, 42, 172
Swartbank, 98

Technological appropriateness, 144
Technology - impact on villagers, 114
Tetraploids, 200
Therere, 115, 119, 120
Tilapia, 170
Tilapia species, 179
Time in rural life, 123
Tomopterna, 197, 200, 201, 203, 204
Topnaar water needs assessment, 100
Topnaar, 91, 93, 96, 99, 102, 103, 105
Total coliforms, 155, 157, 158, 163, 164
Traditional beliefs, 126
Traditional conservation systems, 191
Traditional customs, 121
Traditional family structure, 121

Wetland/watershed area ratio, 50, 557
Wetland/watershed ratio, 67
Wetlands evaluation systems, 39
Wetlands, 4, 39, 83, 209, 210, 212
White researchers, 119
Whole ecosystems approach, 6
Wind direction, 95, 96
World Bank, 141
Wye catchment, 16

Yachiyo Engineering, 80

Zambia - climate, 78
Zambia - rainfall, 78, 80
Zambia - soils, 79
Zambia - vegetation, 78
Zambia - wetlands, 197
Zambia, Department of Water Affairs, 76
Zambia National Council for Scientific Research, 79
Zambia National Water Resources Master Plan, 80
Zimbabwe, 155
Zimbabwe - wetlands, 197